GARVIN OF THE *OBSERVER*

# Garvin of the OBSERVER

David Ayerst

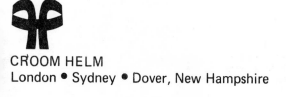

CROOM HELM
London • Sydney • Dover, New Hampshire

©1985 David Ayerst
Croom Helm Ltd, Provident House, Burrell Row,
Beckenham, Kent BR3 1AT
Croom Helm Australia Pty Ltd, First Floor, 139 King Street,
Sydney, NSW 2001, Australia

British Library Cataloguing in Publication Data

Ayerst, David
    Garvin of the Observer.
    1. Garvin, J. L.    2. Observer, The
    3. Journalists–Great Britain–Biography
    I. Title
    070.4'1'0924    PN5123.G3

    ISBN 0-7099-0560-2


Croom Helm, 51 Washington Street,
Dover, New Hampshire 03820, USA

Library of Congress Cataloging in Publication Data

Ayerst, David.
    Garvin of the Observer.

    Bibliography: p.
    Includes index.
    1. Garvin, J.L. (James Louis), 1868-1947.
2. Journalists – Great Britain – Biography. 3. Observer
(London, England) I. Title.
PN5123.G3A9    1984    070.4'1'0924 [B]    84-23767
ISBN 0-7099-0560-2


Typeset by Columns of Reading
Printed and bound in Great Britain by
Biddles Ltd, Guildford and King's Lynn

# CONTENTS

Contents

FOR LAREMA
OUR BOOK

# PREFACE

J. L. Garvin's family papers were kindly placed at my disposal by his grand-daughter, Mrs Patricia Wildblood, for this biography. Other members of his family circle helped in similar ways: Mrs Joan Woods, his stepson's widow, and Mark Barrington-Ward, his godson, provided records which have proved invaluable; so have their personal recollections. Mrs Ursula Slaghek, Garvin's daughter, has taken a continuing interest in the progress of this book. All have left me an entirely free hand.

David Astor, who was then still editing the *Observer*, generously gave me access to the office records, and Tristan Jones supplemented them from his family memories. By far the largest collection of Garvin material is in the Harry Ransom Humanities Research Center of the University of Texas at Austin. I have special reason to be grateful to Mrs Sally Leach, then its assistant librarian, who was generous with private hospitality as well as official help. Most of the references to manuscript material at the end of this book, apart from those to family letters, are to items in Austin for the use of which I am grateful. Exceptions are there recorded. In the concluding section I have noted the main sources of information about Garvin's long life as they become relevant and expressed my thanks to those who have helped me in particular fields.

I have profited from many talks with Professor John Stubbs, who read the early chapters in their original form. Sir William Haley went through the whole of the first draft and made many detailed suggestions. Extensive pruning was then carried out with the help of my wife and of Sir Michael Tippett. Lord Bullock saw the finished product and gave it and me the necessary final impetus. Their help has been great; the faults are my own. I have been saved from a number of bibliographical errors by Mr Hamish Bain and Mr S. E. Taubenheim, two booksellers in Burford.

Nigel Nicolson has kindly allowed me to quote from Lady Sackville's Diary now in the Lilly Library of the University of Indiana. I am grateful for permission to quote to: Collins and A. D. Peters for an extract from *Nancy* by Christopher Sykes; to Constable for an extract from *C.B.* by John Wilson; to Hutchinson's for a passage from L. S. Amery: *My Political Life* and another from Boothby: *Recollections of a Rebel*; to Methuen's for two passages from Robertson Scott: *Life and Death of a Newspaper*; to John Murray for an extract from *Tribal Feeling* by Michael Astor; to *Punch* for an extract from verses by C. L. Graves, and for a poem 'To J. L. Garvin' by A. P. Herbert for which Lady Herbert and A. D. Peters have given permission.

# INTRODUCTION: GARVIN IN HIS TIME

J. L. Garvin enjoyed a long life and a long editorship. He was born in the year of the Second Reform Bill; he became editor of the *Observer* in the year Asquith became Prime Minister; he was sacked in the year Singapore surrendered in the Second World War. The end of his editorship coincided with the close of the Golden Age of the British press. Among a galaxy of great editors four men stand out for the extent of their influence. Thomas Barnes was editor of *The Times* from 1817 to 1841, Delane from 1841 to 1877, C. P. Scott of the *Manchester Guardian* from 1872 to 1929, and Garvin of the *Observer* from 1908 to 1942.

The political influence of the press in their time was bound up with the inability of politicians to make their views known to the country except through newspapers. Before the Great Reform Bill it had not really been necessary for the electors of Eatanswill to be kept informed. After 1832 it mattered what the country knew and thought. There was no way except the newspapers by which what was said in the House of Commons or the Free Trade Hall could be known to those who had not been there. Politicians had reluctantly to reconcile themselves to the unpalatable fact that papers not only reported but commented. Editors distributed praise or blame. They brought out what speakers had left out. They put forward their own ideas. It was here that the particular influence of individual newspapers made itself felt.

Fortunately for the public there were many papers from which to choose, far more than there are today. A paper's influence depended on the quality of its editor, not only his integrity but his imaginativeness. Good editing came increasingly to mean producing a paper that reflected and enriched the whole life of its readers; their interest in sport, in books, in music as well as in politics. Readers identified themselves with their favourite paper, trusting its judgement in one field because they knew it to be trustworthy in some other in which they were expert. Garvin and Scott made their papers a companion for middle-class Englishmen in all their activities.

In Garvin's time there is no doubt that the middle classes ruled Britain. They formed a much higher proportion of the whole electorate than now. In the two fierce elections of 1910, in both of which

Garvin played a significant part, only 58 per cent of all men had votes.

Delane and Scott were both Oxford graduates, born into newspaper families, natural candidates one might say to become editors. Garvin came from the bottom drawer, the son of an immigrant Irish labourer. For many years he was undecided whether his life-work was to be in literature or politics. It was the breadth as well as the depth of his interests that made the *Observer* the newspaper without which no English Sunday was complete.

Before Garvin, there were no 'quality' Sunday papers as we know them now. The *Observer* and the *Sunday Times* were ancient but negligible properties with minute circulations making sizeable losses. Long before Garvin died most respectable middle-class families would have hesitated to admit that they had not seen the *Observer*. Or else the *Sunday Times*; since, as Garvin wrote, 'all can grow the flower now for all have got the seed'. He was writing about Northcliffe, the friend he admired above all newspaper men. It was Northcliffe who first cultivated the seed from which the 'popular' mornings are grown; Garvin that from which the 'quality' Sundays come.

It was not until Garvin had been editor of the *Observer* for three years that the first Official Secrets Act was passed. It made little difference to his newsgathering. Indeed his major brushes with Cabinet Ministers over 'leaks' happened before the Act. Garvin's problems over press freedom were not with the government over news but with his proprietors over views. H. W. Nevinson, who knew all the editors of his time, remarked that all the best had been sacked. (C. P. Scott survived only through the generosity of those who bought his paper for him.) Nevinson's list included J. A. Spender, A. G. Gardiner and H. W. Massingham, an outstanding trio of Liberal editors. Had he lived another four months he would have had to add Garvin. All lost their jobs because they insisted on writing what they believed. The struggle of editors to avoid being muzzled by their proprietors or taken over by a political machine was characteristic of Garvin's time. One might think this a private matter like any other between employer and employed, but in fact the public interest is involved. Garvin liked to contrast 'responsible editorship' with 'ostensible editorship' where the editor took his political orders from the owners. He passionately believed that the readers of any paper worth buying or editing had a right to know what the editor himself honestly thought about any important matter. This was the essence of an implied contract, the basis of trust between paper and reader. It had to be maintained even to the point of resignation or dismissal as Garvin did. Today, when newspapers are few and likely to be fewer, Garvin's intransigence would have been not only brave but suicidal. In his time, or for most of it, he could reasonably hope that, if he fell out with one proprietor, he would find another.

An editor of the Golden Age, who was known to influence his readers, soon found himself in a position to influence directly as well as indirectly the leaders of the government or the Opposition. That was Garvin's position almost from his first day at the *Outlook*, a long dead political weekly, till shortly before he lost the *Observer*. He was on friendly and even intimate terms with most of the leading politicians of his day. Joseph Chamberlain, A. J. Balfour, Lloyd George, Winston Churchill, Ramsay MacDonald and a host of lesser men not only talked freely to him but listened attentively to what he said to them.

The Golden Age was marked technologically by the development of shorthand for recording news, of rotary presses and typesetting machinery for quickly printing it, and of railways for distributing newspapers. Its passing came with the introduction of radio and television. Garvin early saw what was coming. Writing to his son in the trenches in 1915, he said, 'Will science ever give distant vision as it now carries distant sound? I think that must come, and wish we were so far.' His prophecy was realised fifty years later in Vietnam where television coverage had political consequences which no printed words could have achieved. When Northcliffe died in 1922, Garvin wrote: 'Had he been born forty years later he might well have set himself to control the future of broadcasting, but in his day the weapon was the press.' Foresight, and the intellectual curiosity from which it sprang, were among Garvin's strengths as an editor.

The old conditions just about lasted Garvin's time, but before he left the *Observer* the eager audience for the Nine o'clock News and the sudden hush in a crowded pub whenever Churchill spoke to the nation showed that the monopoly of Fleet Street had been broken. A Prime Minister no longer needed a middleman. Since then the general power of the press has declined, though the individual power of a particular newspaper remains for those with skill and courage to grasp it. Remember Watergate and the *Washington Post*. Garvin would have applauded that shining example of 'responsible editorship'.

**Part One:**
**JIM GARVIN TILL FIFTY, 1868-1918**

# BOOK ONE: NORTH COUNTRY APPRENTICESHIP
## 1868-1899

---

'We Garvins are in our nature Northerners and flourish better in the cold weather than the hot.'

J. L. Garvin to his son, 5 July 1915

# 1     AN IRISH BOY ON MERSEYSIDE, 1868-1884

James Garvin was born on Easter Day 1868 at 117 St Ann Street, Birkenhead, a terrace house opening straight on to the road in a poor working-class district not far from the centre of the town. The family in 117 was poorer than most of the neighbours because in 1870 Catherine Garvin was left a widow with two young boys, aged five and two. There was no Social Security, only the Poor Law with its grudging out-relief or hated workhouse to fall back on. Catherine Garvin survived by hard work which can be called heroic. Her stone-floored kitchen was nearly filled with an enormous flat-bed mangle weighted with stones. Somehow she managed to earn enough at the wash tub to pay the rent and bring the boys up in decency. She kept her self-respect. To her sons in later years this was endearingly symbolised by her proud boast of having always bought 'the best tea'.

Mercifully the young widow had her own parents and relatives to help her in small ways and to give her the security which comes from being near one's own folk. They cannot, however, have given her much financial help. Her father, a labourer, had been born in the year before the Act of Union and, of course, had no old age pension. The Garvins lived in a closely knit Irish community. Every seaport and industrial town in the North of England had, and still has, whole wards which are predominantly Irish; communities knit together by the ties of kindred, politics, poverty and religion. St Ann Street, Birkenhead, was such a neighbourhood. It was so thoroughly inturned that it reproduced in miniature the patchwork pattern of the Irish countryside. Catherine Garvin lived in that part of the street which was known as 'Carlow Ann's' so that she was in a sense an intruder since the Fahys came from Cork and the Garvins from Tipperary.

Catherine Garvin had the support which comes from a sincere and deep-rooted faith. Her religion was held with intense devotion and without any hesitation or doubt. It was laced with superstition which on one occasion caused her to take Jim, who was suffering from bronchitis, to Holywell in North Wales and there to dip him in the spring. The dogged determination, the steel in her character, was probably well suited by the temper of the parish priest of St Laurence, Birkenhead. Father Geraghty was long remembered in Birkenhead as a hard, domineering Irishman who 'put the boot in among the boys', by which presumably was meant putting the fear of God into them.

Michael Garvin, Jim's father, was thirteen in the year of the great potato famine. He came over to England leaving his parents at Kilsheen in County Tipperary. Little is known of Garvin's paternal grandparents — nothing in fact beyond the tradition that the family had been millers and that his grandfather had disgraced the family by making a runaway marriage with Mary Kinsley, a Protestant girl who never thereafter spoke to her family nor they to her. In later life Garvin was pleased to think that this quarter-share of Irish Protestant stock made him a complete Irishman. He liked also to explain that the reticence or 'shutness' of character which he believed himself to possess came from his grandmother. Once, when he was twenty-five, he went to the small town at the south of the Slieve Bloom hills, where she lived. 'I haven't written to anybody in Roscrea,' he said in a letter scribbled in the train, 'so that it is quite on the cards that I may find everybody out and shall just have to come back to Dublin.' We shall never know.

When Michael Garvin married in 1861 he had been a labourer. Later he went to sea. I have found in all Garvin's letters only one allusion to his father's death. He told Northcliffe that 'very nearly 40 years ago my father's ship went down under a iceberg in the Newfoundland seas or rather south of them. It was in the winter of 1869 and he was just about my age.' That squares well enough with the loss of the *City of Boston* homeward bound with two hundred passengers and crew, including one Michael Garvin, a stoker.

Michael Garvin is an elusive character. A rocking chair, brought back from one of his voyages, is a sign that he did not forget the young wife he left behind. Persistent enquiries by Garvin's daughters, however, failed to elicit more about their grandfather than that he was 'a decent, respectable man who always wore a silk topper on Sunday'.

That may be, but there was another side to him. Lady Colvin once told Garvin about her own first unhappy marriage to a heavy drinker. 'You helped me more than you could tell,' he wrote to her next day. 'My mother went through it. I was the child of many tears — the consolation for them, she said, and the sole hope.' Strange that it is only in a Campden Hill drawing room in 1919 that one can find a clue to what was probably happening in down-town Birkenhead fifty years before.

The Garvins' situation was unfortunate but not uncommon. What was exceptional was the calibre of the boys. Michael was delicate, 'elegant', immediately likeable, quick to respond, a brilliant talker, and gifted with the ability to catch somebody's features and character-

istics in a rapid pencil sketch. Jim, on the other hand, though consti-
tutionally robust, was physically unco-ordinated — he described himself
as 'the unhandy man', shy and afflicted with a bad speech defect which
those who knew him later as one of the most brilliant talkers of his
generation find it hard to credit. As a boy he was something of a loner:
'solitary, finding sufficient in his reading, studies and imagination to
occupy the bulk of his spare time'. Both boys were mercurial, climbing
high in ecstasy or tumbling into depths of dejection and sometimes of
self-pity. Both were explosive in temper when roused, which was seldom;
neither harboured a grudge. Michael was the admired elder brother,
Jim his devoted follower. Their mother gave them every encouragement, but their minds far outstripped hers. Soon they were on their
own, discovering for themselves riches beyond her knowing. This was
true of the world of imagination and of thought, but not, I think, of
personal emotion. Throughout childhood and adolescence the fatherless
boys were closely knit, some would say too closely knit, to their mother.
There is no sign of teenage rebellion.

The Garvins were fortunate in their school. Years later Jim recalled
'the real inspiring power of a remarkable man called Doogan', the
headmaster of St Laurence's Roman Catholic school. The Garvin
brothers must have been a dream to teach, a rewarding dream when
teachers were paid partly on results assessed by Her Majesty's Inspectors
of Schools. Garvin once told a conference of teachers:

Perhaps the turning point in my life was when I was ten, and, in
answer to some question of H.M.I., I mentioned Demosthenes of
Chaeronea and committed a false quantity. Surprised and amused,
he said 'Chaeron*e*a, Jimmy, Chaeron*e*a! but you know more Greek
history than the ordinary undergraduate.' Innocent enough to think
this a greater compliment than it was, I was encouraged and loved
him for it.

If the schoolroom was a pleasure, the playground was not. W. H. Egan,
a future Labour MP, remembered that Garvin 'used to hold himself
aloof from the worst rough and tumble of the playground and as a
result sometimes got roughly handled by the bully type of lads'. So did
others, and the 'quixotic protection' which Jim extended to a younger
boy, Henry Byrne Jones, was the beginning of a lasting friendship with
the man who became his income tax adviser. Jack Kearney, a future
Manchester headmaster, was another St Laurence's boy with whom
Jim's friendship persisted long after schooldays, kept green by the fact

that he became godfather to Kearney's daughter Una.

These friends encouraged each other, of course, but in Jim's case the real driving force was within. 'I read without control,' he said, 'thoroughly enjoyed myself and found my own food. I would not have had it different for worlds.' He started with fairy stories. At six he began on the fifty-six military novels of James Grant. The great children's classics enthralled him. *The Swiss Family Robinson*, for instance, he must have read ten times. By sixteen he had been through the whole of Dickens, 'not so much a novelist as an extension of life', Scott, Thackeray, George Eliot, Charles Reade and Wilkie Collins.

That surely might have been enough, but it was far from all. Jim had an eight-volume set of Rollin's *Ancient History* which he read lying flat on the floor to trace the retreat of Xenophon's Ten Thousand on a large map. When he was eleven he bought Langhorne's *Plutarch* at a market-stall. He reckoned it was the foundation of his library. Cheap to begin with, dingy to look at, well thumbed, it kept to the end its place among grander editions on his shelves, his 'first teacher in politics and about the best'. An epoch-making purchase.

Gibbon, whom he tackled at twelve, was epoch-making in a different sense. Catherine Garvin, like many an Irish mother, would have felt fulfilled if she could have seen one of her boys a teacher, the other a priest. It was a reasonable ambition. The school turned out many teachers, Michael Garvin among them, and many priests, even a bishop. Grandfather Fahy, who was addicted to phrenology, thought that Jim's 'bumps' would make him either a bishop or a prizefighter. Obviously the 'unhandy man' would never be a boxer, however pugnacious his temperament; but what kept him from the priesthood? There was much that might have led him at least as far as the seminary. He was fired with the ideal of Catholic chivalry. At his confirmation he added Louis, after the crusading king of France, to his baptismal James. Father Robert Silva had so opened Jim's ears to music that years later he pencilled in his notebook these words: 'the empty church, the distant sound of the choir practising Weber in G and a man's voice doing alto solo which Joe Hamlin used to sing when I broke in with the treble — what a sense of romance was in that religion of ours'. Nevertheless the boy who read Gibbon at twelve found there many things which the Rome of the first Vatican Council wished the faithful not to know. He began to think for himself in a way that was likely to lead him to disappoint his mother.

If in his later boyhood Garvin was already drawing a little away from the faith of his neighbours, he was coming more intensely to share their politics.

Jim's love of history fostered patriotism. For an Irish boy on Mersey-side, living among people whose poverty was a constant reminder that they were disinherited, there was only one possible *patria*. One day he heard two old women talking Irish. It suddenly struck him that this was his language and that he could not understand it. He lived in England, he spoke English; but he felt Irish of the Irish, a foreigner in the land whose language he spoke.

When Jim was thirteen he left school. He had already had a paper round, and had begun to weave fantasies about the time when he would become an editor: 'When I am, Jack, you shall be manager,' he told Kearney. It was not altogether fantasy. While he was still at school, he gave up an hour each evening to learning Pitman's shorthand. His later notebooks show that he wrote a clear hand.

Garvin's first job, however, had nothing to do with newspapers. He was employed as a messenger boy or junior delivery clerk by a firm of Birkenhead solicitors. He had no intention of staying in a blind alley job and no hope of escaping one except by acquiring marketable qualifications. This he set out to do in the only way open to him, by evening classes. For ten years or so Garvin carried on his formal educa-tion in this way. It is easy to think of Garvin as a pure Arts man with nothing to show on the other side. It was not so. Mathematics and electricity, which he took at night school, were not only bread and butter subjects to him, they were genuine interests. He won a prize for mathematics from a City company and was proud that he could do cube roots in his head.

About the time that Jim left school, Michael began to train as a teacher. He passed his examinations and got his first appointment in 1884. It was in Hull. The family went with him.

I

Not long after the Garvins moved to Hull Joseph Chamberlain, 'Radical Joe', came to the city to launch his campaign for his 'unauthorised programme' of social reform. He seemed to have a special message that day for Jim Garvin as he denounced 'profitable tragedy' at sea, the practice by which shipowners overloaded and overinsured their 'coffin ships' so that, sink or swim, they made a handsome profit.

> I found [Chamberlain said] that every year more than 3,000 lives were lost at sea . . . And it is not only the men whose lives were lost whose fate you have to consider. What is the fate of their families who are left without resource, struggling against destitution when the bread winner is removed?

Forty-eight years later Garvin recalled in his *Life of Joseph Chamberlain* that 'Every word went home.' It did to him. His own father had been one of the lost legion of 1870. For a short time 'Radical Joe' became almost as much Jim's hero as Charles Stewart Parnell himself.

A general election was close at hand. Hull's senior MP was a Liberal, but a shipowner who had helped to kill Chamberlain's Merchant Shipping Bill. After that, the Irish Radicals of Hull, heirs of Fergus O'Connor and the Chartist tradition, would find it difficult to vote Liberal as they usually did. They were relieved when Parnell, 'the uncrowned king of Ireland', ordered them to vote Conservative this time. It was with conviction and alacrity that Jim Garvin helped to turn out the Irish vote. In Hull the Conservative won. In the new Parliament the Liberals needed Irish support. Parnell's price was Home Rule Bill. Gladstone paid, but Chamberlain and 93 Liberals voted against the Bill. Another general election followed. This time the Irish voted Liberal, but neither in Hull nor elsewhere were they numerous enough to offset the loss of Chamberlain's Liberal Unionists. The Gladstonian Liberals in Hull continued to blame the Irish. In letters to the press Jim Garvin defended himself and his Michael Davitt branch of the Irish National League 'whose members live and work . . . with the Irish population, who saw the enthusiasm, spontaneous and unfeigned, with which they received the Home Rule candidate, who saw their broken and dejected looks on the night of his defeat'. Chamberlain, Garvin's new hero, became his hated foe.

After the excitement of two general elections within twelve months day to day constituency work seemed depressingly unrewarding. Garvin complained to the *Dublin Weekly Freeman* that nowhere were the Irish so apathetic as in Hull. His Michael Davitt branch had a clubhouse with a piano. It subscribed to the best English and Irish papers. There were cards, draughts, dominoes, and all for a 'phenomenally low' subscription. 'Yet not more than twenty use it even with moderate regularity; the debates and readings ... have the same spare attendance; while the purely business meetings of the League scarcely ever draw more than the same dozen faithful faces.' One can sympathise with the young financial secretary. It is the kind of disappointment every ward politician has to experience.

## II

At least Garvin had the consolation of the clubhouse and 'the best English newspapers'. It was at this time that he started his life-long reading of *The Times*, which hated his hero Parnell, and the *Manchester Guardian*, which, side by side with Mr Gladstone, had just been converted to Home Rule. Newspapers were compulsive reading for politicians in those somersaulting years. Garvin's itch to write in them was also strong. Hull, like most provincial cities, had its own daily papers which were safe from competition because London papers could not arrive by breakfast. One of the Hull papers, the *Eastern Morning News*, was much of Garvin's mind. It was there, or in its weekly, the *Express*, that most of his early writing is to be found. Nearly all of it was Irish propaganda, vehemently expressed but often prudently argued. And even at seventeen he had evidently begun to feel the tug of a wider patriotism in which Irish and English could share alike: 'England has given Home Rule to Australia, Canada, Cape Colony and the West Indies, and lo! not only does the Empire stand, but an Australian contingent has just returned from the Soudan.'

A year later a man only six years older than Garvin became editor of the *Eastern Morning News*. At Balliol J. A. Spender had been friendly with Cosmo Lang, a future Archbishop of Canterbury, and had his room wrecked by Edward Grey, a future Foreign Secretary. 'Journalism is not a profession, not a profession, Mr. Spender' had been Jowett's warning. All the same it was a good opening for a man whose uncle owned the *Eastern Morning News*, the *Western Morning News* at Plymouth, and the Central Press, a London news agency. Spender understandably wanted to meet the unknown gifted controversialist who contributed to his paper. Equally understandably Garvin, a gangly eighteen-year-old clerk, was afraid of being laughed out of court or rather out of the paper when it was discovered what a boy the scourge of the Tories was. Spender invited him to call; Garvin procrastinated. At last an appointment was made. Garvin found Spender at his desk, lit by a green shielded light which left the rest of the room in semi-darkness. Spender picked up a speaking tube and asked the front office to send up Mr Garvin. Shyly, from the shadows, Garvin explained who he was. Spender threw up his hand right over his handsome head in a gesture of astonishment that Garvin never forgot. Nor did he forget the encouragement which the future editor of the *Westminster Gazette* gave him: 'It is an immense thing when one who knows says to you, "You can."'

## III

No doubt Garvin would have liked his life to be all politics and newspapers, but he had a living to earn and a better living to prepare for. He was a clerk, at first with Reckitt's, the starch manufacturers, and then with a firm of corn merchants. One day he amused himself with pen portraits of the staff. The manager was a man of thirty with the figure of a boy of thirteen, who tripped daintily upon his toes from stone to stone and arrived on a wet day with immaculate shoes while his underlings' boots were caked in mud. Then there was Varley with his oiled hair smelling of languid perfumes. 'He knows nothing, will learn nothing, and is so independent that he spurns good advice ... and lives upon his mother, a widow in good circumstances.' Another clerk was 'a universal iconoclast, doesn't believe in religion but believes in Darwinism; doesn't believe in God but believes in Huxley ... doesn't read newspapers and doesn't understand politics, but has a strong aversion to the royal family'. Still he was straightforward, good-hearted and industrious when he liked.

It would be good to know what his fellow clerks thought of him, but by the time his daughter tried to find out, no one remembered. This history of Reckitt's, however, records that Garvin studied Gibbon in the dinner hour, contributed to the *Eastern Morning News*, and went to evening classes.

More influential in the long run than all the formal teaching were the hours Garvin spent in Tutin's bookshop. J. R. Tutin was much more than a bookseller; he was a devoted Wordsworthian, writing a book on the poet. He allowed his writing to spill over into talk with the shy youth who haunted his shop. At Birkenhead Garvin had been a devotee of Scott and learnt much of *Marmion* by heart. At Hull Wordsworth became the great love of his life by whom henceforth all other poetic enthusiasms, and they were many, were measured.

Meanwhile there was the all-important question of a career. Since 1870, civil servants had been recruited by competitive examination. Garvin took a correspondence course run by a paper quaintly named the *Civil Service Aspirant*. He failed in the competition for men clerks in 1887 — too much electioneering, perhaps? — but was determined to succeed in the following year. Alas, the date of the examination was changed so that he was just too old to enter. The same thing happened with the Excise examination. He complained in the *Civil Service Aspirant* that it would make the frustrated candidates 'depraved and danger-ous ... cynics, scoffers, and Red Republicans. As for me,' he added, 'I shall wear a Phrygian cap, sing the Marseillaise; and make a demon-stration of *one* in Trafalgar Square.' No doubt Robbie Burns had been happy to become an exciseman, but before long Jim Garvin was glad that he had failed to follow suit.

# 3   GARVIN FINDS A GURU, 1889-1899

## I

When Jim was twenty-one the Garvins moved to Newcastle where his brother had secured a job as a science master. Tyneside had more Irishmen than any other part of England except Merseyside. Moreover Newcastle was a regional capital as Hull was not. Naturally Jim Garvin immersed himself once again in local politics. His Irish nationalism and radical politics still went hand in hand. He soon got to know a trade union official, Arthur Henderson, the 'Uncle Arthur' who became a key figure in the Labour Party's rise to power. To the end both men recognised the bond formed during their early Tyneside experiences in Garvin's 'Jacobinical youth'.

At other times Garvin would speak of his 'Fenian past'. A strain of romance, a flavour of aristocracy modified the proletarian necessities of Jim's early years. One sees the disinherited rather than the *sans culotte* in this reminiscence of Garvin in a Tyneside pub:

> A score of Irish working men sitting round. Mr. James Louis Garvin holding forth eloquently, passionately on the glorious days of Cucullian, or Finn and his Fenians, or pouring out his soul while he held up for our example the great deeds and sufferings of Lord Edward, Wolfe Tone and Emmet.

Garvin's first two years in Newcastle saw Parnell's triumph, fall and death. In February 1889 the *Times* articles on 'Parnellism and Crime' were proved to be based on a forgery. Garvin rejoiced; but in November 1890 Parnell was co-respondent in the notorious O'Shea divorce case. In December the Nationalist Party split. A minority still followed Parnell, but the great majority chose Justin McCarthy as their new leader. The agony in Committee Room 15 at Westminster was also felt in every Irish ghetto in Britain. In Newcastle the anti-Parnellites were set to take over the Irish Institute. The press were carefully excluded from the crucial meeting, but Garvin, who was a member, sent a long report to the *Newcastle Daily Chronicle*.

By this time he was the regular North of England correspondent of *United Ireland*, the weekly Dublin paper which supported Parnell.

14

This, of course, meant a field day for him when Parnell spoke in New-castle Town Hall. Garvin wrote:

> The moment he stood at the rail of the platform one felt . . . that this was the first man of our race as long as life dwelt in his body. . . . It is impossible to describe in words the peculiar impression of fire and force, restrained yet hinting at volcanic depths, which is con-veyed with every word and gesture as the rail before him sounded under his clenched fist and the platform sounded under the heavy stamp of his foot; . . . and when he ended with rare dignity and simplicity by appealing to his countrymen 'to stand by the man in his hour of trouble who stood by them in theirs,' he awoke a feeling in the hearts of those who heard him which will be slow to die.

It lived on in Garvin. To him Parnell always remained one of the half-dozen men of his time whose 'life-work is *heroic* in effect and essence'.

## II

In Newcastle Garvin started as a clerk earning just over a pound a week. In 1890 he got a better job as foreign correspondence clerk with a coal exporting firm. He could manage French and German, but had no Spanish. He bought a grammar and three weeks later wrote his first Spanish business letter, a good one which produced a satisfied customer. Garvin was proud of his success and kept up his Spanish.[1] Then the firm for which he was working collapsed, but on the strength of his record with it he was offered a better job in South Wales. It was a fine chance, but he wanted to be a journalist, not a businessman. He decided to try his luck with the leading Newcastle paper. He secured an interview with Joseph Cowen, the owner of the *Newcastle Daily Chronicle*. Cowen was discouraging as wise men are when young men want to enter a precarious occupation in which success is evasive. 'My advice to you, Sir, is "Don't,"' Cowen said. 'Journalism is a life of drudgery.' Garvin replied that everything depended on drudgery — Bach and cathedrals, for instance. A man should give the whole of himself to anything he undertook. Cowen fell back on an employer's impregnable defence. There was no vacancy. 'What, none at all?' asked Garvin. Well, there was room for a proof-reader at 28 shillings a week. Garvin took it and Cowen accepted the astonishing proviso that Garvin should be allowed to write short editorial notes as well. Perhaps he guessed that in engaging a proof-reader he had discovered a leader-writer. Garvin's first editorial notes appeared on 11 September 1891.

His first big test came in October. He was sent to cover Parnell's funeral. It was his first visit to Ireland. On the steamer from Holyhead Parnellite MPs mounted guard over the coffin. Garvin was deeply moved, but he was already professional enough not to let what he was feeling get in the way of newsgathering. He buttonholed one MP who told him that to surrender now would be to confess that in standing by Parnell the previous year they had been either traitors or fools. The facile talk of reunion in which the English were indulging was, Garvin concluded, 'mere speculation, and it is shallow speculation'. So it was.

At Kingstown, not yet Dun Laoghaire, the coffin was taken out of the rough shell in which for safety it had been encased. The crowd furiously tore the deal boards to pieces – 'every one of those chips will be a simple and affecting monument to Mr. Parnell in a thousand humble Irish homes'. Garvin left the relic-seekers and followed several thousand young men armed with hurley sticks who escorted the coffin to a lying-in-state in City Hall.

Little touches distinguish a good story from a competent one. Garvin had seen something which other reporters missed. As the procession made its way to Glasnevin Cemetery, he noticed how some of the older bystanders took off their hats to a man in one of the many coaches that followed the hearse. The man was James Stephens, the Fenian leader of 1848, who had come home to Ireland after a long exile. The novice reporter had used his eyes to good purpose:

James Stephens stood by the grave, an old man representing an older movement, which the man they were burying in his prime had superseded. O'Connell's monument stood out more strongly still against the star twilight, like a spire whose silent finger points to heaven. It represented an Irish movement older than Stephens. So were three generations of Ireland's ceaseless struggles linked together ... I saw Mr. Justin McCarthy looking very sad and old on the outskirts of the crowd. None of the others, who have been conspicuous in opposing Mr. Parnell, appeared, and it was better so. The people were orderly, but their wrath is deep and bitter. Mr. Parnell is dead, but the dead leader again leads.

Joseph Cowen's gamble had come off. There was no doubt about Garvin's command of words, no difficulty about his politics, but Cowen could not know whether he would stand the prolonged fatigue and achieve the speed and punctuality which a journalist needs. Parnell's funeral involved a sleepless working night followed by a long day crowned by the need to telegraph 2,000 words for Monday's paper. When morning came it was apparent that Garvin could meet a dead-line.

## III

Garvin found in Cowen a hero and a friend, almost a substitute for the father he had never known. Cowen's son was general manager of the paper but was less interested in policy and politics than in technical development — it was the first English daily to introduce linotype machines. The editorial staff were worthy rather than distinguished. Cowen himself, a man of 62 with an ailing wife, must have felt the need for someone to whom he could pass on the tradition which he had received and the memory of the exciting events in which he had played a part. Cowen was unconventional in appearance and style for a rich and successful Victorian public man. He dressed always in a plain black suit — like a miner on Sundays, as a friend described him. Instead of the conventional 'topper' he always wore a 'wideawake', a soft wide-brimmed felt hat. His stocky figure, massive forehead and his 'peculiarly beautiful lustrous and expressive' eyes inevitably caught people's attention. He spoke with a pronounced Northumbrian burr, but when he spoke in public it was with a splendid eloquence that made Garvin think of him as the Demosthenes of the North.

Garvin had reached manhood virtually self-taught. He had never had the discipline which comes from close association with the mature mind of a man who was his intellectual equal. With Joseph Cowen he enjoyed the greatly rewarding relation of master and pupil which no one who has known it will ever forget. 'There is between us', Cowen once told him, 'a community of feeling and thought that is beyond the reach of a mere monetary bond.' Both men felt it. In hasty gossips in the office and in long and intimate talks in Cowen's home Garvin imbibed a living tradition in the same way that a cadet of a great Whig family drank in ancestral politics when the port went round his father's table. Cowen had been president of the Debating Society at Edinburgh University in 1848. He had led the Scottish students to align themselves with the revolutionary students of Vienna, Berlin and Paris. After the old gang had fought its way back to power, Cowen used his father's business connections to keep the liberal cause alive. He smuggled clandestine literature into Europe hidden in the fire-bricks exported by Joseph Cowen and Co. Spies were sent to watch him and to monitor his visitors. For their sake he had to travel south to towns where he could meet his exiled friends more unobtrusively than was possible on Tyneside. Garvin was already familiar with the undercover activities of Irishmen, but his eyes were opened to Europe as Cowen talked to him about Louis Blanc, the French Socialist; Kossuth and Mieroslawski, whose liberal risings had been suppressed by Russian troops; Orsini, who tried to assassinate Napoleon III for betraying Italy; and Garibaldi, whose Thousand had freed Sicily and Naples. The list of Cowen's friends is a roll call of the mid-nineteenth-century European Left. As he told Garvin about them he pushed the horizon of the young man's memory backwards by a whole generation.

Quite as important was what Garvin learnt about the day before yesterday in British politics. Cowen had been a Liberal MP for twelve years, half while Disraeli was Prime Minister; half under Gladstone. Years later Garvin recalled in a notebook how 'Mr. Gladstone liked neither the Turk nor Mr. Disraeli. Others, like Joseph Cowen, liked neither Russia nor Mr. Gladstone.' Doubtless no friend of Kossuth could be a Russophil, but why should Cowen have actively disliked Gladstone? There was much more to it than the recollection that Gladstone had ignored Cowen's maiden speech which Disraeli praised. Cowen's dislike reflected his belief that Gladstone had done so many illiberal things and left undone so many liberal things that there was remarkably little health in him. He had, for instance, sent pickets to prison at a time when Cowen was supporting the engineers in their five-month strike for a nine-hour day. Then again, for four years Gladstone had refused Ireland Home Rule, which Cowen supported, and governed it by Coercion Acts which Cowen detested. Gladstone's conversion in 1886 came in time to secure Cowen's vote, but not to win his heart.

Of course young Garvin's support for Cowen's radical views about Ireland and trade unions was inevitable. Less expected, but ultimately more significant, was his adoption of some of Cowen's other heresies. Gladstone, for instance, was really a Little Englander; Cowen an Imperialist with a difference. He believed that the self-governing colonies were precious to the Mother Country, especially because they were more perfect democracies than England had yet become. He was one of the founders of the Imperial Federation League. In one of Garvin's Newcastle notebooks there is a quotation from Dickens — '"My dear," said Mr. Micawber, "Britannia must take her choice." "Micawber," returned Mrs. Micawber, "there you are wrong. You are going out, Micawber, to this distant land to heighten not to weaken the connection between yourself and Albion."' Garvin gave this extract the title 'Mrs. Micawber and Imperial Federation.' He had caught from Cowen a wider patriotism than the exclusive Irish Nationalism of his youth.

Again, to Gladstone free trade was a fortieth Article of Religion. Cowen was a waverer. Young Garvin's mind moved in the same agnostic direction. He read Ruskin and began to doubt. Neither Cowen nor Garvin had put their imperial faith and their economic doubts together to form the vision of a democratic Commonwealth held together by imperial preference. That final step came for Garvin three years after Cowen's death.

From Cowen Garvin caught a distrust of political machines. The Liberal caucus had opposed Cowen's re-election in 1885, but he beat John Morley into second place. Cowen refused to stand again in 1886, expressing his decision in words that seem sadly up to date: 'I regarded myself as a representative of all the electors, and not as a delegate of a faction ... [This] secured for me the unappeasable animosity of our organised Liberals ... I preferred principle to party, and the constituency to the Caucus.'

## IV

There was no abominable caucus to stop Cowen saying what he liked in the *Newcastle Daily Chronicle*. The city then had three morning papers, three evenings and a host of weeklies. Two of the mornings were straight party papers – the kind politicians love for the same reason that today they love party political broadcasts. The third, the *Chronicle*, under Cowen had become undoubtedly the leading paper of the North-East. Its politics reflected his quirky individualism. This infuriated politicians but delighted readers. Fortunately for Garvin his thinking marched so closely with Cowen's that he could write his mind freely on almost every subject that he touched. The freedom and the responsibility of his time on the *Chronicle* were a splendid training for what he liked to call 'responsible, not ostensible editorship'. Nothing less would ever content him. The *Chronicle* really spoilt him for the 'fitting in' that most journalists have to do.

It remains a mystery how the newest, and possibly the youngest, member of the editorial staff came to have such a free hand. His colleagues are shadowy people today. One wonders how much substance they had then. 'You are the only man on the paper I have close personal relations with,' Cowen once told Garvin — a strange admission from 'the Governor'. Strange too that with so many journalists in Newcastle and with quite a large editorial staff on the *Chronicle* Garvin should have found little to say about them. Perhaps the explanation lies in what he told Stanley Morison:

> I never was a proper journalistic journalist . . . No man who played so large a part through journalism ever had so little to do with it. I never belonged to the Press Club or that kind of thing or cared for journalistic gossip.'

Garvin might avoid journalistic small talk, but he took newspapers seriously. Some time in 1899 Joseph Cowen asked him to put down in writing his suggestions for improving the *Chronicle*. Young journalists like to toy with ideas for re-making their paper to their own fancy. Few ever get the opportunity. Fewer still find that their youthful ideas work. Garvin did. What he put down for Cowen to consider, he carried out on the *Observer* and the *Pall Mall Gazette*.

'The face of the paper has as much effect as the face of a person or the window of a shop.' That was how Garvin started. It was no use a paper being well written if it didn't look well. Readers did not make judicious comparisons between one paper and another. They went by the look of them. The *Chronicle* was making far too much use, Garvin thought, of its new black type for headlines: 'We should be as sparing of them as a musician in a symphony is of the trombones.' Garvin went on to rearrange the sequence of pages, to redesign the leader page, making room each day for a column of 'features' — books, music, drama and art. 'The principal paper of a district ought to be the focus of local intellectual life. We are that in politics. We ought to be so in other ways.' It could all be done without any increase in staff; but of course Garvin was a glutton for work — he proposed to take on a books column two days a week in addition to his foreign and general leader-writing. What on earth would his colleagues have thought of him?

There was something lacking, too, in the *Chronicle*'s politics. It was all very well to be eminent in destructive criticism, but it ought to have something constructive and positive to say about Imperialism and Anglo-American friendship — a pity, then, that its American correspondent had been dropped. Garvin suggested that the paper should be friendly to Conservatives like Salisbury and Balfour and to Rosebery and Edward Grey among the Liberals. He did not mention

Joseph Chamberlain. On most things Chamberlain and Garvin thought alike. Home Rule was now a dead issue, but perhaps neither Garvin nor Cowen could forgive the man who scotched it in 1886.

Garvin was dissatisfied with the *Chronicle*'s business management. He told Cowen so one Saturday, and then spent Sunday in checking advertising over an eight-year period. He found a steady decline. He went on to warn Cowen that there was on the editorial staff 'suppressed mutiny against the open despotism of a family federation', and to plead for 'the emancipation of the editorial department from the Machine Room'. Brave words about Cowen's son, but perhaps Garvin toned them down in the copy he gave Cowen. That was often his intention, less often his practice.

# I

In Garvin's early days in Newcastle his closest friend was John Lavery, a man of his own age, an Irishman and – it almost goes without saying – a follower of Parnell. Just before Lent began in 1893 Garvin was best man at Lavery's wedding. Lavery's mother-in-law, 'that porcupine in petticoats' as Garvin pictured her, thought herself a cut above her daughter's husband and his friends, but she did her social duty and a month after the wedding she gave a party to which she invited Garvin. There, on 15 March, he first saw Christina Wilson, a dark-haired Irish beauty with a singing voice of great quality and clarity which captivated him as completely as did her sparkling eyes and trim figure – tiny by comparison with his six foot. He was, as he put it in verses written for a newspaper competition:

> A pale and lanky figure, who would like his moustache bigger –
>     Which is more than he can truly say about his gloves and boots;
> With good-humoured, awkward ways; and a large and earnest gaze,
>     That seems to find it very hard to trace things to their roots.
>
> He is fond of cats and tea; you'd be quite surprised to see
>     Upon how many matters he's exactly of your mind
> For he doesn't like to differ – but *when* he does, a stiffer
>     Stickler for his own opinion it is very hard to find.
>
> For on hobbies literary or the state of Tipperary,
>     If you once can get the steam up – don't he go a startling pace!
> Strange mosaic of quotation, Irish rhetoric, and information –
>     With an awkward knack of fitting dates and figures to his case.

That night Garvin promised himself, 'By the grace of God that is the woman I shall marry.' It was in a double sense love at first sight. Jim had no sisters and, as far as we know, had had no real friendships with girls. His school, his work, his political life had all thrown him exclusively among men. Now, just before his twenty-fifth birthday, there came an impulsive and total surrender followed by an impetuous wooing. Eight days later Garvin went down on one knee in the street with an Irishman's characteristic grand gesture, told her of his love, and asked if she could return it. 'Well, Jim, I don't mind trying,' she said. On Good Friday evening at Tynemouth 'with the moonlight on the sea you began to feel you could love me', he reminded her in one of the torrent of ardent, tumultuous letters in which in those early days – and later when they were parted – he allowed his love and his desire to fall headlong from his pen, 'tossing off sheets like snowflakes'. Their life together was to be lived on breathtaking heights and in deep depressions, but it was a true marriage.

Garvin, emotionally adolescent, was intellectually full-grown, the rising star of Newcastle's leading paper, a polymath with a head full of history and poetry. 'There is an old poet called John Donne,'[1] he told Tina and quoted a verse, adding: 'I do twenty times a day "catch you in some close corner of my brain" and kiss you and press you a thousand times; but it doesn't do for me long; my passion is stronger than my imagination.' A girl barely turned seventeen in her first job after leaving convent school was unlikely to have heard of Donne. To be wooed with such erudition was flattering, but a trifle overwhelming. Tina, however, was capable of holding her own. In childhood she had always been in escapades. On the day of her first communion she was discovered in her white frock selling rhubarb from the garden in the street. A daughter recalled that she had 'the grave charm and wildness of the Celt'.

So had Jim, and with it a monarchical temperament and the ideas of his time on man and wife. He was still a practising Catholic, but resented the interference of priests. He told Tina how he had interfered in a row between the newly married Laverys:

If you went to priests and paid more attention to them than me – as Mrs. Lavery has done with Johnnie – I should go mad. I want you to promise never to do it . . . You would have laughed if you could have heard me preaching at her last night and seen me thump the table and stride about the room, laying down the law, and Johnnie delighted and crying hear! hear! to every word I said. Thank God, darling, that you have a stronger mind that Mrs. Lavery and trust to my honour and knowledge more than she has done to his.

Next Sunday Jim met Tina's father coming out of his office: 'Told him that you and I were thinking of being married in August twelvemonth. He laughed, and said "All right, my boy, if you can square the old lady." There's a model father.'

## II

August twelvemonth proved to be October twelvemonth. Early in the New Year Michael Garvin was found to be suffering from tuberculosis. The doctors told him that his life would be in danger if he stayed in England, and it was decided that he should emigrate to South Africa. Jim went with Michael to Southampton. 'It nearly burst our hearts as the train steamed out to see poor little mother led away blinded with crying.' The brothers lunched together on board the *Tartar*.

> I was the very last visitor to quit the ship, and then Michael ran up by the upper deck and I jumped upon a box on the top deck of the tender ... I waited and waited until he became a mere speck, and watched again until I could see him no more.'

Jim came back to seek consolation in Tina's arms. Seven years later he gently chided her for forgetting that most precious anniversary.

> How could you forget about March 9th. [1894]? It is the thought of that heavenly evening (there were two but upon the first I had stopped at the gate of Paradise and had not dared to throw them open once and for all ...) We sat in the large armchair and first you were in my arms, I wooing you with the tender grace you remember your lover using when he held and nursed you on his knees, and then you sat in it and I was in your lap for a time like a dear big baby, but at last slipped down and knelt before you, and then in a moment of passion all the world disappeared.

Tina and Jim must, one imagines, have been planning to set up house on their own, but Michael's catastrophe meant that Jim would have to support his mother unaided and provide a home for her as well as for his wife. It could only be done by sharing a house. Michael's illness also involved putting off the wedding. Tina, as a minor, needed her father's consent. Robert Wilson, a superintendent of police, was a hard-headed Ulster Catholic. He probably thought Jim feckless and his economic prospects dubious. The Wilsons certainly thought his health precarious. They probably feared that he would contract tuberculosis − the killer disease which 'ran in families'. Friends were as usual Job's comforters. One put her oar in before Michael was out of the country. 'Darling, I now speak seriously,' Jim wrote to Tina. 'Mrs. Bryson is wrong. I am very strong naturally, but I have not always taken the care of myself that I should, and that I pledge my word to do in the future for the sake of those I love.'

It is difficult to know how serious the Wilsons' opposition was. Garvin's daughter Katharine records that, when her father married, he took nothing from them except Tina's wedding dress. One does not know how near the literal truth this was, but certainly Garvin was a proud man who would hate to be beholden or patronised. After he went to London the only member of his wife's family with whom he kept close contact was a younger sister who was a great favourite with all the Garvins. On the other hand there was no breach. Robert Wilson gave Garvin cigars and lent him money when he was hard pressed in his early years in London. Garvin in return advised Wilson about his pension problems.

## III

Jim and Tina loved the countryside. At first she was the more knowledgeable. There had been no one to teach Jim the names of plants and birds and flowers. His eye had been for the broad sweep of landscape. On boyish walks up Bidstone Hill in the Wirral he could see the Great Orme's Head and the Welsh mountains behind. Northwards Black Combe and the great hills of the Lakes were sometimes visible. That was the kind of view Garvin loved.

Most of Garvin's twenty-mile walks were taken 'in the joy of the solitude that is accepted', often with George Meredith in one pocket and Stephen Phillips in the other. Sometimes, however, he had Tina or a journalist friend, Edwin Wilcox, for a companion. It was from Tina, I think, that he learnt to look more closely at what was beneath his feet or just above his head and to give names to what he saw. 'By Denton Burn celendine, daisies, coltsfoot, dandelions, much furze in bloom ... I am beginning to distinguish one bird from another and was especially pleased to recognise so well the yellow bunting. Flocks of them were in great abundance.'

On one of these walks in 1894 Jim passed a house at Benwell on the edge of open country but within reach of the centre of Newcastle. Then and there he decided that it should be his home. He and Tina were married on 18 October, spent a four-day honeymoon in Harrogate, and then settled down with his mother at 2 St James's Road, West Turnpike, Benwell.

A year later, on 12 October, Tina gave birth to a boy. They called him Roland Gerard. Roland recalled the impulse which had made Jim at his confirmation add Louis to his baptismal name — father and son both bore Crusading names. Gerard came from the hero of Charles Reade's novel *The Cloister and the Hearth*, the first book that Jim lent Tina. Two years later a daughter was born. They called her Viola after Francis Thompson's poem, 'The Making of Viola', and after Alice Meynell's daughter Viola, for whom the poem had been written.

Years later Tina told how, when her son was a toddler, he came running in one day with news of a wonderful white river he had made. While the milkman was in the house he had turned on the tap and drained the milk churn. It took all the money they had to make good the flood damage — a comic loss, but tragic too, so close to the margin did they live. Scenes such as this pressed hard on Jim's mind as, with Tina again pregnant, he faced the problem of their future.

I

Garvin was fond of telling young journalists that they should stay in the provinces until they were thirty. He had, and so should they. He did not tell them that it was against his will. At twenty-five he was hungry for Fleet Street; by thirty he was desperate. The *Newcastle Daily Chronicle*, good paper though it was, was read only in Durham and Northumberland. There could be no permanent satisfaction on it for a man who wanted to be read by the men who ruled Britain.

That was why on the day after he first met Christina Wilson he answered an advertisement for an assistant editor for a new London paper. The paper was not named, but it was T.P. O'Connor's *Sun*. He heard nothing for four months. Then he was asked if he would like to be its leader-writer. If so, he should sent cuttings of his work, including his report of Parnell's funeral, and come for interview. He did, and was offered the job at five guineas a week. 'T.P.' was one of the best informed political journalists of his time, a great populariser of literature, and an Irish Nationalist MP. Garvin was greatly tempted, but reluctantly turned the offer down. He could not support his wife, his mother and his child on the money offered.

In October 1893 he paid his second visit to Ireland. He had a splendid week in Dublin where life was 'so much warmer than in England and the people so much cleverer and more friendly'. He met Yeats and Lionel Johnson as well as all the principal Nationalist leaders. 'Everybody is making a great deal of me,' he boasted. He was not deceiving himself, at least not outrageously, about the impression he was making. In 1896 he was asked to become the *Irish Independent*'s London correspondent. His 'copy' was not to be 'added to or altered' in Dublin, but the pay was only half what he needed. As John Redmond explained, the directors wanted to put Garvin in charge 'but without disturbing Mr. O'Kelly, M.P., who is nominally chief in command there but who does not write a London Letter'. The attempt to get Garvin on the cheap was to cost the Nationalists dear. Had he accepted Redmond's offer he would have found himself in a Fleet Street illuminated by a remarkable group of radical journalists. He seemed destined to become one of them. His opinions were so variegated — he was not Cowen's disciple for nothing — that, whichever party he joined, he would find himself both at home and rebellious. In that sense his choice did not matter. In another, it was decisive. For better or for worse Garvin's rejection of the *Irish Independent*'s offer ended his 'Jacobinical and Fenian youth'.

## II

It was as a contributor to a monthly review that Garvin first became known outside Tyneside and Irish Nationalist circles. Today, listening to the radio, watching television or wading through outsize Sunday papers has fatally eaten into the time which used to be devoted to reading the monthlies. In the eighteen-nineties, however, they really counted. They were found in clubs, senior common rooms, college libraries and country houses; in Whitehall and in Downing Street. They were read by politicians, scholars, bankers and members of the learned professions. Their editors and assistant editors were people of note — a list which includes Sidney Smith, Jeffrey, Lockhart, Bentham, George Eliot and John Morley demands respect. Their contributors wrote with authority on very varied subjects. The daily newspapers carried surveys of their principal contents, and often found in their articles a topic for a leader.

In November 1894 a new editor took over the *Fortnightly Review*. W. L. Courtney, 'tall, dark, handsome in the heavy dragoon manner', was at the beginning of a second career. He had been a philosophy tutor at New College until he was forty. Then he astonished Oxford by joining the *Daily Telegraph*. 'It wasn't only the fact. It was the paper! In Oxford we scarcely knew of the *Telegraph*.' Joining *The Times*, the *Daily News* or the *Manchester Guardian* would have been understandable. 'But the *Daily Telegraph*!' He was a good journalist but he had still to prove himself as an editor.

Each week about twenty to thirty articles intended for the *Fortnightly* came to the desk of Janet Hogarth, supervisor of women clerks at the Bank of England. She acted as 'reader' for Courtney, who had been her tutor at Oxford and was later to become her husband. In April 1895 there was one on 'The Future of Irish Politics' by a man called J. Louis Garvin of whom she had never heard. It fascinated her. She scribbled a note to Courtney, 'You had better look at this at once. It is out of the common.' Courtney decided to give it pride of place. Garvin's article was topical, bold and novel in its insights and judgements. It was sure to be talked about. 'I shan't give him his name,' Courtney said, 'he can't expect it this time. I shall let people think it is by some person of high authority.' They did. It was widely quoted. Garvin had found an outlet where he would be read by the people he most wanted to influence. Courtney had discovered a young, very promising, contributor. For both men it was a break-through.

It was eighteen months since the defeat of the second Home Rule Bill. A general election was imminent. Garvin dismissed the Liberal claim that chivalrous Mr Gladstone had set out to rescue captive Ireland as 'a Perseus and Andromeda version eminently fit for a stained glass window, but wholly superfluous' and indeed 'a sheer perversion of the facts'. Garvin's first electioneering had been in 1885 when the Irish voted Tory. He speculated that just conceivably this might happen again. After all, the Tories needed Irish Catholic votes to help maintain Church schools. Might they not offer Ireland in return 'something that would be Home Rule' from a different recipe than Gladstone's? They were, he argued, 'beyond question the party best able to deal with the problem'. Garvin's mind was on the move.

Courtney must have wondered whether his new contributor would turn out to be a single-subject man. Garvin did not leave him long in doubt. The Independent Labour Party, founded only two years before, held its annual conference at Newcastle. Garvin turned his experience at the press table into an article for the *Fortnightly*. He called it 'A Party with a Future'. Unfortunately, no sooner had he written it than the ILP failed to win a single seat in the general election. Garvin revised his article, analysing the election results to show that the party with no present was a party with a future. He took into account not only the votes polled, but the youth of the voters. The title stood. The Labour Party, Garvin wrote (it is nearer to his meaning to drop the adjective Independent),

is a party which unquestionably commands the emotional force of its adherents as no political movement in Great Britain has done since Chartism, and which, in the opinion of experienced observers ... may ultimately play all the part which Chartism would unquestionably have played in politics under a democratic franchise.

For 'experienced observers', read J. L. Garvin, a perceptive young man.

**III**

Garvin knew Courtney only through the post. Much warmer was his relation to Wilfrid and Alice Meynell, the friendliest and most generous of hosts whose home was the centre of a literary circle remarkably free from backbiting. In 1893 Michael Garvin, 'my twin in taste' as Jim described him, had borrowed a copy of *Poems* by Francis Thompson. While Jim was struggling at home to write a leader about the Russo-German commercial treaty, Michael insisted on declaiming 'The Hound of Heaven'. Jim was irritated and at first reacted against the poem as well as the reading, although he had loved 'The Making of Viola' when he had found it in a magazine the year before. 'Then I opened the book myself and read it right through. Then I began at the first page again and went on to the last ... The poems began to swarm in my head like bees.' He wrote an unsigned review in the *Newcastle Chronicle*. A letter of thanks came from Wilfrid Meynell, inviting him to stay, and another from the poet himself who copied out Garvin's review and kept it among his very few cherished possessions.

From 1894 Jim became a regular guest whenever he could get away from Newcastle, often arriving with a present of girdle cakes and mushrooms from Tina. Soon he was adopted into the Meynells' family circle, but it was not until 1897 that he first met Francis Thompson face to face. He reported to Tina:

> I scarcely know how I can give you any idea of this extraordinary man — a very red and hairy face in a middle-sized man with rather broad shoulders and rather thin legs. Black hair and beard somewhat untrimmed, ambushing a flaming countenance from which two blue and bloodshot eyes look. He had been taking opium and was scarcely in a fit state to be in society. He smiled much, however, and said very little and on the whole I like him. A strange, strange creature.

Acquaintance with Francis Thompson, the junkie whom the Meynells had rescued, did not diminish Garvin's admiration for Francis Thompson the poet.

Forty-seven Palace Court, Kensington, was a house in which Jim Garvin, still a shy, stammering solitary, felt at home. He went shopping with teenage Monny; wrote letters in pencil because 'as Palace Court is a habitation of queer journalists there is only one pen and my host is using it'; and borrowed a white tie to go to his first 'swell dinner

party'. 'When in Palace Court I talks; when outside I ride on omni-
buses,' he told Tina. 'It is, as always, very distinguished and incon-
venient, very quiet and thoroughly happy.'

Jim got to love his hostess as much as he already admired her poetry.
He was captivated by her grace of figure and her long firm rhythm in
walking. Her voice was 'a musical contralto that seemed full of kindness
and sorrow. Her dark, unchanging eyes missed nothing ... not the
difference between the curve of one eyelid and another.' His affection
was returned. On her deathbed she sent him a message to say that his
friendship had been one of the happinesses of her life. Wilfred Meynell
wrote a few days later:

> One of the last things she said, 'with one of her contrite smiles',
> was 'When I was a little girl I wanted to be buried in Westminster
> Abbey.' I trust she knows that you have given her 'honours of
> mortality' exceeding even that. Though I have read it [Garvin's
> obituary] only twice, I know it in my heart (in the real meaning of
> words) and a great deal of it by lip.

At this time Garvin was uncertain whether poetry or politics would
rule his life. To the Meynells it was literature that mattered. They planned to introduce him to Coventry Patmore whose *Angel in the House*
was often on his tongue, but left it too long. Instead of a meeting
Garvin wrote an appreciation which appeared in the *Fortnightly* three
months after Patmore's death. When Alice Meynell read it she wrote,
'Nothing has given me so much consolation and happiness since death
closed the dearest friendship of my life.' Another taste they shared was
for George Meredith's poetry. The Meynells took him to visit Meredith
at Box Hill in 1896, and Alice persuaded Jim to write a major article
about him. He took his time but finally sent it off to Courtney at the
beginning of 1899. It was, I think, the only article by Garvin that
Courtney ever rejected. He returned it with a long letter written with all
the care with which in his Oxford days he must have dissected a promising undergraduate's slightly off-course essay.

> I honestly believe that you have got hold of the right idea in deal-
> ing with Meredith's poetry and that the substance of your criticism
> is both sound and just. On the other hand, since I am going to deal
> quite frankly with you, there is much that I quarrel with in your
> style. There is no reason in writing about Meredith to adopt more
> than Meredithian complexity, quite the reverse.

He ended with a shrewd guess: 'I wonder if you have been reading Mrs. Meynell lately; she is a bad model to imitate.'


**IV**


Garvin's close friendship with the Meynells had whetted his appetite for literary London and given him a foothold in it. There was not, however, a sufficient living to be got in that way. He had hoped that Wilfred would be able to find him an opening on a London paper; but, when he discussed the possibility with his host, he discovered that the world of political journalism was quite outside Meynell's influence. In 1898 he made a determined effort to force his way in. Beerbohm Tree, most successful of actor managers, and Harold Large, Frank Benson's manager, offered to help. Tree promised to get him interviews with Massingham of the *Daily Chronicle*, Cook of the *Daily News* and Douglas Straight of the *Pall Mall Gazette*. The promise was not kept. Garvin persisted. Tree wired that the letters would be ready if he called at the theatre that night. Garvin called. There were no letters. In the end Garvin managed to see Cook, but the interview, though friendly, was fruitless. Large promised to put him in touch with the *Illustrated London News*, but forgot to do so. At the end of a frustrating fortnight Garvin concluded that nothing but his own efforts and his *Fortnightly* work would be of any use to him.

He had not long to wait. He had already sent Courtney another trade union article. He followed it up with an Irish one and then with one on Lord Rosebery. Courtney liked 'The Disraeli of Liberalism' so much that he wrote another long letter in his tutorial manner.

I wonder if you are better as a literary or political critic. I am inclined to think that your literary skill applied to political questions and politicians is more effective than your purely literary criticism ... The whole point of my letter is that I should value it very much if you would write as often as you thought fit political articles for me under your own name.

Three days later Courtney wrote again. 'Please tell me when you come to London. Would you care to become a candidate for a vacant leader-writer's place on the *Daily Telegraph*?'

# BOOK TWO: EMPIRE DAY IN FLEET STREET, 1899-1906

---

'As an augur Calchas had no rival in the camp.'

Homer, *Iliad* I. v. 69

I

And so one July day in 1899 Jim Garvin waited in a room full of green plush furniture for an interview with the editor of the *Daily Telegraph*.

Presently the door opened and Sir Edward Lawson appeared — keen, jolly, slightly vulgar and entirely affable — to look at him 'Punch' to the life as Wilfrid said. I had been very nervous, but when he appeared I was as cool as a cucumber and full of cheek. He put me at my ease in the kindest way in the world. 'Now, Mr. Garvin, tell me all about yourself.' 'Thirty-one,' I began, 'wife, two children, mother; education irregular but extensive' — so it went on until he had the history.

I saw in a second or two that there was going to be little doubt about the issue.

Then it was his turn and he used it to admiration. 'Now,' he said, 'I am going to tell you what I think of you, your good points and your faults.' He did. The shrewd, plain old boy put his finger on my weaknesses — over-elaboration, for instance — with delightful acuteness and geniality.

Garvin left the office with an offer of £600 a year for five years plus an annual bonus. The parting with Cowen was hard. Perhaps Garvin hoped that he would match Lawson's offer or at least raise his salary. At any rate when Cowen's letter came without any counter-offer, Garvin 'broke down and cried like a child, downstairs by myself after midnight, shouting at the alarmed family to go away when they tried to interfere'. But of course he took the job. It was, as Wilfrid Meynell told him, 'a chance against the world'.

It was some time before Garvin felt certain that he had done the right thing. When he heard that Cowen was ill, he wrote, but did not post, a letter full of wistful nostalgia: 'Of course I can write what the *Telegraph* wants, but it doesn't want what appeals above all to you and me. We ought never to have met or never parted.' And he went on to weave a fantasy of what he would do if he had a thousand pounds --

leave the *Telegraph*, provide for his family and 'tramp about the Continent for a year like a poor student, writing by the way, learn Russian and return to write for the *Newcastle Chronicle*, the *Daily News* and the *Fortnightly Review*'. Six months after Garvin left Newcastle, Cowen died. Garvin was on his own.

## II

Edward Lawson, the governing proprietor and editor-in-chief of the *Daily Telegraph*, had been with the paper virtually all his working life. So had John Le Sage, his right-hand man. The paper was their creation, named when the telegraph was new. It was full of news, as it still is, and abundant enterprise. It sent H. M. Stanley to "darkest Africa" and reaped the largest circulation in the world.

In 1899 *The Times*, though the Sick Man of Fleet Street since the Piggott forgeries, was still the paper of the Establishment, but the *Telegraph* spoke for the middle-class voters who kept the Establishment in power. It shared their energy, their confidence, their conviction of an imperial destiny, and reconciled their ambition with righteousness by the weight of the White Man's Burden. But the *Telegraph* was now forty-five years old, not only middle-class but middle-aged. The pace was now set by the three-year-old *Daily Mail*. In comparison the *Telegraph* was old-fashioned, especially in the leader columns. Writing leaders for Lawson confirmed Garvin in the prolixity and pontification that came only too naturally to him.

The *Telegraph* did, however, give him something that the *Newcastle Daily Chronicle* could not provide. From the Reporters' Gallery in the House of Commons he frequently observed at first hand the politicians whom he was soon to get to know personally. There was another more important benefit. In Newcastle he had stood out head and shoulders above the rather colourless men who were his colleagues. On the *Telegraph* his friends were his rivals. Their ability matched his own and their background gave them a poise which he lacked. He learnt to hold his own at the top end of the most competitive occupation in the world. His work had to stand comparison with that of his fellow leader-writers, Iwan Müller and J. B. Firth, both Oxford men with firsts in Greats. Garvin was already deeply concerned with foreign affairs. His work in this field would be scrutinised by E. J. Dillon, the remarkable Irishman who spoke twenty-six languages and had recently exposed the Armenian massacres by going underground, disguised sometimes as a Turkish woman, at others as a Kurdish chief.

Garvin's work was more humdrum. During the 'khaki election' in 1900 Le Sage had to serve two masters and found it troublesome. So, accordingly, did Garvin. 'Mr. Harry', Lawson's son, was standing as a Radical for Bethnal Green; his father was speaking at Tory meetings. Le Sage performed a balancing act, telling Garvin to say 'that the Government must be returned by an overwhelming majority – but that the Opposition were Britons after all'. He found 'the silliness of this kind of thing more disgusting than its dishonesty'.

Such fits of exasperation alternated with spells of elation when Garvin knew he was writing well. He had, too, a genuine affection for Le Sage. For his part Le Sage recognised in Garvin a good all-rounder whom he could trust to make a readable story out of a requiem mass for Lord Russell of Killowen, to write a holiday leader on a day at the seaside, or to handle with insight the siege of the European legations in Peking. At the same time Le Sage suffered from Garvin's slowness in writing and procrastination in getting down to work: 'Would you be good enough to finish your leaders as early as possible?' he wrote one day. 'Last night we were late at Press. The sub-editor leaves me a note that your copy was not complete until 1.20. As a rule we cannot take leader copy later than 12 o'clock at latest.' Garvin was conscious of his weakness, but could not cure it. Part of the trouble was his love for 'an open sea and all canvas spread'.

Lawson, like Cowen, had taken a liking to Garvin. Garvin responded, but with reservations. He was no longer the unformed youngster whom Cowen had moulded, but a man with a mind of his own, who found Lawson's precise instructions irksome. In his *Telegraph* work Garvin was too often just 'His Master's Voice'. Thus, when Lawson ordered a leader on Queen Victoria's birthday 'in plain, terse, vigorous, loyal and most genial words', he did not leave it at that but elaborated:

It should begin with some such phrase as that today all her loving subjects are celebrating her 81st birthday amidst and after circumstances than which none have been so momentous during her long reign. Then you might mark the impressive way in which this great struggle not yet finished connects itself with the marvellous development of Empire which the Queen has witnessed.

And so Lawson went on, ending with the afterthought 'somewhere in the article Ireland should come in and, if you please, Mafeking'. At the foot of the letter Garvin pencilled this comment:

At the same time   (plain, terse, vigorous     )   H'm
                   (loyal, genial, and impressive)
     Let's try.

Eight months later the Queen lay dying. Garvin wrote the obituary leader but, as he told his wife:

> All pleasure in what I thought was a magnificent piece of work is gone now because the old boy and Harry and Courtney and Müller and Le Sage have tampered with the article, and although of course all of it remains mine but a sentence here and there, these interpolations utterly different from my style and thought disgust me. However it can't be helped. The old man sitting in evening dress with his big, bald, polished, fine head like the dome of St. Paul's was enraptured with the leader and said no matter how long I wrote I never would nor could do anything better. Then he showed me with the simplest, nicest old vanity, chuckling and genial, that made you want to hug him, how in the closing sentence he had improved even on me.

Praise is sweet, and in general Garvin found it compensated for the close supervision he received when he was writing for Lawson himself. For the most part the instructions he received hurt his pride rather than his conscience.

## III

We owe these close-ups of Garvin's early days on the *Telegraph* to a family misfortune which separated Jim from Tina for many months. They had rented a house in Elsham Road, Kensington. There their third child was born and christened Una after the Faerie Queen. By that time, however, Viola, aged two, had contracted a tubercular knee as a result, it was thought, of falling off her brother's rocking horse. Her parents blamed themselves as parents will. For Viola's sake Tina took the children first to Deal and then to Cornwall. Jim's letters to her at this time not only show how he settled in to the *Telegraph* office, but enable us to come close to their family life as their marriage completed its first seven years. In page after page Jim poured out his passionate desire. He sent Tina 'a little breviary', telling her, you must be very careful of its privacy and perhaps you ought to put it in the fire when you have learned all the terms by heart ... You see it is a third sphere of love as much beyond the level of mere marriage as that is beyond the plane of just courtship. If you do not want to be my bride in any of those ways, let them be at once dismissed ... your absolutely spontaneous and equal consent and wish are always the first essential of my own perfect felicity with you.

Of course there were rows from time to time. When roundabout gossip told Catherine Garvin what her daughter-in-law thought of her, she complained. Jim wrote to Tina:

Of course, I told Mother that she was herself to blame; but now, my dearest love, do you not think you are? For God's sake end it, and if you cannot say things good and kind of the mother I love ... say nothing either to others or to me.

Another recurrent source of worry was the letters from South Africa that made Jim feel that he might have to support his brother. Garvin had come to London with high financial expectations, which were in the end to be justified, but at the beginning he was often near shipwreck. 'When the rates and gas are paid and the tradesmen's books settled,' he told Tina, 'there will not be five pounds left to begin the month with, so that there is the humiliation of being unable to pay the moiety of the doctor's bill Watts asked for.' A fortnight later things were worse:

They sent us a summons about the rates but Mother went about till she found the collector's house and settled it somehow so that she had not to pay the cost of the summons. There is not a pound in the house over the gas bill and the thirty shillings for you so I am afraid we must borrow again.

Misfortune seemed to dog him. When he took the house in Elsham Road the estate agent had made difficulties because he could not give a banker's reference, having no bank account. Now, when the rent became due, he ran into similar trouble. He counted on using the money from a *National Review* article, but the cheque was marked 'A/C payee only', and Garvin had the humiliation, as he felt it, of asking the editor to alter it. Garvin was driven to petty economies foreign to his nature. He gave up *The Times* and the *Westminster Gazette* and walked five miles home when he missed the last train on the 'twopenny tube' instead of taking a cab.

When he got home it was, as often as not, to a cheerless house. He had to do the best he could with what his mother left out for him — a tin of pilchards, for instance:

> I went down to the kitchen, where the beetles were leading high life below stairs, to get the tin-opener ... After a quarter of an hour hammering, wrenching and twisting which gave mother the dim impression in her semi-slumbers that the neighbours were slamming their doors very late at night, I did not exactly lift off the lid but I made ragged rifts in it and through these I fairly gouged out my supper ... tasted incredibly good ... might have been fished by forlorn fishermen out of Keats' perilous seas and sold to princes.

Jim could make an Irishman's good story out of such incidents and no doubt Tina applied an Irish wife's diminishing glass to his sufferings, but in truth irregular hours, overwork, scratch meals and too many cigars (his addiction was already strong) took their toll. At the office old Goodman, a sub-editor 'always paternally kind' to Garvin, would send out for a glass of brandy for him, while at home Garvin sometimes drove himself to take the hateful remedy of Gregory's powder.

Outside the *Telegraph* office Garvin's contacts were still mainly with people he met at the Meynells or through Michael MacDonagh, who was secretary of the Irish Literary Society. In December 1899 Garvin moved the vote of thanks to Charles Russell for his paper on Curran:

> What I said was very good indeed but the delivery was nervous, halting and constrained. Yeats replied in a tone of suppressed temper and protested that Irishmen must abjure rhetoric and that I was preaching practically the devil's doctrine. I replied in a sentence ... that Irishmen in their reaction against rhetoric should not deprive their work of the very quality of their temperament.

Both Yeats and Garvin seem to have forgotten the speaker of the evening in their private set-to. A year later it was Garvin's turn to read a paper on Irish journalism which was printed in the *Irish Literary Gazette*.

**IV**

Strangers and friends alike thought Garvin's first year in London a striking success. He hid from them the insecurity and the black moods of religious despair that make his notebook poignant reading:

> It was ... turning up towards Westminster with a heart nearly bursting, and almost in the shadow of the Victoria Tower, that the hideous unfeeling apathy which had lain upon the spirit ... was broken at last as if something had given way within me, and I knew ... that the loss even of the old conviction of immortality does not mean the forfeiture of the divine sense of things, but gives the last tremendous sense of mystery and leads the soul, prostrate, humble, aware of its own weakness and loneliness at last, to pray for nothing but that it may walk in the presence of God through this life, asking nothing but his presence here, nor questioning him in anything upon the hereafter. Whether I shall ever go beyond this I do not know.

But only a day later he wrote:

> Again the dark time, one of the darkest of my life and the lowest point of spiritual, mental and therefore of literary disability I have reached since the autumn of 1895. This is the reality of what external observers regard as success.

There follows a note on casualties in the Peninsular War and then in penetrating analysis:

> Trying to pray again, the second prayer after many months prayer-less. Again the soul flows out into the old forms of words, while the cold mind questions how much it believes or whether it believes anything – devotion, scepticism, the struggle of the two. The eye for copy all the while, the revolt against the consequences of the eye for copy, and the neat perception that this too has been registered and must be written down.

## I

In Newcastle, though Garvin was awake to German ambitions, he had considered that Russia in Asia and France in Africa were a greater danger to British interests than Germany was. In London in the first fortnight of December 1899 he recalculated the odds. The Kaiser had been in England. Chamberlain was confident that he had achieved a political understanding. 'The natural alliance is between ourselves and the great German Empire,' he said, insisting that 'the character of the Teutonic race differs very slightly indeed from the character of the Anglo-Saxon'. He expected that the German Chancellor would back him up. Instead Bülow announced that the German navy would be doubled. In future, Germany would be 'the hammer and not the anvil'. Garvin copied extracts into his notebook, adding: 'Von Bülow lied of course when he said that Germany had no other object in the world than to defend herself against an attack; he laboured the protest too much for the nations to feel easy about it.'

Certainly Garvin did not. When he was dealing with this incident in his *Life of Joseph Chamberlain* he inserted one of his rare covert autobiographical allusions:

> From that moment in the conviction of a new and growing school of English thinkers — Chamberlain even yet was unwilling to belong to them — the future peril was foreshadowed; and the necessity of settling our differences with France and Russia made only too plain.

Only too plain, that is, to Garvin, but not to Edward Lawson. Garvin was not allowed to make the point editorially in the *Telegraph* — it was his one serious and recurring disagreement with the paper. It might well have led to his resignation if he had not found a safety valve in the *Fortnightly*.

At first Garvin had been a little over-awed by Courtney, eighteen years his senior and 'a swell'. Before long, however, Garvin felt, quite rightly, that 'Courtney is getting to cotton to me rather affectionately'. Moreover in the field of foreign affairs what was plain to Garvin proved to be plain also to Courtney. Garvin wrote on 'The Crux in Foreign Policy' in the July *Fortnightly*. As a result Leo Maxse asked him to write for his *National Review*. In October Garvin drew attention in the *National* to 'The German Danger in the East' and in the *Fortnightly* provided the answer: 'Why not an understanding with Russia?' From this time on Garvin had at his disposal two monthly reviews anxious to publish whatever he sent them.

'The Crux in Foreign Policy' proved to be the first of a continuous series which ran in the *Fortnightly* from July 1900 to March 1911. They dealt with home as well as foreign politics and were much talked about because Garvin's words were memorable. People chuckled when they read about 'the extravagant hypothesis or extraordinary fact that twenty per cent of the governing genius of the country should exist within the Prime Minister's immediate family circle'. In November Courtney decided that Garvin's articles ought to be signed in order to give them cumulative impact. It would have to be a pseudonym, partly because of the *Telegraph* and partly because Garvin was a political nobody.

'Do you mind taking the name of Calchas?': Courtney asked. The Homeric reference was plain:

> As an augur Calchas had no rival in the camp. Past, present and future had no secrets from him; and it was his second sight, a gift he owed to Apollo, that had guided the Achaean fleet to Ilium ... 'Nine is the number of years that we shall have to fight at Troy, in the tenth its broad streets will be ours.' That is what Calchas prophesied.

For Troy, read Germany.

## II

Here, then, is the world as Calchas saw it at the turn of the century, a world in which the British Empire, the German Empire and the United States struggled for supremacy. The victor would have to settle with Russia, but that would be 'at a date which need not interest contemporary speculation'. Britain had long overshadowed other nations, but it could not expect to maintain that ascendancy, nor indeed should that be its object. World leadership would lie with the United States

destined to the inevitable attainment of a supremacy in production as overwhelming as Niagara ... She has infinitely more
material, more labour, more mechanical inventiveness, more transport and shipping facilities, more means for reducing the cost of
manufacture to a lower point than can be possible anywhere else in
the world.

Calchas looked benevolently on the American navy at a time when
most Englishmen did not — relations between the two countries had
recently been very strained. It did not worry him that pre-eminence
in trade and sea-power would inevitably pass to 'the other branch of
the Anglo-Saxon race'.

But would Britain or Germany take second place? Although Garvin
admired Germany, he looked at German politics with a realistic eye
and with an Englishman's patriotic instincts. He saw Germany 'stretch-
ing out her hand to the trident, avid for Empire, believing that colonies
belong as of right to those who can fill them, and markets to those
who can excel'. She had hoped to secure South Africa and the Philip-
pines and to have colonies in South America where her emigrants
could settle under the German flag. 'It was the Anglo-Saxons that
blocked the way everywhere, and it is against that race, but obviously
against the more assailable branch of it, that the naval and commercial
policy of the German Empire is directed.' Garvin visited Germany in
1900 and came back horrified at the extent to which Anglophobia had
'become a fixed idea in the land of fixed ideas, and something which
craves to show itself in acts'.

The danger, Calchas thought, was a Continental System, like Napoleon's, which would unite Europe against the 'Anglo-Saxons'. In 1900
it was not so improbable as it later seemed. His worry was that a breach
between Britain and France or Russia would drive both these Powers
into the arms of Germany:

Her industry would be supreme within the Continental blockade;
and the military force of Russia, Germany, and France together
might hope to redress on land the worst chance at sea and to find
their account in a new partition of Asia from which the English
flag would have disappeared ... Our sailors and too many of our
statesmen regard a triumphant conflict with the fleets of the Dual
Alliance [France and Russia] as the ultimate business and destiny
of the British navy ... We leave Germany out of the reckoning.
She will be very much in the reckoning.

Calchas, therefore, investigated the prospects for an Anglo-Russian understanding in spite of the U turn involved.

If there is again to be a movement like the Reformation or the French Revolution which would transform the spirit of the world, we should expect the revolution to break from this immense, un-formed, obviously ardent [Russian] people, rather than from any of the countries within the more stereotyped system of modern civilisation.

That was far from being the orthodox Marxist expectation in 1901, but it was what Calchas foresaw and what came to pass.

He based his argument partly on the Russian character and partly on the way in which the government's policy of industrialisation was being carried out. A landless proletariat was being driven by economic pressure to work in the new factories and to live, often in barracks, 'under conditions more effectively designed to promote a revolution than any which have ever prevailed in other countries'. These new factory workers, moreover, did not lose touch with their homes, but returned to infect the villages with the Socialism they had learned at work. The danger that threatened the Russian state came more from the workers than from the students with their old-fashioned Nihilism.

In the long run the industrial revolution might bring prosperity to the towns, but in the meantime it had brought disaster to the country-side: 'Disease rages in the track of hunger . . . Yet Russia's chief export is food, and famine would cease if she could afford to keep the corn which must be sold to pay the tax gatherer.' Of course the government view was that, once industry was developed, there would be capital enough to restore the land to fertility. Then the peasant would enjoy better prices, lower taxation and cheaper machinery. It sounds extra-ordinarily like the official propaganda put out thirty years later to justify Stalin's man-made famine. Some immediate relief, however, was possible, or so Calchas thought. The new railways could take half a million peasants a year from the exhausted lands of Russia to the virgin soil of Siberia.

'The virgin soil of Siberia.' Calchas returned time and again to Russian expansion in Asia. It was, he thought, so deeply misunderstood and so bitterly opposed in England that we ran the risk of throwing Russia into the hands of Germany. There was no reason of any sort why the Cossack adventurers should have been aware when they crossed 'the insignificant line of the Urals three centuries ago that they had thereupon begun to approach India and had entered upon a career of Russian aggrandisement'. It was inevitable that Russia should push on to the sea and to an ice-free port. She had now reached the end of the empty lands. Southwards lay China's densely packed millions. Russia's eastward expansion was complete.

There were still two possible lines of advance — south-westwards to Constantinople, and southwards to the Persian Gulf. Both involved a Russian confrontation with Germany. 'The Persian Gulf is the nearest outlet upon ocean of the region including Trans-Caucasia and Central Siberia which will be the centre of gravity of industrial Russia.' If Britain accepted Russia's presence on the Persian Gulf the whole Anglo-Russian controversy would be settled. 'Why not?' Calchas asked. Why not, indeed? In 1900 it was coal, not oil, that drove trains and powered ships.

## III

Garvin was very much the pioneer in 'the new and growing school of English thinkers' who saw in Bülow's Navy Bill the need for a diplomatic revolution. He had published the main lines of his diagnosis and prognosis in 1900. It was complete by the summer of 1902. In the following year 'Vigilans sed Aequus' took up the same theme in the *Spectator*. There is nothing to suggest that Garvin knew that 'Vigilans' was W. T. Arnold, who had for many years been C.P. Scott's right-hand man on the *Manchester Guardian*. It is even more unlikely that Arnold, a dying man in 1903, knew the identity of Calchas or that, if he had, the name would have meant anything to him. Had they met, however, he would have warmed to the young man from the provinces, newly come to London, who knew nobody, had no private sources of information, worked on his own and drew his own conclusions from a knowledge of German books, newspapers and public documents as wide and deep as Arnold's. Both men were in a position to measure the new Germany against the old to which they owed so much. Both found the contrast frightening.

If Garvin had a mentor on Bülow's Germany, it was George Saunders, the Berlin correspondent of *The Times*, whom he had never met. Saunders reported with meticulous care the aggressively anti-English sentiment on which the German government both had to reckon and on which it could rely when it wanted more warships and more colonies. Saunders' own view, though he could neither express it in his reports nor persuade *The Times* to advocate or even accept it, was that an Anglo-Russian understanding was both possible and desirable as an offset to German hostility. Quite independently Garvin had come to the same conclusion without, of course, knowing what Saunders had been writing privately to his chiefs. The same facts led both men to the same conclusions.

In 1943 Stanley Morison, the typographer who devised 'Times Roman' and became the 'grey eminence' of Printing House Square, was busy with the third volume of the history of *The Times*. He was anxious to determine Saunders' influence in England. He could trace his enemies, but not his friends. Morison turned to Garvin for help: 'My position, is yours, as you describe it, when you were in the company of Joseph Cowen.' Garvin told him how he used to read every word of Saunders — 'You could never admire him more than I do' — and how he decided in 1900 that war was coming:

A slow view forced reluctantly on my mind . . . Germany reckoned on the continuance of our old quarrels. I wanted to close them every one; to be free and with friends to grapple with our coming antagonist, the most formidable we had ever met.

The Entente with France came in 1904 and with Russia in 1907. Garvin's share in preparing public opinion was the first, and by no means the least, of his achievements. In later controversies he was aided by the accumulating strength of the Garvin legend. In these early years he could count only on the force of his arguments.

On a Friday evening in October 1902, after dinner at Gatti's and 'a boy and girl parting' from Tina on Charing Cross station, Garvin set off on the longest journey of his life, his only exploration of the Empire about which he wrote so much. He was away for the best part of five months on an assignment for which an editor today would allow at most a week or ten days. He went to cover the Durbar which the most magnificent of India's viceroys, Lord Curzon, held at Delhi in honour of the new King-Emperor. The India that Garvin saw as he travelled from Bombay to Calcutta, from the Khyber Pass to Rajputana was still ruled by the old benevolent despotism of the days before the Morley-Minto reforms. To judge from his exhaustive letters home — one was as long as a page and a half of the *Telegraph* — he met on equal terms only one Indian, a Parsee merchant on his way from Aden to Bombay.

The weekly 'Peninsular and Oriental Express' from Calais to Brindisi was 'a foreign train running over foreign ground [but also] a shuttle that goes backwards and forwards weaving the web of Empire'. The passengers were either ICS or army:

careless men, daredevil men, irritable men gnawing at the conviction of an unjustly disappointed career, one or two of the quick and gentle type of British officers, full of courtesy and manhood who is about the most admirable type of man in the world.

Such was Colonel Younghusband with whom Garvin later spent twenty-six hours in an Indian train.

I blurted out 'I wonder if you would mind telling me if you are the author of The Heart of the Continent.' 'No, my brother's book,' said he. 'Then yours is the one about the Phillippines,' I went on. He replied, 'That is so,' from which moment we talked hard for about ten hours. I asked every kind of question about the Indian army.

Garvin still found the social round exasperating and, I think, intimidating. 'You know what the smart crowd of conventional first-class passengers is,' he told Tina, 'the very embodiment of what I do most hate.' On the voyage he had to endure it, but in the Press Camp at

Delhi he found 'Every table is interesting and every table is gay. I never have known anywhere such a level of excellent talk all round one.' He discussed Meredith and Francis Thompson with a Foreign Department wife during the immensely long dinners — 'hors d'oeuvre, soup, fish, two or three side dishes of the quail and jelly type, joint, pudding, jelly coffee, fruit'. In his mess too was Valentine Chirol of *TheTimes* with whom in the future he was to have much to do.

Inevitably Garvin's mind went back to the Mutiny. He wrote to Tina:

> Here where I sit the guns thundered and smoked all day and flashed all night until John Nicolson led the storming columns through the breach that remains to be seen in the shattered wall and fell at 34 in the squalid lane ... [Did Tina remember that Jim was 34?] I took off my hat beside the plain marble slab that covers him, and the native cemetery keeper gave me there a rose and two chrysanthemums which I have kept. To please me read at once Lord Roberts' 'Forty Years in India' and you will understand all I feel. But when I think that the Coronation Durbar is arising upon the same scene which was the cockpit of the Mutiny it is impossible not to have fresh faith in England and her star.

Garvin's imagination swept him back far beyond the coming of the British. From the age of ten he had longed to see the Taj Mahal, where Shah Jehan laid his bride. It did not disappoint him — 'beautiful as when she was beautiful and cold as when she was dead'. Garvin climbed one of the four minarets,

> like tapers set with reverence round a shrine ... Beneath you on the riverside the wide Jumna sweeps in misty silver away towards the holy Ganges. And this was ours and every city and plain and river steeped in the moon throughout India that night was ours. I never understood the greatness of England till that hour.

'This was ours' — the past imperfect tense, grammatically odd in its context, proved to be the past prophetic. Six months after Garvin died, the King of England ceased to be Emperor of India.

A biographer in page-starved days dare not follow Garvin round India, but he must go with him to Benares, 'the most solemn, profound, fascinating spectacle that the whole earth can have to show'. Male sexual symbols were all around. He wrote to Tina:

I am convinced ... that they are far less indecent in effect and intention than are the average of French novels or the after-dinner anecdotes in which nearly all civilised men delight. The ideas of birth and death, change and reappearance, growth and decay are the mysteries which master the Hindoo mind.

Though Garvin made no Indian friends on this journey, he was saved by his historian's long sight and his aesthetic sensibility from assuming that Britain's current excellence in governing would endure for ever, or that it implied a natural superiority in other respects. Homesick, he cut his journey short and sailed for England on 14 February 1903, bewitched by India and intoxicated by the feel of a divided sub-continent united by the *Pax Britannica*. Once home, other interests banished India to the background of his mind. In London, however, he made three friends who kept his Indian interests alive ready to be brought forward a quarter of a century later. The three had given India outstanding service – Theodore Morison in education, Sir Edward Law as Finance Member of the Viceroy's Council, and Lord Roberts as Commander-in-Chief. For Garvin's understanding of Gandhi's India one can only regret that their service, like his journey, belonged to the period of benevolent despotism.

I

A month after his thirty-fifth birthday Garvin came to the turning point of his public life. Since Parnell's death a dozen years before he had been a leaderless man in politics. He had hesitated between the fascination of Rosebery and Chamberlain's astonishing power of command. Both were Imperialists in Cowen's meaning of the term, which was also Garvin's, but they belonged to different parties. Garvin was still undecided when he came back from India. Indeed, as 'His Master's Voice' on the *Daily Telegraph*, there was no need for him to make up his mind. Sir Edward Lawson would do it for him. He did. He decided to give all the support he could to the campaign for imperial preference which Joseph Chamberlain launched in Birmingham Town Hall on 15 May 1903. Lawson assigned Garvin to that job. He went to see Chamberlain in his room at the House of Commons on 25 May. The Colonial Secretary gave him an hour's interview and put at his disposal all the information that the Board of Trade could supply, which was little more than the Customs returns. Economic policy was then conducted in a fog where statistical visibility was virtually nil.

It was the first time Garvin had met Chamberlain face to face. To Chamberlain it was a routine interview with an unknown journalist. To Garvin it was much more. He no longer hesitated between Chamberlain and Rosebery. He was meeting his leader. 'It was the question of Canada more than anything else', he later told Northcliffe, 'that made me throw in my whole lot with Chamberlain.' In the summer before Garvin's Indian visit the Prime Ministers of the self-governing colonies had had a meeting in London, the second in the series of what are now called Commonwealth Conferences. They had asked for preferential treatment for their exports to the United Kingdom. Canada had taken the lead because her trade was suffering from German retaliation against the preference she gave British manufactures. Her request could be painlessly granted in the 1903 Budget because there was in existence a corn duty which had been imposed to pay for the Boer War. It could be removed from the Empire but retained for foreign countries. Chamberlain persuaded the Cabinet to do this, but in his absence the decision was reversed. Defeated in the Cabinet,

Chamberlain appealed to the country. The Birmingham meeting was the first shot in his campaign. Alarmed by the split in his Cabinet, Balfour put Ministers into quarantine. They were to think things out, but not to talk in public.

## II

Meanwhile the campaign went on, doubtfully in the Cabinet, reasonably well in the party, favourably in the country. The Lawsons gave Garvin his head and he raced home an easy winner from the field of tariff reform propagandists. His most effective economic critic was J. A. Spender, his friendly patron of Hull days, who was now editor of the influential *Westminster Gazette*. Garvin was undoubtedly right, however, in picking out Spender's cartoonist as the best populariser of the free trade case: 'If a Free Trade Cabinet was formed upon the principles of Constitutional realism, the person to be sent for would undoubtedly be Mr. F. C. Gould.' It was a shrewd jest. At the beginning of the century Gould was as strong a political influence as David Low between the world wars.

The style of Garvin's campaign was set in his opening leader in the *Daily Telegraph*. He did not argue that free trade was wrong in itself, or that Cobden had been mistaken. It was simply that times had changed, and so must policies. 'The books of the Cobden Club are not the Koran, and much less are they the Bible. The higher criticism is not confined to theology alone.' Then, in a more emotional vein, 'it concerns the welfare of generations yet unborn whether this Empire, unique in its character as unrivalled in its opportunities, is knit close into one homogeneous whole, like a planet, or is broken up into a mere meteoric shower'.

The special articles which followed, day after day, week after week, were closely argued, free from hyperbole, direct and to the point — one point, on the whole, to one day's reading, often with a brilliantly selected statistical text in bold type at the top of the column. It was a perfectly designed and executed newspaper campaign.

'There is only one man in London who could have written it,' a delighted Harry Lawson told Garvin about one of his campaign articles. People talked about them and, like Lord Milner, wanted to meet the writer. Henry Chaplin, a former Cabinet Minister and a close friend of Edward VII, told Garvin (and Lawson) that his *Telegraph* articles were the best things he had ever read in any newspaper on any great question. He had passed them on to the King at Marienbad. 'He read twelve of them there and before I left I got him an advance copy of them reprinted to read on his travels.'

Garvin's contribution to the inter-Empire trade campaign was not confined to the *Telegraph*. He devoted four long Calchas articles to it in the *Fortnightly* during the second half of 1903 and wrote regularly in the *National Review* as well. He argued that without Empire preference the colonies would drift away, making their own regional arrangements and very likely erecting tariffs to keep British goods out. The September *National Review* carried a fifty-page supplement on 'The Economics of Empire' by 'the Assistant Editor', a title designed to give Garvin's writing editorial authority. Just before the editor, Leo Maxse, set off on holiday he wrote delightedly to Garvin:

> Joe caught sight of me as he was driving away from [Lord Salisbury's] memorial service, stopped his carriage, jumped out and said 'This Supplement is splendid. I have been asking the Duke [of Devonshire] and the Prime Minister to read it. If we can't win on these lines, we can't win at all. I have read it once and shall read it again.' There!!!

A few days later Garvin insisted on seeing Chamberlain because he suspected that Chamberlain was on the point of resigning. Garvin asked him point blank. According to Amery's diary,

> Joe was at first extremely surprised, then acknowledged that it was true and added that, to show that he was not going in a hostile spirit, he was going to leave Austen to become Chancellor of the Exchequer, to which Garvin replied: 'I hope to God you don't find that a fetter on your freedom of action.' Joe was dead silent for a full minute afterwards.

No doubt Chamberlain was considerably annoyed for, as Garvin recalled:

> At my second and most daring interview with Mr. Chamberlain he was just upon the point of devouring me when I told him for the first time that I was Calchas and various other pseudonyms and anonyms, who had been like a whole train of followers. He said to me across the table 'I did not know you were my unknown supporter,' and all was right and a great hour followed.

Garvin's leader had become his friend.


## III

Of course Garvin was right. Chamberlain had fettered himself to the Conservative Party by leaving Austen as a hostage. He was not only proposing a major shift in taxation, but a revolution in economic thinking. For half a century free trade had been an axiom of British politics accepted by all parties. Chamberlain was challenging economic laws that seemed as self-evident as Euclid. Latterly, however, a number of men, Garvin and Joseph Cowen among them, had begun to have misgivings which, for the most part, they expressed only tentatively and in a low voice. Doubters were to be found in all parties. Lloyd George himself seemed at certain moments to be a possible convert. The Tariff Reform League, Chamberlain's chosen instrument, was aware of this widespread interest and wanted to appeal to men of all parties. 'Many of us Tariff Reformers in the East End are Liberals,' Maxse was reminded by his chairman at a League meeting. The situation was in some respects similar to that in our own time when there are Europeans and anti-Marketeers in all parties.

Why then was there no significant movement of 'Liberals for Empire Preference'? Why in the end were its supporters found almost exclusively in one wing only of the Tory party? Various reasons suggest themselves. There was no referendum, such as we have had over the Common Market, to separate this issue from all the others that influence a general election. Then, among many Liberals there was still an unforgiving dislike for what they saw as 'Radical Joe's' treachery in 1886. Moreover Joe, having left Austen behind as Balfour's hostage, could not free himself from his association with a divided and increasingly discredited government. And, because Joe was fettered, Garvin felt himself bound in the same way.


## IV

The day after Chamberlain's Birmingham speech Leo Maxse, 'aggressively truculent, sardonically witty, and always lovable', had burst into Leo Amery's room at *The Times* and, 'seizing both my hands in his, waltzed me round the room as he poured forth a paean of jubilation at the thought that, at last, there was a cause to work for in politics'. Garvin shared their elation. It was natural that they should found a club to bring them together and to propagate their views. And so in January 1904 Amery gave a dinner party in his rooms in the Temple at which 'The Compatriots' was founded. Its members were democratic Imperialists who shared Earl Grey's outlook — 'My country is the Empire; my home is England.' In India, Garvin had felt with pride 'all this was ours', something Britain possessed. Now, when he spoke of the Empire, he meant something to which we belonged, not something belonging to us.

Another of the Compatriots with whom Garvin soon became intimate was F. S. Oliver. Oliver, who liked to describe himself as a mere draper — he was a partner in Debenham's — had one of the most penetrating political minds of his generation. His books about the eighteenth century set men thinking more deeply about the twentieth. Maxse, Amery, Oliver, Garvin — four men in their thirties — formed a strong bodyguard of writers and thinkers round the old radical statesman in his last campaign.

A fifth member of the group was to become Garvin's closest friend. Edward Goulding, a southern Irishman, was a bachelor five years older than Garvin. He was neither a writer nor a thinker, but the skilful chairman of the Tariff Reform League's organisation. Lord Riddell called him 'Joe's Man Friday'. *The Times* recorded that 'for forty years no back-bencher in the House of Commons had greater influence'. Garvin soon found that Goulding's 'pernickety affectation of cynicism conceals enough human goodness and active charity to stock a mother's meeting'. To both men imperial preference was a means of uniting the Empire and paying for social reform at home, not of propping up failing industries or enriching greedy manufacturers.

**I**

For Garvin the autumn of 1904 had the promise of spring. He had made his name as a campaigning journalist; he was about to try his luck as a campaigning editor. Chamberlain's views were well represented in the daily papers and the monthly reviews. The Sunday papers in those days hardly counted with the men whose minds he had to win, but the political weeklies did. He lacked support among them. The *Spectator*, then at the height of its influence, was owned and edited by the Conservative Free Trader, St Loe Strachey. Garvin's friends, including Chamberlain himself, thought he was the man to take Strachey on if a paper could be found for him. Two men were willing to put up the money. Garvin could choose between them.

William Robinson, who owned *Gardening Illustrated*, was anxious to start a new political weekly with Garvin as editor. Sidney Goldman wanted him to edit the *Outlook*, which he had recently bought. Amery favoured Goldman; Maxse at first was doubtful because Goldman, though sound on preference, was 'a well-meaning little German Jew . . . not to be trusted on larger matters'. Garvin hesitated, but finally decided for Goldman.

Goldman did not deserve Maxse's denigration. He was a good citizen of what Chamberlain and Garvin, meant by the Empire. He had been born in Cape Town in the year of Garvin's birth and was finally to settle in British Columbia. He had lived as an Uitlander in the Transvaal and built up a fortune in mining. During the Boer War he had been a war correspondent and got to know Lord Roberts. He was now heart and soul with Chamberlain in his Empire policy.

The *Outlook* sold for threepence and for that reason was not in the same class as the sixpenny *Spectator* and the other leading political weeklies. Its price would have to be raised if it was to compete. Goldman was prepared for that. It would also need a new editor. There was a difficulty here. Filson Young had only recently been appointed. Like Goldman he had been a war correspondent in South Africa, was a splendid descriptive writer, an Imperialist, but not a Tariff Reformer. And so Garvin was to be brought in as co-editor to put that right. But 'can two walk together except they be agreed'?

**II**

Garvin had not finally committed himself to Goldman by 21 October. It was to be the strangest Trafalgar Day since Nelson fell. Russia was at war with Japan. Its Baltic fleet was steaming down the North Sea to the Pacific when it mistook some Hull trawlers for Japanese torpedo boats and opened fire. Twenty British fishermen were killed or wounded. There was a violent outburst of anti-Russian feeling in Britain. Garvin was on a short holiday in France, well placed to observe the disastrous effect of British Jingoism on French opinion. After his return he wrote to Maxse: 'Had war broken out, she would have been against us to a certainty – and the German game would have been won. Is it quite impossible to make *The Times* see our policy towards Russia from that point of view?'

Calchas saw his hopes disappearing, his worst fears materialising. The Entente with France was barely six months old; that with Russia was still three years off. Both were endangered by the hysterical British reaction to Russia's hysterical blunder. Garvin came back to England to consider his future in a determined mood. He must be the master of his pen as he could never completely be on the *Daily Telegraph*. He would write nothing that he did not believe; he would say everything that he felt needed saying. That was what he understood by 'responsible journalism'. For him it could only mean responsible editorship.

He settled with Goldman on 22 November. The terms were good – £1,500 a year for five years. He understood he was to be in complete control, but he wisely asked Goldman to define his relation to Filson Young, whom he seems to have envisaged as his assistant editor. Goldman brushed Garvin's request aside with an airy 'Don't give the matter any further thought. *Alles zal recht kommen.*'

From Young's point of view things were going wrong, not coming right. He was saddled with Garvin, whose position was undefined, whose work he admired but over whose opinions he had no control and, worse still, about whose movements he had little knowledge. Garvin was not on the telephone and lived at Bromley. (He had moved there in 1902 for his family's sake.) A series of pained but half-playful notes from Young tell a story to wring any newspaperman's heart. The last is dated Wednesday, 4 January 1905: '3.45 p.m. and nothing received. The paper has been late every Friday since you started writing for it. I shall have to have a ghost set of leaders ready unless you can absolutely guarantee delivery – and that would be absurd.'

Before Friday came, Young was sacked or walked out. His staff went with him. Garvin was on his own without so much as a note to tell him what articles had been ordered. He turned to Leo Amery, who thoroughly enjoyed an emergency. Tina shut Jim up to write the political articles, while Amery and a few friends wrote the rest of the first *Outlook* for which Garvin was solely responsible.

In spite of everything the two Irishmen, Garvin a Catholic born in Birkenhead, and Young a Protestant born in Manchester, could appreciate each other. A year later Young wrote: 'There is no other weekly paper – politics apart – that I feel has behind it a mind with which I am so much in sympathy.' Later he was to write regularly for the *Pall Mall Gazette* during Garvin's editorship.

## III

Garvin's first need was an assistant editor, not only 'one of ours' in politics, but a man with the classical education Garvin lacked. In 1904 that mattered, or Garvin thought it did. Amery suggested young Ned Grigg. As personal assistant to the editor of *The Times* he had the world more or less at his feet. Garvin offered him £600 a year; Grigg, oddly quoting his mother's opinion, asked for £700 and got it. The friendship thus begun, endured.

Within a few weeks Garvin recruited other young men whose work gave the paper distinction. Gerard Fiennes, a cadet of a famous family, wrote knowledgeably about Service matters. Sydney Brooks, 'a writer whose pen is equal to my own', as Garvin told his wife, came from Joe's Birmingham via the United States. E. C. Bentley had already the touch which invented the Clerihew. The best journalist and the closest in friendship to the editor, the first to call him 'Garve', was Beach Thomas. His green fingers held a golden pen. 'I must get him to teach me about birds,' Garvin thought. He was still anxious to learn as well as eager to teach. For music Garvin had E. A. Baughan, and for art, Arthur Symons. Charles Whibley wrote about plays and was ready to cover a theatre 'if there's anything that's good, but not Alexander, Tree or Irving', the famous actor managers.

These were Garvin's regulars. He needed special contributors for special occasions. Nineteen hundred and five was the centenary of Trafalgar. The second sixpenny *Outlook* had an article by Chamberlain on 'Nelson's Year and England's Duty'. As Trafalgar Day drew near Garvin hunted for a poet to celebrate it. With less than a fortnight in hand he wrote to A. E. Housman only to be told: 'As you anticipate, I am not able to compose a poem on Trafalgar. I am afraid too that I admire Napoleon more than Nelson.' Next he tried Thomas Hardy, who was already a contributor. The answer came by return of post: 'Nothing occurs to me beyond what I printed in the first part of The Dynasts.' He turned to George Meredith and was rewarded. Meredith sat down, and wrote a poem. He was seventy-seven, but 'the feeling is strong yet'.

A campaigning journalist who becomes an editor runs the risk of boring his readers. Garvin's catholicity of interests reduced the risk. With such a team as this he avoided it. Most of his own writing was political; but when he did write about books, his readers asked for more. His job, however, was the honey-bee's — to fertilise other men's flowers. This he did so well that his *Outlook* was an instantaneous journalistic success.


## IV

The *Outlook*, on the other hand, was not a business success though it came near to it. Garvin put the circulation up from 3,000 a week to 4,000 in spite of the doubled cover price. He reduced the loss from £650 a month to £125. There was more to do. He and Goldman disagreed about what that should be. Goldman wanted to reduce expenditure, Garvin to spend more in order to reach a circulation of 6,000 which he reckoned would be the break-even point. He was right, but it is easy to be right when someone else is paying the bills. He was right, but he might not have made good had he been given the chance. Both men were so much babes in the wood of newspaper management that there was probably no way of making the paper quickly profitable except by calling in expert managerial experience. Instead editor and owner fell out.

They quarrelled about the non-existent profits. Goldman was prepared to give Garvin a fifth share of any profits that might be made during his editorship. Garvin wanted a quarter share of the equity. Financially it might have made little difference, but to Garvin a share in the ownership was a symbol of editorial independence. This quarrel reached its peak during the disastrous 1906 election which ended in a landslide Liberal victory. Goldman arranged for special articles in the *Standard*, according to Garvin 'for the purpose of advertising the *Outlook* with my brains since you could not do it with your money'. Chamberlain intervened to make peace. Garvin told Goldman that he had promised Chamberlain to cooperate better in future, adding, 'I have given that promise and I mean it.' Goldman for his part suggested that they should both forget that there had ever been any difficulty.

The *Outlook* was still losing money. The two men devised a scheme which they put to Chamberlain. By the use of his name and the party machine they hoped to enrol 20,000 annual subscribers who would not only receive the *Outlook* but contribute to party funds by a delayed discount on their subscriptions. It sounds too clever by half and entirely out of character for Garvin. It is strange that he did not see this, but in 1906 he was so much the party politician himself that he forgot that the value of a free press depends on its keeping its distance from party machines.

Chamberlain was on holiday but made time to warn Garvin: 'I do not believe in bribing subscribers; in such a case they will take the bribe and then leave you ... wait for a fortnight until I return – then come and see me and talk everything over quietly.' The scheme was shelved. The losses continued.

In July Chamberlain had a severe stroke. He was never able to speak in public again, though he remained an oracle who could be consulted. For Garvin he was the irreplaceable leader.


# V


A cascade of personal and family troubles threatened to drown Garvin during his *Outlook* days. They had started while he was still undecided whether to accept Goldman's offer or Robinson's. He had gone off on his own to Skye for one of his prodigious walking holidays. For a man who paid so much attention to anniversaries it seems pointed to leave his wife alone for their tenth wedding aniversary. They had quarrelled before he left; she kept it up by letters. A spate of telegrams and crossed letters only made things worse. In the end a penitent but exasperated Garvin cut his holiday short. Part of the trouble seems to have been about money. 'If you would like to show that you really can manage the money matters', he wrote, 'you shall do so ... with [my] regular help by going every week or month with you into the accounts.' Behind the housekeeping problems there clearly lay a deeper misunderstanding. Jim was writing as one would write to a child. He does not seem to have realised that Tina was no longer the girl barely out of her schooldays whom he had married. He loved her dearly, but his letters suggest that he was unable to put himself in her place. Later on, she was able to make allowances, and in letters to her son treated her husband both as a great man and an overgrown small boy; sometimes magnificent, sometimes ridiculous, always lovable. It is doubtful whether she was as detached at twenty-seven.

That autumn there was a crisis over Viola's tubercular leg. A succession of expensive specialists advised amputation. Three days after Christmas, Garvin, a proud man, brought himself to confide in Goldman, who not only gave him an interest-free loan but introduced him to his brother, a specialist in Freiburg-in-Breisgau. Tina took Viola to him. He operated and saved Viola's leg.

Tina was torn between her duty to her six-year-old daughter and her husband. Viola was in hospital in a foreign country. Jim, though outwardly successful, was on the verge of a nervous breakdown. Tina realised that he was almost as dependent on her as Viola was. For his part Jim knew that Tina's place was with Viola, but he made a guilty, half-hearted attempt to bring her home, saying that he feared he was 'on the brink of the great breakdown at last'. Without her he was a lost soul, 'not your husband, but your orphan'.

Meanwhile in Germany Tina dreamed that Molly Smith, a Newcastle friend, was replacing her in Jim's affection. He wrote:

Oh do not, do not tear my heart by telling me of your poor foolish dreams, or rather tell me always but try, try not to have them or to think the thoughts that bring them. Molly is to me what my sister would have been if I had ever had one.

Tina's instinct, however, was sound. She had cause for jealousy, for Molly Smith was attractive, attentive and a sympathetic listener.

In the spring Tina was away for six weeks on a West Indies cruise. She fell ill in Bristol on her way back and had to stay there. Meanwhile Jim's threatened nervous breakdown had come. Goldman − 'that little man is one of earth's rarest' − came down to Bromley, saw Garvin, sized up the situation, and called in a Harley Street specialist who packed Garvin off for a rest cure where he was not even allowed to see *The Times* in spite of his plea that it was 'not an exciting organ'. After a month Garvin was allowed to go. He set off by himself for a vigorous convalescence in the Engadine.

## VI

Perhaps Garvin and Goldman would have made a lasting success of the *Outlook* if the latter had not sailed for East Africa at the end of April

1906 with nothing settled, and if Garvin had not become impatient, Goldman left his partner in charge. Willoughby did not share Goldman's affection for the wayward editor, and was pained to find that Garvin's office was not as methodical as a merchant's counting house. Worse still, Goldman's third partner turned out to be a Free Trader. The prospect was dismal.

Garvin felt that he must do something for himself. He turned to Northcliffe, explaining that Goldman was away for a long time — rumour said possibly for two years. He asked Northcliffe to buy Goldman out and take full business control of the *Outlook*, giving Garvin the coveted quarter share. The two men met twice in three days at the end of June. Nothing came of it because Willoughby was determined that nothing should. Garvin asked his Empire friends to seek further capital. In the end Sir Rowland Blennerhassett, Garvin's gossip on Balkan politics, found an apparently satisfactory solution. He enlisted the help of Walter Long, who got a promise of new money from an undisclosed source. Long's private secretary, Gerald Arbuthnot, a naïve and likeable young man, was thrilled to be entrusted with negotiations between the fascinating Garvin, the elusive Goldman and the unnamed man who was willing to buy the *Outlook*. Before the end of August Garvin knew that sufficient new money was available. The next thing was to find out if Goldman would sell. Willoughby would not provide his address so Arbuthnot and Garvin had to wait until Goldman returned at the end of October. He agreed to sell, but, since he still believed in Garvin, he wanted to keep 15 per cent of the equity. The buyer refused. It was not until 3 November that Garvin learned that Lord Iveagh had bought the paper for his son, Walter Guinness.

Arbuthnot thought that he had secured the two conditions on which Garvin had insisted — editorial independence and a quarter share of the equity. He was wrong. Garvin had two or three completely unsatisfactory interviews with the new owner. Almost everything that he had done with the *Outlook* was to be undone. It was once more to become a threepenny paper under a new editor, though Garvin would continue as a regular weekly contributor, or so Guinness expected. Guinness told him that the staff were extravagantly paid and there could be no possibility of a share in the equity. Garvin replied, as might have been expected, 'Your letter ignores every promise with regard to share, interest, tenure and the continuity of the character of the paper made by Mr. Arbuthnot upon the security of Mr. Long's word and support.'

Long, an honourable man, was shocked and deeply apologetic: 'I am miserable. In losing you and Grigg we are losing the bravest and best of champions and I feel strongly that both of you must be very sore and angry.' They were. Garvin put it tersely to Leo Maxse: 'Long is a muddler; Goldman is a Jew; and Guinness wants my Pierian spring to run like his porter and to smell like the Liffey. Hence the final break.'

Discriminating readers mourned the loss of Garvin's *Outlook*. The Governor-General of Canada, Lord Grey, plaintively enquired, 'Where now can I get my sound wine of Garvin?' He was soon answered. North-cliffe sent Garvin New Year greetings: 'I hope 1907 will be less anxious for you than 1906, and I thank you for the great pleasure my wife and I derived from the *Outlook*.' That was an encouraging message to receive from the man who, above all other men, had the power to make the hope come true.

# BOOK THREE: THE NORTHCLIFFE YEARS, 1907-1911

---

'Garvin, a man of eloquence and originality, whose role in Opposition politics over the next two or three years was almost equivalent to that of a parliamentary leader.'

John Grigg, *Lloyd George: The People's Champion*

I

The day after Garvin left the *Outlook* he asked Northcliffe to make him his right-hand man. It was a cool suggestion, but not as brash as it sounds. Northcliffe had asked him the year before to become editor of the *Observer*, but he had felt bound to Goldman. Since then there had been discussions about Northcliffe buying the *Outlook*. Northcliffe was certainly well disposed, but even so Garvin's was a remarkable letter. He wrote:

They tell me you tire of men and throw them over, and would tire of me and throw me over . . . In spite of all they say I am personally drawn to you, and your creative genius fills me with amazement. I have dreamed for hours often and often of what might be done were I your political right hand. You might have vast power, and you have not got it ... I don't know whether you are satisfied that I am your man. If you were not, better not experiment. But this is the truth. On my side with many defects and inconsistencies, with a touch of the poet, a touch of the prophet and a touch of the wire-puller too (for I know what politics are and must be) there is knowledge, experience, yet unquenchable fire, courage, incarnate, considerable common-sense, and entire sincerity. On yours, – you say, when Joe is gone, where is the man? You are the man. You can do through your papers if you like what no man could through any other medium.

Northcliffe replied at once, suggesting that Garvin should go to South Africa to cover the first election since the Boer War. It was a tempting offer, but his wife saw that Garvin needed a long break before he went back to work. Northcliffe agreed. Instead of South Africa, Tina and Jim took three months' holiday in Italy.

This Italian journey opened a new epoch in Garvin's personal life. He had put behind him his wayward attachment to Molly Smith. Tina was happy again, and Jim rejoiced in the rebirth of his marriage. Both were enchanted with Italy – the moment and the mood were right, the lovers were expectant and satisfied. Their youngest child was conceived there and named Ursula for the memory they had of the great Carpaccio in Venice. The 'year of Italy', as they called it, coloured Garvin's feeling and influenced his thinking for the rest of his life.


## II

Garvin was back in England by the middle of April. He returned temporarily to the *Telegraph* to Burnham's delight as a nightly contributor of leading articles, though not as a member of the staff. He was also writing three or four articles a month in the *National Review* and the *Fortnightly* for which he now undertook a monthly review of foreign affairs. In the autumn he was to start a new series for the prestigious *North American Review*. There was no shortage of work.

Meanwhile Garvin debated his future with Northcliffe. They spent five days together in early September at Elmwood, Northcliffe's unpretentious country home in Thanet. After a short break they were together again in the Tudor splendour of Sutton Place. Northcliffe wanted Garvin primarily for the *Daily Mail*. He offered him £3,000 a year for five years and a share of profits. Garvin reluctantly turned down 'the most splendid offer ever made to any journalist in this country' because, as he told Goulding (he was writing as Irishman to Irishman),

> Northcliffe's health and various interests compel him to be often away, and Kennedy Jones ('a master of all the lower journalistic arts') has the real grip on the machine ... Kennedy Jones comes from Newry; Marlowe, the editor, from Waterford – they are both in my conviction anti-Imperialists at heart. That explains everything. On the *Daily Mail* I should have had enemies all about me, and when Northcliffe was not there, they would hold the cards.

Northcliffe, however, owned the *Observer* as well as the *Daily Mail*. He renewed his offer of the editorship. Garvin asked for a 20 per cent share in the paper ('this would decide me at once') instead of the third share suggested sixteen months before. Garvin was usually inclined to think that his proprietors were trying to get the better of him, but on this occasion he felt that the lower figure offset the paper's heavy losses in the interval.

It is characteristic of Garvin's personal relations with Northcliffe that he began this important business letter with a disquisition on his youngest daughter's birth, 'comforted beforehand with stories of Uncle Joe and afterwards by Lady Northcliffe's grapes'. It was the beginning of an intimate and lifelong friendship with Molly Northcliffe in which Tina shared.

The final decision was probably made at Sutton Place in mid-September, but, before it could take effect, it was necessary to dispose of the existing editor whose contract had three years to run. Austin Harrison was not an easy man and had an important father. Northcliffe wanted to avoid trouble so he preferred indirect action instead of his normal direct attack. Harrison continued as the *Observer*'s main reviewer and became also the *Daily Mail*'s dramatic critic. This satisfied neither Garvin nor Harrison, but they had to put up with it. On 12 January 1908 the *Observer* announced that at the end of the month Garvin would become editor of the paper 'in which he has acquired a proprietary interest'. He had already on 29 December contributed the first of the series of articles of which the last appeared on 22 February 1942.

## III

The business success of Garvin's *Observer* was as predictable as the failure of his *Outlook*. He now had behind him Northcliffe's drive and the tremendous resources of his organisation. Garvin still had much to learn about editing; but his tutor, a very diligent tutor, was the most gifted newspaper publisher of his day, perhaps of all time. The tutor, moreover, both liked and admired his pupil. In such circumstances pupils learn fast.

Northcliffe had bought the *Observer* for £5,000, a price which sufficiently shows its expectation of life. It was the oldest surviving Sunday newspaper, but it had gone rapidly down hill under the eccentric and lackadaisical direction of Mr and Mrs Beer, who also owned and edited its rival, the *Sunday Times*. Their readers had good addresses, but were few in number. The *Observer*'s net sale was 2,000 in winter and 4,000 in summer (the reverse of the usual pattern) when Northcliffe bought it.

Its circulation was already well on the way up by the time Garvin became editor. Austin Harrison's regime, backed by Northcliffe's business management, and a reduction of the cover price from twopence to a penny, had brought the net sales up to just under 20,000 a week. Twice as many readers were needed to make it pay. Garvin knew that the money was there to bring them in if he could provide the kind of paper they wanted.

Of course he could. Of that he was confident. Rightly so. He did it in eighteen months. The following year the net sale was 57,000 a week and the year's profit nearly £4,000. Since he became editor circulation had gone up by 185 per cent, revenue by 162 per cent, and expenditure by only 50 per cent. There was room for his kind of Sunday paper.

Garvin's dream could be realised because its time had come. The Victorian Sabbath was giving place to the Edwardian weekend, although there were still many middle-class households in which Sunday papers were banned as works of the devil. It soon became difficult to regard Garvin's paper in that light. People wanted to read it, and found they could with a good conscience. In the end it became almost a pious duty. Englishmen and women, like God, rested on the seventh day and found it good. They had time to relax and reflect. Garvin invited them to do both in his company. Sunday gave them time to read. He gave them something worth reading on Sunday. Politics fell into place beside music, books, the countryside. Pages 4 and 5, he said, must be kept 'quite free from the faintest suggestion of the existence of politics. The public must feel quite safe from them in that part of the paper.' Even in politics the *Observer* ought to look at the passing world in the timeless light of the weekend pause. Sometimes it did.

In the early days Northcliffe was constantly at Garvin's elbow or looking over his shoulder. His praise was worth having because it was offset by criticism and suggestions. The letters that passed between them are the letters of men who understand one another and feel free to say what they think. Time and again Northcliffe recurred to the need for more news, more varied news, not only political news but news of the 'man bites dog' variety. Most lacking of all was material to interest women readers. Garvin had to learn that, while the *Observer* and the *Outlook* were alike in appearing once a week, the *Observer* had to be a newspaper while the *Outlook* could remain a simple review.

Two contrasting letters dealing with successive issues show Northcliffe at work. He took a generally poor view of the *Observer* of 1 March 1908. Its politics were too heavy and took too much space. Apart from that, he complained of a story about a 'millionaire murderer'. There was nothing in the copy to justify the headline, a fair criticism even if it came from a man whose income of £200,000 might be expected to make him touchy. If Garvin wanted sensationalism − 'but personally I don't like it' − why couldn't he have settled for the mad innkeeper who killed a customer in the presence of a deaf mute, the only witness? The news generally, Northcliffe went on,

> needs much more careful measuring out and allocation. I don't know whether you make a plan of the paper on Saturday afternoon, but it is a wise thing to do. I suggest you write less this week and spend more time on this planning ... Will you also hold an expense meeting?

A week later Northcliffe congratulated Garvin on his best *Observer* yet: 'The tone of your criticism is one that I wish I could get my other papers to adopt. It is none the less forcible because it is so friendly to everyone and because it shows such complete independence of party.' Northcliffe showed his eye for detail. The quality of the paper varied between copies. The manager must examine every roll every Saturday: 'Will you sometimes give an eye to this yourself?'

All was well where there were direct dealings between Northcliffe and Garvin. Yet their close association began at a time when Northcliffe was already becoming increasingly irritable; when, as his biographers put it, 'the current of his warm and friendly nature ... would suddenly fuse in a violent flash, destroying the good will of years'. They go on to say, and the record bears them out, that 'there were men close to him, J. L. Garvin, for instance, and Norman Angell, who never saw that side of his temper perhaps because they could answer back'. Garvin felt that Northcliffe was his partner, not his employer. He succeeded in keeping himself editorially free from Carmelite House, the headquarters of the Harmsworth Press. He refused Northcliffe's invitation to join the daily meetings of the *Daily Mail* editorial council in return for an additional fee, although he was never a man lightly to turn down money. He quoted Chatham's decisive words: 'I will be responsible for nothing but what I direct.' Indeed the idea of Garvin as a member of a committee is ludicrous. Northcliffe saw the point and acquiesced.

It was neither possible, nor would it have been sensible, to keep the managerial side of the *Observer* equally independent. It was in second-rate hands. Northcliffe put in Alfred Butes, his secretary, as non-resident manager under George Sutton at Carmelite House. For a short time indeed Butes moved into the *Observer* office, taking direct control. These were necessary steps if the paper was to pay. They were part of Garvin's training as an editor-manager fit to control the whole working of a paper. Nevertheless he did not like them.

**IV**

Almost before Garvin was established at the *Observer,* Northcliffe was busy buying *The Times.* Garvin knew nothing about it. He was North-cliffe's political counsellor, not his business confidant. Like all the world he thought that Northcliffe's rival, Pearson, had succeeded. He commiserated with Northcliffe, congratulated Pearson and thus innocently lulled him into a false security. It was probably not till Sutton brought Garvin an article for the *Observer* called 'The Truth about *The Times*' that he guessed what was happening. He asked who had written the article. Sutton smiled and said, 'It just blew through the window.' Three weeks later Northcliffe owned *The Times.*

The purchase drastically altered the position of the *Observer* among Northcliffe's possessions. It had been his one card of entry into the handful of newspapers which those who governed England took seriously. Compared with *The Times,* however, the *Observer* was nothing. In a way this left Garvin more freedom than he might otherwise have had; on the other hand it meant that resources were diverted to *The Times.* In the spring of 1909 Garvin asked Charles Russell, his solicitor, whether Northcliffe could sell the *Observer* without consulting him. 'Legally, yes; morally, no' was the answer. Garvin suspected that Northcliffe wanted *The Times* to take over the *Observer* as a Sunday edition. *The Times* would never agree to share ownership. Garvin would be bought out. He would lose the magic feeling of ownership, but so it would have to be. He wrote to Northcliffe, 'Fond as I am of the *Observer,* never think for a moment that I want to keep it for my own purposes like a log tied to your leg.'

Meanwhile Fleet Street and Whitehall gossiped about the next editor of *The Times.* Rumour went that Northcliffe regarded Buckle as expendable. Who would take his place? Garvin was a possible candidate; many thought the candidate with the best chance. As early as May 1908 Spender of the *Westminster Gazette* told friends that Garvin was to succeed Buckle. Rumours multiplied. Garvin denied them. They persisted. At last in January 1909 Lord Esher, a close friend of Edward VII and one who had been greatly interested in the *Times* ownership question, asked Garvin to see him. It was their first meeting. Garvin reported the conversation to Northcliffe:

> We talked for two hours, and a very astonishing conversation it was. In the course of it he said as follows: 'If Northcliffe did the right thing he would make you editor of *The Times.* He *won't.*'

These last words were simply trumpeted as though he were giving me a facer. I told Esher very very quietly my withers were unwrung and why.

Nevertheless as late as 1910 Garvin seems still to have half-expected, or at least hoped for, an offer. Reluctantly he had to admit to Tina:

In spite of the vague suggestions from time to time I have not the slightest faith in any intentions of Northcliffe's as regards *The Times* and me, and it irritates me intensely when I think I am being played with in any way.

One may doubt whether Garvin would have made a suitable editor for *The Times*. He was an innovator, an individualist, a skirmisher in front of the line; *The Times* was not only the newspaper of the Establishment, but its communications centre. Garvin probably lacked the patience and self-discipline needed to organise and control a large office with a world-wide staff. It does not seem his style. Perhaps Northcliffe shared these doubts. At any rate he left Buckle undisturbed.

Nevertheless Northcliffe's liking and admiration for Garvin were unabated. Politically they were as close as ever. They shared too a love of books and music — Northcliffe was far from being the uncultured office boy of Salisbury's gibe. He and Garvin were much together. In 1908 they spent a fortnight in Seville; in 1909, but for a sudden political crisis, they were to have toured Canada and the United States together. In 1910 Garvin spent a month with Northcliffe at Valescure, and later he and Tina were at Elmwood for six weeks. The *Observer* meant less to Northcliffe, but the Garvins more.

## 12    GREVILLE PLACE, 1908-1922

**I**

The King of Portugal was murdered as Garvin was sending his second *Observer* to press. He did not leave the office until four in the morning. Special edition followed special edition, the last appearing at seven on Sunday evening. He had edited the *Outlook* from Bromley, but the *Outlook* was only a review. The *Observer* was a newspaper and must carry Saturday's news as thoroughly as *The Times* had carried Friday's. If it succeeded, Monday's *Times* would have a jaded look, since Sunday was still the Lord's Day when nothing political was allowed to happen – at least in public. Garvin decided to move nearer the office. He had hankered after St John's Wood when he first came to London, but could not then afford it. Now he could. He took Number 9 Greville Place which remained his home until he moved to Beaconsfield after the First World War.

Greville Place runs from Maida Vale to Abbey Road. It was a quiet neighbourhood where professional men lived in houses built sixty or seventy years before. Round the corner was Edward Hutton whom the Garvins had met during their 'year of Italy'. He was a prolific writer of travel books for a more leisurely age. Other neighbours included Madame Marchesi, an opera singer; Frank Dicksee, the artist; and R. C. Hawkin, secretary of the influential Eighty Club.

**II**

In Newcastle, when the children were very young, Jim had had time to play games with them and tell them stories. In Kensington and Bromley he gradually lost touch. A Newcastle friend thought he had grown cold. Jim indignantly explained that 'like poor Swift whose heart was so very much like mine, I play the part of hypocrite reversed'. Nevertheless a fews days later he confided to Tina, 'I wish to God I could find out what kind of boy Gerard really is. He is most difficult to gauge.:'

After the move to Greville Place things were easier. As his children grew into their teens they began to sense what their father was at in

74

his study and to feel that they were in a way kindred spirits. To the younger ones, though, he seems for a time still to have remained a mysterious figure to be approached with a trepidation that was really quite unnecessary.

In St John's Wood there were friends for the children, and there were really good schools within reach. The girls were within walking distance of South Hampstead High School, and Gerard's journey to Westminster School was easy. The Garvin children got on well together. They produced family magazines with childishly esoteric titles. They wrote their own plays and acted them in a sham Greek temple at the bottom of the garden. The house was well suited to the interlocking pattern of childish and adult living which went on there. It had:

> three storeys, a roof you could walk on, and a semi-basement kitchen much lighter than many ground-level kitchens of to-day [1948] There was a small garden that seemed large, in which grew a pear tree and a wild damson ... Garvin's study was on the ground floor, looking out on to the prim lime trees that made the hedge between the front garden and the street. Across the hall from the study was the dining room, and next to it the 'little study' where the first telephone stood. He used in this small room to receive people he did not want to keep for long ... It was lined from ceiling to floor with the dullest books in the house. The attractive books were nearly all in his own study.

This is how Katharine, Kit in the family, remembered her childhood home. She was only four when the family left Bromley.

Most people go out to work and come home to relax and live their private lives. There is a divorce between home and office or factory. Garvin's life was run on different lines. The *Observer* office was, as far as he was concerned, an out-station of his study, where the paper was really edited. This would have been impossible for the editor of a daily paper; one would have said it would be impossible for any editor if Garvin had not done it for thirty-four years. His wife sat beside him as he wrote. To the children he was an unseen but very real presence. Much later a grandchild would sometimes curl up beside him in the great chair quietly reading, careful to make no sound that could disturb his concentration. Grandchildren have liberties denied to children.

## III

If the need to be near the *Observer* office on Friday and Saturday had been all that was at stake, Garvin could have stayed in Bromley. What made the move essential was his wish to live near the centre of things. He was in great demand by hostesses with political or literary interests. They invited him not only because he was editor of the *Observer*, though of course that came into it, but for himself, and because of the pleasure that his conversation gave. There were, of course, people who thought that he talked too much. More would have agreed with Lady Leconfield, who longed for another chance to hear Garvin's talk. His was the best she knew, though she had 'spent open-eared hours with Harry Cust and George Wyndham'. Men as well as women enjoyed listening to Garvin. Sidney Colvin, whose double reputation in art and literature matched Garvin's enthusiasms, was asked by his wife what he would like for his birthday. 'Garvin for dinner' was his immediate firm reply. Garvin's talk was not just a monologue. He loved a good set to. Sir Edward Law had been Finance Member of the Viceroy of India's Council. A nephew was present one day when Garvin came to dinner. To his astonishment host and guest fell into violent argument, stalking about the room, contradicting each other, speaking at the same time. To the nephew's still greater astonishment, when the party broke up the two men told each other quite unselfconsciously what a pleasant discussion they had enjoyed.

There is a curious contrast between Garvin's passionate fluency on all questions of public concern and his entrenched reticence about the private places of the soul. Behind the glittering flow of metaphor there was the sense of a deeper layer of his personality about which he never spoke, but of which the sensitive were aware. They found it a guarantee of his integrity. His friends turned instinctively to him for comfort in bereavement or in trouble. As Viola wrote, 'My daddy's courteous silences helped his daughter more than he can guess.'

The shy young man had come to enjoy 'good society'. Greville Place gave him the opportunity. Northcliffe, confronted one day with a below average *Observer*, taxed Garvin with 'too much wining and dining', but of course he recognised the value to a journalist of coming across important people without having to ask for an appointment. Meeting people at dinners and receptions helped Garvin not only to get news, but to get things done. He could say to a man what he could not publish to the world. It was influence he sought. He found it through the *Observer* and in conversations with men and women who had power. He used it to further the causes he had at heart. He knew, too, that the friendships he made would be useful in an age of political patronage if he decided to stand for Parliament as he had half a mind to.

## IV

Garvin enjoyed pitting his wits against Lady Londonderry's in a friendly though serious encounter; his wife must have found such occasions a strain. Hers was the more difficult role. Hostesses invited Garvin for himself; they invited Mrs Garvin as his wife. The change in her life was enormous. It can be inferred from the figures she jotted down at one end of an account book. The page is simply headed 'My Clothing'. It shows that in Newcastle she spent £14 a year on clothes and only a little more when they lived in West Kensington. When Garvin became editor of the *Outlook*, she spent a little over £80 a year. From the time they moved to Greville Place her annual expenditure almost doubled. A list written apparently in 1914 puts the value of her jewellery at just under £750. It includes an emerald necklace worth £165 and an opal one worth £190.

Tina certainly enjoyed much of her new London life. She loved music, and found Lady Northcliffe anxious to lend the Garvins her box at the opera almost as often as they could wish. The prospect of an evening with the First Sea Lord might well have daunted the policeman's daughter, but she found 'Jackie' Fisher's boyish personality infinitely endearing: He wrote to Jim:

> *My best love to your wife.* Tell her I have got the very best seats (for 'What Every Woman Knows') 7.15 sharp at the Carlton Restaurant and, don't say a word, – we'll make a night of it afterwards at my club (the ladies' part of it of course) ... *grilled bones and mushrooms at 4 a.m.* 'We won't go home till morning!'

Tina was completely at ease with Jim's few close men friends.

She was glad of guidance and reassurance from Frances Colvin as she struggled to find her feet in the great world. Even so the innumerable shallow acquaintances she was forced to make were a trial. Her health never seems to have been good, and then in 1909 she suffered a serious mastoid. Soon she began to find relief in drinking too much. Normally she was still a gay companion, a welcoming hostess and a welcome guest, but storm clouds began to gather over Greville Place.

# 13    THE DEFENCE OF BRITAIN, 1908-1911

## I

In 1908 Garvin was more convinced than ever that Germany was willing to go to war with Britain if it could not assert its will by the threat of war. Throughout 1908 and 1909 his main concern was to convince his countrymen of this danger and to persuade them to take effective counter-measures. 'The one way of making an Anglo-German conflict not inevitable is to act as if it were certain to occur,' he wrote in the *Quarterly Review*. The editor, G. W. Prothero,[1] had commissioned the article because he too accepted the reality of 'The German Peril'. Garvin thought the German Chancellor 'as vain as a peacock might be supposed to be if it could appreciate a mirror'. Prince Bülow read the article, marked 125 passages with queries, exclamation marks and comments, and then exploded in an interview he gave to the *Standard*. Its ferocity suggested he had something to hide. In the next *Quarterly* Garvin dismissed the German Chancellor as a light-weight, but treated with serious courtesy the comments of Professor Hans Delbrück in the *Preussische Jahrbücher*. Garvin's counter-attack on the Chancellor was conducted in the body of the article while the more serious argument with the historian was relegated to lengthy footnotes which provide, as it were, a descant to Prince Bülow's pomp and circumstance. The whole makes a singularly impressive political argument, the effect of which is enhanced by the fact that the main body is Garvin moderated by Prothero, while the footnotes are Prothero with 'telling additions' by Garvin. Garvin-cum-Prothero, or such another, would on occasion have been more effective in the *Observer* than Garvin *solus*; but who can edit the editor?

The point of Garvin's warnings was at once underlined by an astonishing interview which the Kaiser gave the *Daily Telegraph*. He explained that his people were bitterly anti-English, but that he was our friend. In a sense both statements were true, but the Kaiser's friendship was so pathological in its nature, and expressed in such offensive terms, that the hate outweighted the love in his ambiguous relation to his grandmother's country. When Count Metternich, the German ambassador in London, read the interview he told his staff, 'Now we might as well shut up shop.'

## II

A great body of British opinion now reluctantly believed in the threat from Germany's expanded and accelerated naval building programme. It had been very different when Calchas wrote his first articles. There was, however, still a strong element in the Liberal and Labour parties, and indeed in the Cabinet, which shied at effective counter-measures, partly out of pacifist sentiment, partly out of other priorities (battleships would cost money needed for social reform), and partly out of a belief that there would be no war because it was economic nonsense. Norman Angell's *The Great Illusion*, published in 1910, is typical of a wide body of opinion.

One might have expected Garvin to launch a whole-hearted onslaught on the Liberal government. In fact he supported its naval measures while opposing its army policy. The line he took arose naturally from his relations with Sir John Fisher, the First Sea Lord, and Lord Roberts, the retired Commander-in-Chief. They had been journalistic contacts in *Outlook* days; they became his friends. They liked Garvin a great deal better than they liked each other.

First, then, the Fisher-Garvin axis. Garvin thought Fisher 'the least like any other man' as well as the most fascinating of his contemporaries: 'He seemed to the orthodox brilliantly insane, while he, with more reason, thought they were respectable imbeciles.' That was Garvin writing about Fisher; it might just as well have been Fisher on Garvin. Fisher was as much of a democrat as a natural autocrat can be. So was Garvin. Both had 'a touch of the prophet and a touch of the wirepuller'. In both men a flamboyant manner was combined with a sober mastery of matter. Although Fisher was old enough to be Garvin's father, he retained the effervescence of a high-spirited and mischievous boy. They played a glorious game together and enjoyed it thoroughly. The stakes were high. They put their careers at risk, confident that they were playing for England.

In 1908 the navy was as popular with the public as the army was unpopular, but it was an intensely unhappy service. The First Sea Lord and the Commander-in-Chief, Home Fleet, Lord Charles Beresford, were bitter enemies. As Fisher's friend, Garvin had access to much confidential and probably to some secret information. As a Tory, and already an influential one, he could use it to prevent Admiralty policy becoming the straight party issue that Beresford would have made it. This was Garvin's value to the Admiralty which had its work cut out fighting off the left wing in the Cabinet and the party.

When Garvin took over the *Observer* he went to Fisher for a thorough briefing. All through the nineteenth century the navy had been unchallenged at sea, deployed in all the oceans of the world, always ready to enforce diplomacy by gunboats. That world was passing. Germany was building a fleet which would match the latest British ships. The navy's superiority in older ships was irrelevant. Fisher's policy was to keep ahead in modern ships and to concentrate them where they could perform their only probable fighting task, the destruction of the German fleet. This made one side of Garvin's next article. There was another side as well. Beresford had got his Tory friends in the House to demand an enquiry into the Admiralty which left-wingers on the government side would have supported. After talking to Fisher, Garvin was able to say with authority,

> There will be no enquiry. There can be no enquiry. If it were instituted, it is notorious that the strongest Board of Admiralty we have ever had would instantly resign as a body to the infinite joy of the German nation.

There was no enquiry.

The First Lord, however, was furious at the leak. Fisher asked Garvin 'as a matter of the very highest importance' to come secretly to his house that afternoon. Together they drafted a letter from Fisher to Garvin asking who wrote the article and what papers he had seen. With tongue in cheek the co-authors proceeded: 'The inference is that the writer . . . has been given secret and confidential facts.' The rebuke, as Garvin and Fisher drafted it, thus concealed an admission that Garvin's facts were right.

Garvin refused on principle to name his source and published Fisher's letter and his own to prove that the facts in his article were right. That Sunday Fisher lunched with the Prince of Wales: 'The talk was about little else than the *Observer* and he was greatly pleased.'

The old admiral and the middle-aged journalist kept up their close collaboration. Official papers, which one might expect to have been carried 'by hand of officer only', were at least on one occasion carried from Greville Place to Queen Anne's Gate by the two eldest Garvin children, aged twelve and ten. They were rewarded by an apple each from the admiral's sideboard, and given a letter to take back to their father. It said: 'Remind me to talk to you about three things — a scene in the Committee of Imperial Defence, War Plans, and the remarkable range of wireless.'

At the beginning of April 1908 Reginald McKenna succeeded Tweedmouth at the Admiralty. The First Lord and the First Sea Lord agreed that eight more battleships would probably be needed in 1909. McKenna needed all the toughness with which Garvin credited him to get his programme through the Cabinet and the House. The Tories shouted, 'We want eight and we won't wait,' but the Liberals were hungry for defence cuts. McKenna and Fisher had to smuggle the programme into the Estimates by a back door.

On the face of it, the Estimates provided only for four dreadnoughts. The pacifists seemed to have won, but Fisher warned Garvin to read carefully the footnote on page 252. He did and wrote, 'As a lady's letter finds its meaning in a postscript, the most significant part of Mr. McKenna's proposals is contained in a footnote.' It said that four more dreadnoughts might be needed. The First Lord's contingent word was not, of course, the Chancellor of the Exchequer's bond. The half-promise had to be made what Fisher called 'parliamentary sure'. In this Garvin played a part.

The debate on the navy Estimates was dominated by fierce Tory attacks on Fisher. Garvin edited a Conservative newspaper. He served an impulsive owner. It could be make or break for him as well as for Fisher. He had to show his fellow Tories that, far from being a traitor, Fisher had in fact won their victory for them against the opposition of two of the most powerful men in the Cabinet, Lloyd George and Winston Churchill, and probably against the wishes of most government MPs. Fisher put the decisive trump card in Garvin's hand when he told him that Sir Edward Grey, the Foreign Secretary, had had such unsatisfactory talks with the German ambassador that he had made up his mind that nothing less than the whole eight battleships would do. Garvin used his knowledge in the *Observer*:

> The whole eight Dreadnoughts ... are secured by the notorious certainty that otherwise Sir Edward Grey's resignation would break up the Government, and that in his resignation he would carry with him the members of the Board of Admiralty, civil and professional alike.

Fisher had given Garvin the certain knowledge. Garvin made it 'notorious' and thus 'parliamentary-sure'. Fisher telegraphed: 'All splendid Piscator'. Northcliffe too was delighted and gave Garvin's article a prominent place in Monday's *Daily Mail*.

On the other hand Grey was furious. He sent a 'very awkward letter' to Fisher, saying that he had heard that Garvin was claiming him as his source. Fisher sent Grey's letter on with the comment that 'no one has a right to know of an absolute private conversation between us two and perhaps you would kindly send me a letter to Sir E. Grey to disclaim me as an authority for your statements'. This Garvin did at once. It was a typical Garvin defence written more in anger, or at least pained surprise, than in sorrow: 'My aim was to do what one man on my side in politics could do to prevent this business becoming a mere party-squabble or a mere personal vendetta.'

Grey recognised the truth of Garvin's remark and replied in a conciliatory way. A public man's 'unexpressed opinions are matters of fair speculation in the press', he conceded.

> If he himself speaks indiscreetly in private he himself must bear the responsibility for his views appearing in public but what is intolerable is that others, who are in official and confidential relations, should make statements upon his individual views upon which statements can be founded in the press ... contrasting his position with that of his colleagues.

In other words Grey had no complaint to make of Garvin but plenty of Fisher. What mattered to Garvin was that Grey did not deny the truth of the *Observer* story.

Fisher had won his victory but got no thanks for it. The hero of the hour was Lord Charles Beresford. Two days after the *Observer* article his appointment as Commander-in-Chief, Channel Fleet, ended. When he landed at Portsmouth, and when he reached London, he received the rapturous welcome usually reserved for the victor in a decisive battle. He wrote a formal letter of complaint. This time he got the enquiry he had been denied the previous year. It was conducted by the Prime Minister and four Secretaries of State, dragging on from April to July. The report was a typical Asquithian document. The Admiralty was cleared of Beresford's serious professional charges, but his face was slightly saved by the suggestion that the Admiralty's public relations could be improved. It was less encouraging to Fisher that he had been led to expect, but not sufficiently so to be a resigning matter. On 9 November he became Lord Fisher of Kilverstone. He was still First Sea Lord.

McKenna had been in almost as deep trouble as Fisher. He had incurred the hostility of his most powerful colleague in the Cabinet. Lloyd George was as much opposed to a big navy as McKenna to 'the

people's budget'. Both gave way in the interests of Cabinet responsibility. Six years later, when McKenna himself was Chancellor of the
Exchequer, he told Garvin how grateful he was

> for your gallant defence of me in an Opposition paper at a moment
> when my fortunes were under the blackest of clouds. A very dear
> friend of mine said to me as recently as a few days ago 'You owe a
> great deal to Garvin. He stemmed the tide.'

## III

If Garvin was right about the international situation, the army needed
strengthening as well as the navy. There were rival schools of thought
inside the army as well as the navy. Garvin had to choose between
them. He let his readers know where he stood. This was good journalism. But he was by temperament too much a player of the game
himself, too anxious to be in the thick of the action, to stand back and
see how things looked from the other side. This was a weakness. His
*Observer* suffered from the restricted vision that a single observation
post provides. He saw the navy entirely through Fisher's eyes, the
army through Roberts'. There was, moreover, an important difference between the situation of his two guides which affected their vision
and his. Fisher was First Sea Lord and exercised great power; Roberts
had been Commander-in-Chief and retained considerable influence.
He had resigned in 1905 to lead a campaign for compulsory military
training.

Roberts was ideally fitted to be the hero of Garvin's romantic
imagination. A fellow Irishman, born in the year of the First Reform
Bill, his career embodied the legend of Empire. He had spent forty-one
years in India, winning the VC in the Mutiny. He had been with Napier
in Abyssinia in the year that Garvin was born. In South Africa in 1900
he had turned defeat into victory. The title he bore and the nickname
he earned — he was Earl Roberts of Kandahar and Waterford, but
'Bobs' to the troops — epitomise the breadth and the humanity of the
vanished Empire.

He gave no dinner parties like the one at which Fisher's guests drew
lots to decide who would be lucky enough to sit next to the Duchess
of Sutherland. Emphatically it was not his style. Instead Roberts would
turn up on his own in Greville Place, or Tina and Jim would go down
to Ascot to dine, consult and stay the night. There were presents for

her and a signed photograph for her son, but nothing apparently for the girls, who are never referred to in his letters. Perhaps the fact that Roberts' only son had been killed in action in South Africa gave him a special interest in the shy, talented schoolboy who was becoming a crack shot and a champion fencer.

Given the strength of pacifist sentiment inside the Liberal Party and among its Labour allies, and the need for money to pay for new social services, Fisher and Roberts could not both hope to secure what each considered necessary for the defence of Britain. Indeed both might have failed. For this reason Fisher could not afford to act as Roberts' ally even had he felt inclined.

'Too big for a small war; too small for a big war.' That was Fisher's view of the British army; and, since he was opposed to a land-war in Europe, he thought it was too big. Roberts drew the opposite conclusion. Garvin agreed with Roberts. He took the threat of invasion seriously because he was convinced that Germany had it in mind. She was by far the strongest military power in the world. The German Admiralty, he believed, counted on the British navy becoming involved in Asiatic waters. At such a moment, given the German shipbuilding programme, her navy might hope for a local supremacy in home waters, and that was all she would need to mount an invasion.

The risk was serious enough for the Committee of Imperial Defence to study the possibility. The invasion sub-committee took nearly a year to reach a compromise. It decided that a 'bolt from the blue' was impracticable, given British command of the sea, but that a Home Defence army was needed. Much of the regular army was needed in India; the rest was earmarked for an expeditionary force. Once that had sailed, Britain would be defenceless against an invader. Fisher talked freely to Garvin and the King and many others about the desirability of 'Copenhagening' the German fleet. Had he been allowed his way, we might not have needed a Home Defence army; but Copenhagen was a hundred years behind us and Pearl Harbor still a generation off. In 1908 Fisher's idea was fantasy.

On the need for a Home Defence army Garvin parted company with Fisher and supported the government. Haldane, the great reforming War Secretary, proposed to rely on a part-time, volunteer Territorial Army. Garvin believed that it would be impossible to recruit enough men or give them enough training to be battle-worthy. On this he parted company with Haldane.

The two men differed only over means. Both saw the German danger with clear eyes because both knew the Germans with affection, admiration and despair. Haldane had deliberately chosen to go to the War Office, a notorious political graveyard, in the confident hope of securing a joyful resurrection for the British army after the exposure of the Boer War.

It was unfortunate that there was nobody to bring Haldane and Garvin together. Theirs would have been as fruitful a partnership as Garvin's with Fisher. Garvin, however, was already Roberts' man — he had been his speech writer on national service since 1905 — and Roberts was out of favour with the government. Campbell Bannerman had long before written him off as 'a good soldier, a capable administrator, most conciliatory towards the civil population, but a most arrant jobber and intriguer and self-advertiser, and altogether wrong in his political notions'. It was inevitable that Garvin should approach the Admiralty with sympathy and the War Office with distaste.

On the broad issue Garvin was right about what was required, but wrong about what could be obtained. It is possible that, if Britain had had compulsory military service in 1908, there might have been no war in 1914. The Kaiser felt he could disregard Britain's ridiculously small professional army.[2] He could hardly have left out of account a nation trained to arms.

Haldane was right in the sense that compulsory military service was not practical politics in Edwardian England. No government, right or left, would have dared to propose it. In these circumstances he did the best that could be done. He established the General Staff for which reformers had argued in vain for twenty years. He organised an Officers' Training Corps in schools and universities from which the New Armies of 1914 recruited many of their junior officers, including Garvin's son. He gave the new Territorial force a structured organisation so that it became a properly balanced army-in-embryo with its own services instead of the unconnected assembly of yeomanry and volunteer units it replaced. It was a remarkable achievement in the face of Cabinet colleagues who insisted on, and got, a reduction in the cost of the army. Alas, the damning best that Garvin found to say about the Territorial Army was that 'The architect has been exceedingly ingenious. But we are not a whit nearer having a house we can live in.'

It is pleasant to recall that, when the First World War came, Garvin stoutly defended Haldane against those who blackguarded him as a man whose 'spiritual home was in Germany'. They became firm friends and greatly enjoyed each other's company.

I

In his early forties Garvin was closer to the centre of political power than at any other time. Between 1909 and 1911 his role, as John Grigg puts it, 'was almost equivalent to that of a parliamentary leader'. They were revolutionary years. In 1909 both Houses of Parliament had real power. By the end of 1911 Britain was already a single chamber democracy-in-embryo. The Lords had lost their power to hold up an incoming government's legislative programme until the electors had thought again. Future Prime Ministers would in practice have to be commoners. In the first and last acts of this constitutional drama Garvin was a counter-revolutionary leader. In between he was a peace-making *deus ex machina*. Of course his own reading of his part was nothing like as clear cut, but this was the prevailing impression he made on his contemporaries and, through them, on events.

Before the revolution began Garvin had worked hard not only for McKenna's battleships but for Churchill's labour exchanges and Lloyd George's old age pensions. His only complaint was Oliver Twist's. He wanted more. He was anxious that workhouses should be abolished, that we should stop rearing paupers and 'give every child a chance'. In this he went further than the Liberal government was willing to go.

Lloyd George had to find the money to pay both for old age pensions, which he wanted, and for extra dreadnoughts, which he did not. Garvin suggested one way to do it; Lloyd George chose another. Both saw taxation as a method of social reform as well as of raising money. To Garvin, tariff reform with imperial preference was a means of uniting the Empire and providing the base for an economy that would produce more wealth, give more employment and make social insurance less 'like drawing water through a sieve'. The new taxes on income and capital that Lloyd George proposed were ways of redistributing property, especially in land, as well as paying bills.

Neither Lloyd George nor Garvin spoke for a united party. McKenna, for instance, heartily disliked 'the People's Budget', but acquiesced. Conservative Free Traders were vehement against tariff reform. Garvin told them truly that 'If Tariff Reform be wrong, this Budget must be, in the main, right;' but he could not convince them.

The crunch came at a time when the government seemed to have lost the confidence of the country. Shrewd judges gave the Conservatives a possible majority of a hundred at a general election. In the spring of 1909 it would have been fought on the defence of Britain. The Liberals would have lost. By doing so much to secure the famous eight dreadnoughts for his country, Garvin had unwittingly helped to lose the election for his party. Lloyd George and a little navy would have been unpopular. The House of Lords would have spoken for the country on the navy; it spoke only for itself on the Land Tax.

## II

The people's representatives in the 1906 Parliament were certain to pass the Budget, but the people might repudiate their representatives. Garvin thought it likely. The only way they could get the opportunity was for the Lords to reject the Budget. The power was there, but rusty through the disuse of centuries. Garvin thought it should be used because there was no other way of preventing a procession of People's Budgets, smoothing the way to socialist confiscation by creating a 'perennial bribery fund'.

It was essential for Garvin to carry Northcliffe with him. His support would guarantee that of the *Daily Mail* and, Garvin hoped, *The Times* as well as the *Observer*. Northcliffe would need convincing. After an Empire Day[1] lunch with Chamberlain Garvin was able to assure Northcliffe that Chamberlain advocated the bold course. 'If I were there, I would do it,' Joe had said. The trouble was that Joe could not be there to give the campaign a positive twist, to show that there was a better way than the People's Budget to pay for unemployment insurance and other reforms. Instead the great landowners put forward a purely negative defence which impressed nobody but themselves. They thought themselves popular among their own tenantry. They were not. Northcliffe reminded Garvin what the village grocer in Woburn had said to them about his neighbour, the Duke of Bedford. He admitted that trade wasn't too bad, but added, pointing towards the Abbey, 'considering I live in the shade of the upas tree'. The upas tree kills all life beneath it. Well might Garvin say, 'Let the Dukes keep off the grass.' The Lords were useful because they alone had the power to make sure that the people were consulted. They were dangerous because they would not keep their thoughts to themselves. And their thoughts were selfish.

The dukes made an easy target for Lloyd George when, at Limehouse, he opened a campaign that in its effectiveness ranks with Gladstone's Midlothian campaign. Next morning Edward Goulding and Garvin were in the train on their way to Cowes as Jacky Fisher's guests to witness the arrival of the Tsar in his imperial yacht. They should have been relaxed and excited like schoolboys at the end of term. They were excited, but far from relaxed. The papers were full of what Lloyd George had told the dockers about dukes — that a duke was a duke merely because he was 'the first of the litter'; that a duke cost as much to keep up as two dreadnoughts, and much more to the same effect. The dockers cheered; Cabinet colleagues flinched, the King was furious. Lloyd George's words had the same carrying power that Nye Bevan's 'We are the masters now' were to have forty years later. They divided the nation.

When Garvin got back to London he was worried about Northcliffe's position. The *Times*' Lobby correspondent had been writing about 'the turning of the tide' in favour of the Budget. What he wrote must have had the editor's approval, but possibly Northcliffe had not been consulted. Garvin therefore wrote him 'a Pauline epistle' of six foolscap pages of typescript containing an apostolic message to stand firm and be of good courage. The true ground for rejecting the Budget was constitutional. A Budget should be confined to raising the money needed to pay the nation's bills. This one went further and proposed to redistribute property. Garvin thought the land clauses ought not to have been 'tacked' on to the Finance Bill. 'If the principle of doing by Budget what ought to be done by statute is once admitted, almost anything whatever might be done by the same means.' Rejecting the Budget, he continued, would bring a general election but not win it. 'Without a great social programme the Conservative and Unionist parties have never prospered long.' Let the dukes keep of the grass, indeed.

Alas, Thursday's *Daily Mail* was infinitely worse than Wednesday's *Times*. It contained an enthusiastic account, exclusive to the *Mail*, of a new fund that Lloyd George was going to set up to provide roads fit for a motor age. It was Northcliffe's own scoop. Lloyd George had given him the text of his unpublished Development Bill. It was an irresistible bait for a man whose journalistic flair was greater than his political awareness.

Garvin was convinced that his 'Pauline epistle' had been in vain. He was wrong. Northcliffe had sent it on to Balfour with an invitation to lunch at Elmwood. There Balfour met Garvin and found the lunch party 'in the highest degree entertaining'. The three men paced the lawn, Northcliffe and Garvin arguing across Balfour, who was in the middle. Northcliffe kept asking for advice about leading articles, Garvin responded with general onslaughts on the Budget. Balfour sent his intimate friend and secretary, Jack Sandars, a long account of an afternoon that had been 'as good as a play'. A day or so later Sandars made an excuse to renew a fleeting acquaintance with Garvin. Thus began a collaboration that became as close as any in Garvin's life. Balfour's account of what was agreed at Elmwood followed closely the lines of Garvin's 'Pauline epistle', but made no reference to an advanced social programme. Was the omission a Freudian slip? At any rate he soon received from Garvin a carefully worked out paper on social reform.

At the end of the week Garvin sent Frances Colvin his own estimate of what had happened. His opinion of Northcliffe, 'the supreme Wobbler', had gone down. On the other hand he thought much better than he had done of Balfour: 'Balfour was admirable and won my allegiance quite. For the rumour that the suggestions of surrender came from him there was never the least justification.' An alliance had been made.

## III

The Lords rejected the Budget on Tuesday, 30 November. Parliament was prorogued on Friday. That same day Lloyd George opened the election campaign. At Limehouse his quarry had been the dukes; at the National Liberal Club it was Garvin. All the weightiest Tory papers, he pointed out, had advised the peers to accept the Budget: 'Who was on the other side? Practically only one able but ill-balanced journalist', 'a wild man', 'an ex-Parnellite', 'a mad Mullah'. There was just enough substance in Lloyd George's attack to make it plausible. The Conservatives lacked a party leader who could move the public. Balfour was superb in parliamentary skill, but had little appeal outside Westminster. The rest of the Front Bench were indifferent in and out of Parliament. The only speaker with real democratic force was F. E. Smith, a back-bencher distrusted by many including, at this time, Garvin.

Accordingly leadership fell to the party's journalists. Two men stood out head and shoulders above an otherwise not very distinguished bunch, St Loe Strachey of the *Spectator* and Garvin. They alone were the equals of a great generation of Liberal newspapermen.

On the crucial election issue of the Lords and the Budget, Strachey and
Garvin disagreed. That left Garvin.

His greatest strength was paradoxically his greatest weakness. His
dazzling metaphors, which set friendly readers chuckling, seemed to
others a mere 'extravagance of phrase'. Lloyd George picked them out
that Friday at the National Liberal Club as a sign of superficiality. In
fact Garvin used metaphor to clinch in one phrase whole paragraphs
of close reasoning. Isolate the metaphors, skip the reasoning, and
Garvin could well be represented as an empty and sometimes offensive
windbag. That is what Lloyd George did. Garvin felt the need to
remove the impression. Fred Oliver sent him a letter showing him
how to do it:

> See you rub this in well ... the temper of the opposing armies —
> our people conspicuously quiet and rather grieved at the course
> it has been necessary to take; quite aware of its gravity and risks,
> the spirit of the Scots who knelt to pray before Bannockburn ...
> P.S. I suppose you realise that what has happened is mainly *your*
> doing. Whether we win or lose I shall bless you.

It was good advice. Perhaps Garvin thought he was following it,
but Oliver did not feel like blessing him when he read the *Observer*.

> Mon cher d'Artagnan [he wrote] You ought not to have called 'the
> cad of the Cabinet' by that most suitable name ... And you ought
> not to have paid any attention to his gibes at you, not a single
> word. I'm sure Mrs. Garvin has told you so, only you won't listen
> to her ... Yours, Porthos (for I am grown very fat.)

Once again Garvin had given unnecessary gifts to the other side. In
the *Guardian* C. E. Montague joyfully remarked, 'When they are shouting "Liar!" "Epileptic!" "Ananias!" "Plunderbund!" at the top of
their voices, they thank Heaven for having made them men of moderate
speech, and not as these Liberals.'

For six weeks the campaign ran relentlessly on until the first constituencies voted on 12 January. Garvin had already written off his early
hope of a decisive victory. In the end he expected a hung Parliament.
He was right. In the new House the Irish held the balance and could
dictate their terms. Garvin had almost certainly been wrong in urging
the Lords to reject the Budget and using his great influence with
Northcliffe and his growing influence with Balfour to persuade them

to think as he did. Garvin got his election, but he could not win it. He had counted on a triple programme of tariff reform, social reform and imperial preference sweeping the country in the same way that it had recently won over such unlikely constituences as Haggerston and Bermondsey in London's East End. Perhaps, if Joe had been there to lead, it might have been done; but Joe could only look on while Churchill and Lloyd George roused expectant crowds to delirious enthusiasm as once he had done. The finest leader-writing could not match the physical, face to face impact of a packed meeting. On platform after platform the radical pair buried Garvin's 'Tariff or Budget?'[1] under the bolder cry of 'Peers or People?' It was in vain that Garvin argued that the Lords were defending the Constitution by refusing to pass a Budget to which legislative clauses had been 'tacked'. The point was too subtle for the hustings. He should have known it. Perhaps he did.

At the end of the election the Liberals had lost 125 seats and their absolute majority. The Conservatives had gained 115 seats, but were still two fewer than the Liberals. No government could survive without Irish Nationalist support.

# 15  A TRUCE OF GOD, 1910

## I

In the spring Garvin and Charles Whibley spent five weeks with North-cliffe at Vaucluse. They cracked jokes and talked books and argued interminably about Burke and Cicero and other matters that put the ephemeral electioneering of the recent past into the perspective of Lilliput to Gulliver.

Only once did current politics intrude. One day at Cannes Garvin ran into Balfour as he was about to set out for golf. They talked for a while about what would happen when the new Parliament got down to business. The Irish Nationalists were now not so much the allies as the gaolers of the government. To win them over the government must ensure that Ireland actually got Home Rule. The Irish had little sympathy with the other Liberal policies. They had voted against the second reading of the People's Budget and they strongly objected to a tax on whiskey. Garvin remembered with distaste how twenty-five years ago he had helped to deliver the Irish vote to the Conservatives. He was glad to find that Balfour was determined not 'to eat dirt as in 1885'. He would form a government if the King sent for him, but he would make no 'profligate barter with either of the Irish sections'.

Northcliffe's health gave cause for alarm. There were good days at Vaucluse when he was delightful company, but the bad days grew more frequent as the weeks passed, especially after that ambitious hostess Mrs Colefax arrived. Like Taper and Tadpole in Disraeli's *Coningsby* she wanted electioneering talk; Garvin's mind was on the stars. He was glad when Northcliffe's specialist, Bertram Dawson, descended out of the blue and ordered his patient complete rest and quiet. The party broke up.

By the time Garvin got home, Asquith had bought the Irish Nation-alists by the promise of Home Rule in spite of the Lords. The Irish let the Budget pass; they presented their promissory note. Asquith could only honour it if the King agreed to create five hundred Radical peers at one fell swoop.

**II**

Early in the afternoon of Friday, 6 May, King Edward had a heart attack. Before midnight he was dead. It was press day for the *Observer*. Garvin sat down at once and, without consulting anybody, wrote 'A Plea for a Truce of God' — the close season for private baronial wars that the monks of Cluny had sponsored nine hundred years before. In simple sentences he poured out his own shock, his own grief, his own resolve:

> If we may apply a homely phrase to as great a matter as could engage the purposes of a people, the nation must see fair play for the King . . . Let there at least be the suspension of arms — a truce of God proclaimed on behalf of the King as the first public event of his reign.

Garvin's emotional plea was immensely influential because it precisely caught the public mood. Sometimes a single voice can start an avalanche. That Sunday Garvin's did. His demand for a Constitutional Conference proved irresistible. Seventy years later John Grigg, Lloyd George's biographer, recognised its paternity. 'The Truce of God (or Garvin)', he wrote, 'was now in being. It was to last four months.'

Of course the idea of a conference was not a sudden inspiration. Garvin had argued for it before, but in vain. Now the time was ripe. He portrayed the calling of a conference as a legacy from King Edward to King George: 'The whole spirit of his reign may guide us in this matter almost as accurately as if we possessed assured knowledge.' Perhaps Garvin did. It was only a few days since Lord Esher, Edward's intimate friend, had sent for him.

Within hours Garvin knew that he had made an impression on the Liberals. He had a neighbour whom he had never met. R. C. Hawkin was a close friend of the Lord Chancellor. As soon as he had read his *Observer* he sent round to ask Garvin if they could have a talk. They got down at once to working out ways of breaking the constitutional deadlock.

Oliver too recognised at once that Edward's death changed all. While Garvin was busy with his 'Plea for a Truce of God', Oliver wrote an article 'On the Need for Calling a Conference' which he signed 'Pacificus' and sent to *The Times*. His Lowland Scots canniness gave his style a pawky, salty wit that was as devastating as Garvin's headlong onslaught, but *The Times* refused to break Court mourning. 'Pacificus' was held over for a fortnight. Wiser than Buckle, Garvin had recognised that it was the suddenness of Edward's death that had stopped men in their tracks. Their will to fight was paralysed, but could soon return. If Garvin had not published his 'Plea' within twenty-four hours of the King's death, the propitious moment might have passed unrecognised.


## III

Garvin had put his professional life in peril. His position depended on Northcliffe's affection, admiration and support. 'The Chief' was still forbidden by his doctors to attend to business. Garvin's letter went unanswered and probably unread. There was no means of knowing Northcliffe's reaction. The omens were bad. His lieutenants at Carmelite House were hostile. Kennedy Jones thought a political armistice would help the extreme Radicals. Marlowe, the editor of the *Daily Mail*, agreed with him. In his depression Garvin had even talked, half seriously, of emigrating to Canada.

It was a lonely man who sat down at the end of the week to follow his appeal to the heart by an appeal to the mind. What Garvin wrote was audacious, even outrageous. He started with the premise that constitutional reform was necessary, which seemed like treason to many on his side in politics; and that successful constitutional reform needed a wide basis of consent. He thought that in the new circumstances this consent could be obtained in a round table conference. The way would then be open for an agreed programme of social reform, including the transformation of the Poor Law and insurance against unemployment and sickness; in fact for all the items high on Garvin's personal agenda.

> It would mean in the sum not only a conciliatory work of constitutional settlement, but a creative work of social progress; and over both the present Government might preside with the full consent of their opponents. Who doubts that, if reason and patriotism prevailed, this would be done?

But who was willing to do it? Garvin named six Liberal Ministers, starting with the Liberal Imperialists, Asquith, Haldane and Edward Grey — no surprises there. He added two Radicals, Morley and Loreburn, the Lord Chancellor, C. P. Scott's intimate friend. Then came the name, which to most of our readers, will be the most unexpected of all — we mean Mr. Lloyd George. It is definitely said, and we see no reason to doubt it, that the Chancellor of the Exchequer, though no one would suspect him, any more than ourselves, of being for peace at any price in this matter, is not for blind war.

The talk with Hawkin was bearing fruit.

Garvin ran the risk of being utterly discredited, denounced and disowned by Balfour and Lloyd George, and in deep trouble with Northcliffe. He had taken a public stand. He waited anxiously for private reactions. They were encouraging. Lloyd George had read the *Observer* 'with great care' and was much impressed with its good sense. The Master of Elibank, the Government Chief Whip, was 'most sympathetic' and liked Garvin's article 'very much'. Both messages came through W. T. Stead, the most flamboyant of serious journalists, the man who had gone to prison for exposing the white slave traffic in his 'Maiden Tribute of Babylon' articles in the *Pall Mall Gazette*. Stead made two suggestions on his own account. He proposed 'a conference of our own' to prepare the way for a conference of leaders, and he invited Garvin to lunch to meet the Master.

Garvin consulted Oliver, who advised him to have nothing to do with a mini-conference. Stead, he said, was a born liar 'only fit to meddle in the affairs of the other world'. Julia, his spirit guide, 'would certainly be present and ditch everything'. The same objection applied to the lunch. It was excellent that the Master wanted to meet Garvin, but he would not want the world to know that he had done so as it certainly would if Stead were present. By devious manoeuvres behind Stead's back his lunch party was turned into a *tête à tête* breakfast at the Master's home. Garvin made amends to Stead by giving him a memorandum to send on to Esher. Esher liked it. So far, so good.

Meanwhile Garvin had been careful to keep in touch with Sandars and Balfour, who did not discourage him, though they thought success unlikely. Oliver had got a similar response from Austen Chamberlain.

**IV**

The crucial period began on Wednesday, 1 June when Garvin had lunch with Joseph Chamberlain: 'He was flatly against the Conference policy. I explained it fully to him and showed that I had carefully thought out all the possibilities and had two strings to my bow. He was at length largely converted.' It was therefore in a cheerful mood that the Garvins went that night to dine alone with the Olivers. They had much to discuss since, as Oliver said, 'You and I are after the same hare and I think we shall catch it.'

But at breakfast with the Master next morning Garvin learnt that the prospects for a conference were not good. It was getting on for a month since King Edward's death; nearly a fortnight since he was buried. All this time there had been talk of a conference, but no sign had come from the Opposition leaders, no approach had been made by the government. It must soon be now or never.

That same evening Sandars told Esher that, if the Crown moved, Balfour would feel it his duty to respond. It was welcome, unexpected news. On Saturday afternoon the King went to see Joseph Chamberlain at his London home. They spent over an hour in 'much intimate talk, especially on Empire subjects'. The King already knew that a majority of the Cabinet were in favour of a conference and that Balfour would agree. 'If Chamberlain said the same speaking in his own person that may very well have settled the business,' Garvin told Northcliffe. Certainly Hawkin on the Liberal side thought that 'something happened' that afternoon between Joe and the King.

Meanwhile Garvin was busy on his *Observer* article. He set out to show that there were various ways in which Asquith and Balfour could live in relative happiness together: 'At least one plan could be devised for preserving the historic form in the House of Lords while giving Radicals, whenever the country is with them, a fair chance in it.' Oliver was upset by the article, thinking it no business of outsiders to offer blue-prints to members of a Conference — and anyhow he didn't like Garvin's. Two days later he delightedly ate his words: '*Mon fils*, You builded better than I knew; . . . Anyway you have done the trick and all is well.' Oliver's writings, too, had had more than a little to do with tipping the balance. The second 'Pacificus' article had finally appeared on Monday, 6 June, the third two days later. Garvin's congratulations so pleased Oliver that 'I hugged your *Private* letter: didn't even show it to my wife, but just told her you valued my prominence for one forenoon as high as Roosevelt's.'

The Conference met in private a week later. Oliver and Garvin could sit back, happy that they had had something to do with bringing together men who could set parliamentary government on a new collison-free course.

**V**

Early in October Garvin came back from six weeks in the Cotswolds, where he had left the *Observer* unread and steeped himself with 'extraordinary joy' in the minor Elizabethan dramatists. He returned to find everything outwardly the same, but in extreme privacy a revolutionary *coup* was being prepared. Lloyd George had let Sandars know that he wanted to talk to Balfour about a coalition. Sandars met Balfour's train at King's Cross and told him what was in the wind. A private memorandum by Balfour records the substance of the talks that followed at 11 Downing Street during the week beginning 10 October. Lloyd George suggested that Asquith should remain Prime Minister with a seat in the Lords while Balfour led the Commons. The programme he suggested – a strong navy, national service on the Swiss model, Poor Law reform, social insurance, devolution at home, imperial preference, Welsh Church disestablishment but not disendowment – reads very much like Garvin's on 15 May. What was new was the proposal for a coalition in place of Garvin's suggestion that the Liberal government should carry out an agreed programme. Such a proposal could only come from the government side.

An envelope containing Lloyd George's proposals is endorsed by Sandars 'N.B. Those who knew of this besides members of Conference were F. E. Smith, Bonar Law, Garvin.' When Balfour complained about leaks, Lloyd George said, 'Garvin knew everything, but gave nothing away.' In the *Observer* on 16 October Garvin prepared his readers for a Messianic future without betraying his knowledge that there was a Messiah waiting in the wings. He elaborated proposals for devolution showing how important it was for the sake of the Empire to solve the Irish problem. If the opportunity were missed, the Unionist Party 'would be deprived of the sympathy of the Dominions. It would be dead and done for.'

He sent his article and a long explanatory letter to Balfour, who had gone back to Scotland. He wrote also to Austen Chamberlain. He got a catalogue of awkward questions from Balfour; and, from Austen, long and kindly letters too full of saving clauses for comfort. Oliver, busy with more 'Pacificus' letters, got a similar response.

**VI**

Balfour came back on Monday, 31 October. While he slept in the train,

Garvin and F. E. Smith talked deep into the night. The two Merseyside men now found not only that they could work together, but that they liked each other. That night their nerves were on edge. So were Jack Sandars'. 'I am *very* anxious,' he warned Garvin. Balfour 'has gone back a bit. He shrinks from the Federal issue.'

Balfour and Lloyd George met next morning. The Conference assembled in the afternoon: 'They didn't finish. They didn't break,' Garvin reported to Northcliffe. Far into the night private discussions went on. Bonar Law, 'ludicrously lugubrious', Edward Goulding and Garvin waited impatiently in the Constitutional Club. About eleven o'clock F. E. joined them. He was 'very audacious and gay or devil-may-care'. Before long he rang up Churchill. The position was 'extremely critical but still on'. Soon after midnight he and Law left and let themselves in by the back door to Churchill's house. Asquith was there with Lloyd George or Edward Grey, perhaps both.

Next day Garvin told Northcliffe: 'I fear the great business is "bust" though some people cherish a last second of the eleventh hour sort of hope. I'm very sorry. A strong man on our side would have done the thing.' On Thursday evening F. E. told Garvin that all was over. Later, however, he rang again to say that 'his inevitable friend on the other side', presumably Churchill, had told him that the lesser solution was still open. Next day Sandars confirmed that, though the Federal plan was off, there might still be an agreed scheme for resolving differences between the Lords and the Commons. Early the following week Balfour was to put the proposal to that 'gruesome miscellany', the members of the last Unionist Cabinet. Balfour and Sandars hoped that the *Observer* 'would be tinctured by a sufficient but not unguarded pessimism'. It was. It could hardly have been otherwise.

The 'Unionist Sanhedrin' met on Tuesday afternoon. At about half past six Sandars sent Garvin an express letter:

> The Chief has not returned from the Olympians who have held council for more than three hours. But I am somehow persuaded that those who want to die in the last ditch will have an opportunity of being gratified. It is very, very sad.

The end had come. On Friday it was announced that the Conference would not meet again. The Truce of God was over. A general election followed. 'What a pity that it had to take place!' the Master of Elibank wrote to Garvin. 'I shall always recall the patriotic part you played when during the Conference you genuinely worked for a great national settlement.'

I

Fred Oliver's next letter was signed 'Your devoted Belliconissimus née Pacificus'. Garvin was of the same mind. Papers and speeches were suddenly full once more of war talk (an election campaign is what its name implies), designed less to persuade opponents than to strengthen the faithful. Garvin denounced 'dollar domination' when John Redmond returned from the United States 'with the gold of America to wipe England out'. Redmond himself regretfully admitted 'Garvin is the best fighter of you all. I wish he was one of my boys — and he used to be once!'

Garvin, however, was not only an effective rabble-rouser but, as C. E. Montague called him, 'the Unionist Moltke'. Hard thinking, patient negotiation and the capacity for swift action lay behind the 'foaming at the mouth'. If the government won the election, the people would lose their privilege of 'sleeping on it' before coming to a final decision on fundamental changes. They would wake up to find Home Rule enacted in a form about which they would not have been consulted. The Nationalists would see to that. They demanded, and would be able to extort, Home Rule within the lifetime of the new Parliament.

The only way to prevent this was for the Unionists — that was the Conservative Party's alternative title — to drop anything and everything that might lose them the votes of men who agreed with them on the constitutional issue. Food taxes would have to go, even though they were the key to Empire unity. For seven years Garvin had unswervingly followed Chamberlain. He had helped to bring Joe's vision so near to realisation that only a fortnight before firm hands might have grasped it. Now it must be put out of mind lest worse befall.

His mind made up, Garvin went to see Balfour. He asked him to put food taxes into cold storage for the period of the election, and to promise not to introduce them without a referendum or a general election specifically on this issue. Balfour seemed to accept his diagnosis, but reject his prescription. Garvin went away dejected. In fact Balfour had been impressed. Next morning he told Austen Chamberlain how he had been lobbied in quick succession by a Black Country MP, by the editor of the *Daily Express*, the editor of *The Times*, and by Garvin. 'Garvin of all men!' Austen sorrowfully reported to his father.

Meanwhile Garvin decided that there was still time to smuggle an unrelated paragraph into his 'dollar domination' article. Most readers would skip it or find it meaningless, but the Tapers and Tadpoles would wet their fingers and declare they detected the first whisper of a change of wind. Lancashire was the traditional home of the Tory working man. It was also the sacred birthplace of the Anti-Corn Law League. Garvin prophesied 'interesting developments which will be an election inspiration to thousands not only in Lancashire but throughout the country'. Thus obscurely and without authority Garvin gave the first public hint of 'the dodge to sweep Lancashire'. 'Bravo, the *Observer* — you have fairly started the ball rolling,' Sandars wrote.

Monday should have been Garvin's rest day. Instead he spent the afternoon with William O'Brien. O'Brien had been the hero of 'The Plan of Campaign' in Garvin's Nationalist youth, but was now president of the moderate 'All for Ireland League'. While they were talking, Moreton Frewen came in. He had collected £4,000 for O'Brien in the States. 'Dollar domination' in reverse? Frewen not only had money for O'Brien but also a proposition for Garvin. He wanted Garvin to stand with Carson's blessing as the O'Brienite (Independent Nationalist) candidate for South Armagh. 'I put it aside at once,' Garvin told Northcliffe, but perhaps not without a certain regret. Of course, the very idea would have ruined both Garvin and O'Brien had it become known. It would have seemed the worst sort of political opportunism. There was indeed an element of mere Unionist tactics in Garvin's support for O'Brien — a desire to split the Nationalists and break the government majority. There was also a strategy in it which had nothing to do with party. He sincerely believed that their plan for Federal Home Rule was right, necessary and would be healing.

The exciting afternoon led on to a session at the Constitutional Club where Garvin defended his food tax proposal from eleven at night to one in the morning. Carson sympathised, but kept quiet. Sandars longed to support him, but could not without committing Balfour. The Chief Whip said Garvin's plan would ruin Balfour. Bonar Law seems to have agreed with Garvin in principle, but said that only Highbury[1] could make it acceptable, and that Highbury would not do it. Although Garvin meticulously explained to Austen what Highbury's duty was, Bonar Law's judgement proved right.

## II

On Friday Garvin went to the House of Commons to hear Asquith announce the date of the dissolution. Balfour happened to look up at the Gallery, saw Garvin, smiled 'with cherubic benevolence' and invited him to lunch in the House. This was apparently a new experience for Balfour who was delighted to find how small the bill was — 'three and eightpence for the two of us, he drinking lager and I brandy and soda'. Balfour had long suspected that members must be eating and drinking at the public expense. Now he knew. The two men 'had a most excellent talk'.

Balfour had just had a great success at the party conference. In his speech he had closely followed the line Garvin had taken in the *Observer*. 'Three times the whole audience rose to their feet and yelled: and the Dukes were delirious. I have never seen Arthur really get hold of a crowd before.' That was the private verdict of the *Daily Mail* man who had covered the meeting for the *Observer*. More important than the dukes' delight was O'Brien's verdict after scrutinising the speech: 'It was pleasant to find traces of your struggle for cheap food in Balfour's speech. On the Irish question too he kept an open door most satisfactorily for better times.' So far, so good. Garvin went on working for O'Brien. From a fellow devolutionist he collected another £5,000 to be paid over in notes; but, as he told Northcliffe, 'the splendid old O'Quixote is still considering whether he can accept even that'. He had turned down £10,000 of Tory money.

## III

The election campaign had been in full swing for a fortnight when Garvin decided to devote his third successive article to 'dollar domination'. Balfour was still too undecided about food taxes to make it wise from an electioneering point of view for Garvin to come into the open with his cold storage proposal. He changed his mind at the last moment because of a telegram from the editor of the *Textile Mercury*. The telegram said Lancashire could only be won if Balfour announced that a tariff would be subject to confirmation by a referendum. It ended: 'Will you seek Balfour's approval and advocate it tomorrow. Mr. Bonar Law supports last proposal.' A fortnight's electioneering in northwest Manchester had convinced Law that Garvin was right.

Garvin's moment had come, but he nearly missed it. The telegram had reached the *Observer* office before midday. It did not reach Greville Place till late in the afternoon. An unpardonable delay; but yet, '*O felix culpa*'. Garvin had no time to consult Balfour and risk his disapproval; there was time to scrap the existing article and write a five-column exposition of his plan for the London edition.

The gremlin, which had so nearly sabotaged the telegram, moved to the Guardian office. A leader on Monday dared Bonar Law to do what he had just done, advocate a referendum on food taxes. The *Observer*'s London edition had made a political sensation. Is it possible that the London office had not told Manchester? It is more likely that the leader was C. P. Scott's. He was chairman of the North-West Manchester Liberal Association. Few *Guardian* men would dare to tell that most formidable of editors that his leader was out of date before it was written.

Garvin waited anxiously for Balfour's reaction. Sandars' Sunday report was hesitant: 'A.J.B. jibs a little . . . I have a half-promise that he will tackle the point on Tuesday at the Albert Hall.' Throughout Monday the pressure on Balfour grew. By the evening he had decided to give the referendum pledge. On Tuesday he told his audience, 'I have not the least objection to submitting the principles of tariff reform to a referendum.' Garvin wrote ecstatically to Sandars, 'Men are shaking each other's hands and saying he is out and out and out a leader and a man.' The *Observer* explained 'to Mr. Balfour alone belongs the lasting fame of a triumphant act'.

## IV

The Liberals would not have it so. It was not Balfour they attacked, but 'Balfour's master' as W. T. Stead called Garvin in a mischievous and not unsuccessful effort to belittle the Leader of the Opposition. It was about Garvin that the *Daily News*, the *Daily Chronicle*, the *Morning Leader*, the *Westminster Gazette* and the *Manchester Guardian* wrote day after day. Never before or since has an ordinary working journalist occupied so continuously the centre of the political stage. For fifteen months, from the autumn of 1909 to the end of 1910, he was quoted, applauded and attacked in all the papers of both sides. His power base of course was his influence with Northcliffe. As long as that alliance held, he could command a wider audience for his ideas than any other man in England. Politicians had to reckon with him. Moreover they were fascinated by the daring young man with audacious ideas. Lloyd George had opened the first election campaign by poking fun at Garvin; he closed the second on the same note. What right had a Unionist Party led by a great Scotsman (a snide acknowledgement of Balfour) on ideas supplied by a great Irishman (a mocking salute to Garvin) to turn up its nose at the Celtic twilight enveloping Scotland, Wales and Ireland? After all, it was supposed to be a United Kingdom.

The 'dodge to sweep Lancashire', as Garvin's opponents called it, failed. Substantial gains were made in the North-West, but they might have come without the promise of a referendum. There had already been Liberal losses there in January. The process might have continued in any case since the fear and fact of surtax and higher income tax influenced business people as Garvin had seen that it must. To introduce the idea of a referendum right at the end of the campaign was to risk the familiar sequence of 'order, counter-order, disorder'. In fact the new gains in Lancashire and Cheshire were offset by losses in the south.

The election had been lost; the parliamentary revolution had been completed; only the formalities remained to be carried out. At the beginning Garvin's had been one of the strongest voices that emboldened the Lords to throw out the 'People's Budget' and provoke a revolutionary situation. A fair measure of responsibility is his. In the second stage he regained the ground lost in the first. He preached a Truce of God which men on both sides accepted. During it they came near to finding an agreed solution to the constitutional troubles which beset Britain and Ireland. He has no blame for their final failure to turn the Truce into a Peace. From that failure there stemmed directly the third stage. No 'dodge to sweep Lancashire', no promise of a referendum could hide the fact that the parties and the electors had returned to the positions they had been in before the Truce. Predictably the second general election proved a carbon copy of the first.

I

'Northcliffe only respects those who stand up to him,' Garvin once told Frances Colvin. 'The only basis of my influence is my readiness to put on my hat and walk out.' The first sentence is certainly true; the second, a half truth. Northcliffe admired the master political journalist; Garvin, the Napoleonic newspaper proprietor. Together they believed they could achieve great things. That was the origin of their relation and its continuous basis. It deepened into family affection deep enough to survive business and political disagreements. Garvin's determination to be his own man, whatever the cost, appealed to Northcliffe. Without it, they would never have got on. In the end, they could not get on because of it.

Garvin felt that Northcliffe was surrounded by his rivals, jealous Carmelite House men who envied his semi-independent status and his wholly independent ways. They resented his growing national and international reputation. Northcliffe had foreseen the danger. When he announced Garvin's part share in the ownership, he warned him: 'There is always great jealousy against a journalist who becomes a newspaper proprietor. You must be prepared for it.'

Perhaps Garvin was too much on his guard. George Sutton had been with Northcliffe since the beginning of *Answers*, the first of all the Harmsworth papers. During Northcliffe's illness in 1910, Garvin quarrelled with Sutton about his share in the *Observer* profits. Was the calculation to start with Northcliffe's purchase of the paper, or from Garvin's becoming editor, or from the time that loss was turned into profit? It made a considerable difference. Northcliffe was prepared to write off the £29,000 the *Observer* lost before Garvin took over. He, or Sutton on his behalf, was not prepared to disregard the £11,400 lost during Garvin's early days. The row was strongly reminiscent of Garvin's dispute with Goldman four years before. Nothing could persuade Garvin that he was not hard done by. He suspected sharp practice. His solicitor had to come to his rescue by taking over the negotiations and handling in an impersonal way what Garvin had made a personal matter.

The solution was the creation of 4 per cent preference shares to the value of the £11,400. Northcliffe and Garvin's holdings of ordinary shares were reduced in proportion and the preference shares allocated to Northcliffe. Russell thought the offer a very fair one. It ensured Garvin some dividends whereas, if Northcliffe had insisted on a cash settlement, it might have been years before there was any money for the shareholders.

The tone and temper of Garvin's business letters at this time, and no doubt of his conversation, exasperated Northcliffe and infuriated Sutton, who resigned his *Observer* directorship. Garvin was storing up trouble for himself and poisoning his own mind with possibly unfounded suspicions. He began to make plans about what he would do if he and Northcliffe fell out. He investigated the possibility of reviving W. E. Henley's extinct *National Observer*. He had it in mind to run, if he was driven to it, an *Observer*-in-exile under a recognisable title. The need did not arise. In November the dispute over profits was settled. Garvin and Northcliffe went into the December election as firm friends as ever.

## II

Their St Luke's summer was brief. The lost election brought their partnership to a rough end. Northcliffe had been a late, half-hearted and backsliding convert to imperial preference in so far as it involved a 'stomach tax', likely to alienate readers and lose voters. To him the referendum was not 'a dodge to sweep Lancashire', but a way to brush food taxes under the carpet. To Garvin it was simply a device to concentrate the minds of the electors on the supreme issue of the election, the constitution. There was bound to be a conflict between the two men. It could not be long delayed. The Imperial Conference was to meet in London in May.

After the first of the two British general elections the Canadian Prime Minister had lost hope of getting a preference for Canadian wheat in Britain. He therefore turned to the United States, and negotiated a Reciprocity Treaty which was published on Saturday, 28 January 1911. It provided for Canadian wheat to enter the United States duty-free in return for low, reduced duties on many American manufactured goods entering Canada. The day the treaty was published the *Daily Mail* started a bitter attack on imperial preference and kept it up day after day.

Northcliffe went down to Elmwood, explaining to Garvin that he was rather tired. Garvin pursued him with a letter of sad protest:

> My only feeling is 'God help the Empire!' ... We were right out and out about the food tax in relation to that election; but it is over and I, for one, never dreamed of dropping Imperial Preference altogether. For the *Daily Mail* to appear to be the advocate of the 'banged, barred and bolted door' seems to me as bad as bad can be ... I stick to my whole political faith. Like Luther, 'Ich kann kein Anders.' ... And I love you all the same and hope that Elmwood will do you heaps of good.

Northcliffe telegraphed asking Garvin to come to Elmwood 'before anything definite is done'. It was, he said, a matter he thoroughly understood and felt very strongly about. Garvin tried to put the visit off to the following week. This brought him a straight warning:

> I cannot possibly be associated with a policy that I believe by its hopeless ignoring of new facts will certainly help to lose Canada. This is a very hasty message dictated by telephone sent in hope that you can come tonight for good discussion tomorrow morning.

This reached Garvin shortly before dinner on Thursday. He did not go to Elmwood. It was an uncharacteristic refusal. Instead he wrote a long letter which Tina copied, a sure sign that he recognised the seriousness of what he was doing. He had made up his mind what the *Observer* would say, and had no intention of being talked out of it. Perhaps Garvin realised that he and Northcliffe had come to the parting of the ways and did not want to mar their personal friendship by a painful scene: 'I beg you to relieve me from what, in these circumstances, could only be a miserable and futile ordeal for us both.'

Garvin's article was headed 'Empire Yet; Canada and the States; Preference or Impotence'. It began with a frontal attack on the *Daily Mail*. The *Mail* had brought joy to every German journal that feared Chamberlain's policy. It had brought utter contentment to American apostles of annexation, and dismay to Canadians who had given the best years of their life to Imperial Union. Its arguments were fallacious. Canada had not abolished the preferences it gave to British goods. The Reciprocity Treaty had not yet been ratified. Though 'we have received an unmistakable warning of infinite gravity ... Canada even now is giving us another and a last respite.'

This was altogether too much for Northcliffe. He made no further attempt to see or talk to Garvin. As he told Max Aitken, 'I am extremely fond of Garvin, but I think he acted with great unwisdom in declining to take a mere two hours' railway journey.' On Monday Northcliffe resigned his *Observer* directorship. The paper was for sale. He gave Garvin an option to purchase within three weeks. 'So far as I am concerned the *Observer* is nothing; to Garvin it is everything,' he told Aitken. It was a magnanimous gesture worthy of their friendship. Northcliffe showed unusual generosity in allowing his junior partner an opportunity to buy him out at a reasonable price and carry on in their paper a policy of which he had always disapproved. Lady Northcliffe, who hated the separation, wrote: 'Garve, my dear. It is not going to make any difference to my friendship — and love — for you two people. Of that I am determined and so is the Chief — I have just seen him and he knows I'm writing . . .' For the first time she signed herself Molly.

The Northcliffe years were over. The personal wrench was great; the loss of influence considerable. Gone for ever was Garvin's power to influence the *Daily Mail*, which had made him so attractive an ally to the Unionist leaders. Northcliffe, too, lost more than he realised. The political influence of his papers was at its peak during his association with Garvin. Their separation made no difference to his business success; in that sense the *Observer* really was nothing to him. But it was Garvin who had made the Harmsworth papers important politically as well as journalistically. No one took his place.

# BOOK FOUR: GARVIN AND THE ASTORS, 1911-1914

'We might at any time have difficulty with Garvin having full political control.'

Arthur Steel-Maitland, chairman of the Unionist
Party organisation, to Bonar Law, 7 August 1914

I

The day after Northcliffe gave Garvin an option to buy the *Observer* he approached Max Aitken. Aitken was thirty-one, a Canadian who had settled in England only a few months before and was, as Bonar Law told Blumenfeld, enormously rich, anxious to have a political career, and would be glad of a paper to back him. Aitken promptly lent Blumenfeld £25,000 to save the *Daily Express* for tariff reform. Might he not do as much or more for Garvin and the *Observer*? When Aitken promised to consult Goulding, his close business associate, Garvin naturally felt encouraged. There was, however, a fatal obstacle. Aitken shared Northcliffe's view about the effect on imperial prefer-ence of Canada's Reciprocity Treaty with the United States, the very point on which Garvin and Northcliffe had parted company.

More promising was the approach Lord Roberts made on Garvin's behalf to Sidney Goldman. Goldman consulted the South African financier, Abe Bailey, about a syndicate to buy the *Observer*, leaving Garvin his share in the ownership. Meanwhile Garvin himself had had talks with Waldorf Astor, Aitken's precise contemporary, and, like him a Tariff Reformer who had won a seat for the first time in the recent general election. Astor was more interested in getting Garvin as editor of the *Pall Mall Gazette* than in buying the *Observer*. If that was the only way it could be done, then he would buy the *Observer*, but he would buy it outright or not at all. The Astors never took partners. It took a long time to settle the terms. Until that was done, Goldman's syndicate remained a possibility. It says much for both Goldman and Garvin that, in spite of their row over the *Outlook*, they were willing to work together again.

At last on 5 April Charles Russell concluded negotiations for the sale of the *Observer* to William Waldorf Astor, Waldorf's father. Garvin was to become editor of the *Pall Mall Gazette* as well as of the *Observer* but to surrender his 'proprietary interest'. It was a sacrifice he made with extreme reluctance and always regretted. Apart from the financial angle, Garvin felt, and the world agreed, that the *Observer* was in a special sense his paper. His fifth share in it symbolised this.

His friends, who had been holding their breath for anxious weeks, rejoiced. His own relief shines through a letter to Sidney Colvin:

> Bless you for your letter and all understanding of the neglectful who is never forgetful. Young Waldorf Astor rang me up suddenly yesterday evening with the news ... *Ich kann kein anders* is a terrible voice to arise in one. It must be obeyed but I don't want to hear it again for a while.

## II

Astor, of course, had had to buy out Garvin as well as Northcliffe. Inevitably, Garvin being Garvin, there was a tussle over the price. Northcliffe had fixed £40,000 as the price of the paper, Garvin insisted on £45,000. He justified his demand by complicated arguments about the difference in the value of the paper with or without himself as editor. Alternatively, he argued that his contract still had two years to run and that at the end of the period the *Observer*'s value would have increased. He conveniently forgot that by disobeying North-cliffe's instructions he had himself broken his contract. He appealed from Coode Adams, Astor's man of business, to Coode Adams' master in a characteristically tortuous letter, ending 'Don't think whatever comes of it that it will make the least difference to my personal relations. I know I have had a friend in you. You will have a friend in me always.' It is doubtful whether William Waldorf Astor bothered to follow Garvin's involved reasoning. He knew he wanted Garvin and must pay his price. And what was £5,000 to the Astors?

It was a great deal to Garvin, who had never had any capital. How ought he to invest it? He consulted Bonar Law, who brought in Aitken. There could have been no better advisers – and between them they took a deal of trouble. Meanwhile Astor had satisfied himself that Garvin was politically sound and religiously acceptable. Coode Adams reported that 'G. had been a R.C. but had become a Protestant with his wife and was bringing up his children as Protestants.' This satisfied Astor but was at best a half truth. Certainly both Jim and Christina had ceased to be practising Roman Catholics, but they could only be regarded as Protestants if that word embraces all lapsed Catholics.

Garvin's contract stopped him from writing for other papers without Astor's previous consent in writing. And so Calchas had to die, while Garvin's regular writing for the *Daily Telegraph* also came to an end. More serious was Astor's insistence that the control of the paper should remain entirely and absolutely in his hands. This involved managerial supervision by Coode Adams. Garvin had fretted at Carmelite House influence over the *Observer* management, but at least the Northcliffe men were experts. Coode Adams was not. He was a lawyer and an admirable businessman, but his management of the *Pall Mall Gazette*, a tiny and unprofitable fraction of the Astor empire, had not given him the special touch which newspapers require.

Managerial control was odious but endurable; editorial supervision was entirely unacceptable to Garvin. He had, however, to agree to this awkward clause, knowing how Astor had used his power to sack Harry Cust from the *Pall Mall Gazette*. According to Cust this is what happened:

Astor: American crisis very severe, my position very delicate . . .
Cust:  . . . I telegraphed to you for instructions. You answered maintain judicious attitude . . . Has the paper gone wrong?
Astor: Not at all, perfectly satisfied; moderate and judicious, but acute crisis requires new editorial arrangements. You and Iwan Müller must go, and in a week. Salary paid of course in lieu of notice.
Cust: Why?
Astor: Well in such case prefer dictated policy week by week and day by day.
Cust: Why the devil didn't you do so?
Astor: Knew no use.
Cust: Why?
Astor: You wouldn't have followed my wishes.
Cust: Did you express them?
Astor: No.
Cust: How could I follow them?

One wonders how Garvin dared risk a disaster which seemed a near-certainty. The odd thing is that Garvin and William Waldorf Astor never had a quarrel. The difference in age helped. Garvin liked men old enough to be the father he had never known. They took to him. Joseph Cowen, Edward Lawson, John Le Sage all warmed to the young man whose impetuosity recalled the ardour of their own youth. Garvin's relation to William Waldorf Astor was less intimate, but they got on well.

There was much in the elder Astor's career and character to appeal to Garvin. His sense of history was touched by a man who had served in the New York State legislature and been American Minister in Rome. Italy, Italy of the Renaissance, was a passion they shared. Garvin was a writer; Astor aspired to be. His two historical novels were bad books, but Garvin would never deride a man who aspired to cultivate a talent which the gods denied. Fortunately for Garvin, Astor, who in his forties had pestered Harry Cust with unusable manuscripts, had outgrown his literary ambitions by his sixties. Garvin admired the use to which Astor put his fabulous wealth. To own and inhabit a villa near Sorrento was to purchase semi-Paradise; to give Cliveden as a wedding present to his eldest son was a princely gesture to capture Garvin's romantic imagination; to withdraw, a lonely melancholy widower, to the medieval glory of Hever Castle was to ensure a sympathetic understanding from Garvin who guarded so closely his own innner privacy. Something of Garvin's feeling for the old man comes out in a family letter after a visit to Hever when he found his host

> far more human and intimate than ever before ... At lunch he was particularly proud of his concoction, traditional in the Astor family I fancy, a sort of iced claret punch in a silver bowl and dispensed with a gold ladle. Well, we thoroughly enjoyed it and liked him, the strange, lonely, powerful-natured old eccentric as we have always liked him.

There was between them a natural meeting of spirits. It flourished best when Garvin was in a die-hard mood, but survived the times when his cross-bench longings were uppermost.

## III

William Waldorf Astor bought the *Observer* and lent the use of it and the *Pall Mall Gazette* to his son as a kind of political coming-of-age present. Garvin and Waldorf were helped in their early dealings with one another by the fact that old Mr Astor remained the owner. The loan to Waldorf covered the political policy of the papers, over which he and Garvin agreed. It did not extend to management and finance, over which they were in the future often to disagree. Father and son notoriously found it difficult to get on. The fact that Garvin usually agreed with the son, but got on with the father, smoothed the first four years of their association.

They made an unlikely pair. Waldorf had scraped a fourth at Oxford. It is as rare a degree as the first he might conceivably have got. Certainly he was worth a good second; but then, as Lady Edward Cecil noted with surprise in her pen, he is 'not at all stupid as he has every right to be if he chooses'. He owed his fourth to the way he chose to spend his time. He fenced and played polo for the University, he rowed, he was Master of the Drag, he started a stud which later became famous. Days in the field and evenings at the Bullingdon left little time for books. Then, in 1905, he was told that he would be a semi-invalid for the rest of his life. He had angina and a tendency to tuberculosis. That year he met and courted Mrs Nancy Shaw, a Virginian whose first marriage had ended in disaster. They were married in May 1906.

As heir to one of the world's great fortunes Waldorf had no need to do anything. A man who owns one of England's great country houses, a town house in St James's Square, a 'cottage' near Sandwich, a house on the Hoe at Plymouth, and a place in the Highlands can pass his time agreeably enough. That was neither in Waldorf's nor in Nancy's nature. They both wanted an active life of achievement. Christopher Sykes, Nancy Astor's biographer, writes of them at this time:

> Waldorf Astor was not a respectable version of Macbeth: he was not a man who was only galvanised into action by the ambition of his stronger-souled wife. His ambition was as vigorous as hers, and he was possessed of as stern a will, but a rational will, and he sought for a rational outcome. She had the irrationality of a wilful appetite, and she sought not the reasonable or unreasonable outcome but the one which satisfied it. She had the instinctive wisdom which makes those who have it defy fate, and he was gladly led by it.

Waldorf was led by it into politics. Balfour was told of their decision; Waldorf was offered a safe seat. He turned it down. The rational man calculated that it is useful to work one's way up. He went into the Conservative Central Office. In 1908 he became prospective candidate for Plymouth. Next year he bought a house on the Hoe. In 1910 he fought Plymouth in the two general elections, losing in January but winning in December.

Nancy canvassed busily for Waldorf. If a voter protested that he was a Liberal, she replied that so was Waldorf really, but that he happened to think the Conservative policy was better. That was about the truth of the matter. Waldorf's beliefs on social and imperial matters were almost identical with Garvin's. Like Garvin he was 'a conservative revolutionary'.

If Waldorf was to work as closely with Garvin as he planned, Garvin would have to see a good deal of Mrs Astor. What they thought of each other and how they got on would be important. Both revelled in the centre of the stage; but to begin with they enjoyed meeting on the superficial level of relaxed, easy banter, untouched by the deep affection which, for example, Molly Northcliffe and Garvin felt for each other. Garvin gave his wife a revealing picture of dinner at St James's Square in the early days:

> Mrs. Waldorf was mischievous but more womanly: we were very merry and irresponsible and riotous and epigrams flew, and it was nearly twelve before Waldorf simply seized his wife, suppressed her and with great firmness carried her off to bed. She struggled but loved it. That young man has great strength of character. In her heart she is as fond of him as anything, is a bit afraid of him too and for all her mania for being admired doesn't really care a button for anyone else.

Few young men enter Parliament with half Waldorf's advantages. He controlled two newspapers and the pen of the liveliest political journalist of the day. That was one way of looking at it. It was not, however, how either Waldorf or Garvin saw it. Garvin would never have consented to be any man's PRO – not even Joe's. Waldorf would have coiled up at the idea of having one. They saw themselves as companions-in-arms, fighting for causes which mattered more to them than their careers. If the younger man had the money, the older one had the ideas; had had them in fact long before Waldorf was politically aware. It would be a serious mistake, however, to regard Waldorf as Garvin's protégé. A young MP who in his first session entertains Lloyd George and Lord Grey to lunch and on the same day Austen Chamberlain and Curzon to dinner is already somebody. Waldorf was nobody's man. His wealth ensured the independence which his character demanded.

Garvin's association with Waldorf soon ripened into a friendship strong enough to endure for thirty years many self-inflicted wounds. These arose more often because they were temperamentally poles apart than because they differed in opinion. The circumstances of their association sharpened the contradiction of their natures. They worked together in a field for which Garvin was suited, Waldorf incapacitated. Newspapers cannot effectively be edited by committees, where Waldorf felt at home. Garvin had a field commander's instincts. He could, of course, write to a brief, and had done so cheerfully on the *Newcastle Chronicle* and the *Daily Telegraph*. But he would not edit in that way. He refused to sit down with Waldorf or with a committee — that was a later suggestion — to conduct hypothetical arguments, reach abstract conclusions, and apply them in the paper despite rapidly changing circumstances. In newspaper work time presses, a late news flash alters a whole perspective, new decisions must be quickly made, and can only be made by the man on the spot. Let him be judged afterwards, not ham-strung in advance. Waldorf found it difficult to appreciate these controlling circumstances of newspaper production, and the habits of mind and work with which successful journalists respond to them. 'He wrestles with Garvin all Friday afternoons,' wrote Lady Edward Cecil, 'which would, I should think, send his temperature up.' It must, I should think, have made Garvin apoplectic. Friday is a more than usually arduous day for a man who edits both an evening and a Sunday paper.

Waldorf's interventions were well intentioned but ill-judged; Garvin's reactions prickly and provocative. Very early in their association Waldorf objected to one of Garvin's articles. The more he thought about it, the less he liked it. The two men met and disagreed. Then Garvin sent Waldorf a letter which was part curtain-lecture and part ultimatum. He reminded Waldorf that an editor never takes a strong line which upsets Whitehall or other powerful interests without provoking attempts to check him: 'When they succeed, journalism is devitalised. The public at once feels the difference.' Then came the ultimatum. Garvin would stop his 'big articles', although they put up the circulation. Almost as a postscript he added:

> There is one thing I have to beg. It is that in cases where you wish a policy to be overruled or checked or limited you will instruct me in writing, so that I may be able to place my own view on record.

Garvin's purpose, I think, was to prevent Waldorf trying to edit the paper while admitting his right to curb the editor. Waldorf was not to say 'Do this,' though he might say 'Don't do it again.'

Meanwhile Waldorf had gone down to Cliveden to think things over. He came to the conclusion that Garvin had been right, and thanked him 'for having removed the cobwebs which for a long time obscured what ought to have been patent'. Garvin responded with affection: 'I never read anything more generous and whenever it is my turn to give way you shall find how fully I can reciprocate. Now I don't want any letters of instruction or things in writing.' But neither did he want, though he did not say so, the endless discussions that Waldorf loved. Waldorf had all the time in the world; Garvin had to meet a deadline.

I

There are two ways of looking at the zig-zag political route Garvin
followed during the years of the Astor-Garvin triumvirate. Garvin
might have put it, like Humphrey Pump in Chesterton's *The Flying
Inn*,[1] 'I write under a great disadvantage. You see, I know why the
road curves about.' It curved about because it followed the guidelines
so nearly agreed between the party leaders in October 1910. Party
managers took another, but equally Chestertonian, view: 'The wild
thing ran from left to right and knew not which was which.' But
of course Garvin knew. When the Conference failed, the negotiators
retired to their party lines and withdrew the concessions they had
been willing to make. Garvin remained in No Man's Land because
for him Lloyd George's proposed package had not been a compromise,
but was a creed. He was prepared to live and die by it.

Early in 1911 two friendly enemies, Winston Churchill and F. E.
Smith, founded The Other Club. So far from having a creed, its purpose
was just to dine. A rule provided that 'nothing in its intercourse is to
interfere with the rancour and asperity of party politics'. The creedless
club provided Garvin with the institutional base he needed. He was
among friends. Edward Goulding and Waldorf Astor were members.
The club was made up of twelve MPs, drawn in equal numbers from
either side of the House; nine peers; and nine others, including Garvin,
whom the club called 'distinguished outsiders'. They got an inside
view since of the original dozen MPs, three became Prime Minister, two
Lord Chancellor and one Viceroy of India. Dining together once a
fortnight they were likely sometimes to 'talk the treason that claret
inspires'. The Other Club did not put into Garvin's head the cross-bench
ideas that he expounded with passion, but it gave him regular contact
with the men who alone could carry them out.

Take a look at the membership from this point of view. Lloyd
George was Chancellor of the Exchequer; Churchill became First
Lord of the Admiralty soon after the club was founded. Both had
tried their best to turn the Truce of God into a Peace. F. E. Smith
and Bonar Law had not been members of the Constitutional Conference, but had known what was going on and wished it well. So,

too, did Lord Esher. He always knew everything; and, besides, he was, apart from Ministers, the civilian most closely and powerfully concerned with defence policy. If there had not been an Other Club, Garvin would have had to try to invent one, and in that he would have failed.

## II

Just how unorthodox Garvin's position was became apparent as soon as the new Parliament met. It had two main Bills to consider. The National Insurance Bill laid the foundation of our Health Service; the Parliament Bill castrated the Lords. Liberals damned the dukes and demanded doctors. Tories blessed the Lords and, since they dared not curse the idea of health insurance, they double damned Lloyd George's version. Garvin, half Tory and half Red, wanted both doctors and dukes — though dukes only so long as it took to put something better in their place.

Take the dukes first. The electors had made sure that the Parliament Bill would get through the Commons. The Lords were still legally free to reject the Bill, but not in practice. The Tory peers could either abstain and let it pass or watch 500 new 'puppet peers' outvote them. The preamble to the Bill promised a reformed Second Chamber later. Garvin believed, rightly as it turned out, that if the Bill slipped quietly through, 'later' would prove to be 'never'. He hoped that the torrent of 'puppet peers' would drown the House so deep that 'later' would have to be 'sooner'. He therefore declared himself a diehard like old Lord Halsbury (b. 1823) with whom otherwise he had hardly a thought in common.

Garvin argued his case privately with Sandars, who was half inclined to agree, and with Balfour who was half inclined to disagree. He argued it publicly in the *Observer*. Only once did he hesitate. At the time of the Coronation he suggested to Sandars that a magnanimous gesture might be worth while. Nothing came of it. A month later he was back in his most bellicose mood, the mood old Astor loved. Young Astor accepted Garvin's reasoning but recoiled when he told abstainers that their names 'would be framed in black as the names of men politically dead and damned'. They read their *Observer*, but let the Bill pass. It was time to be off to the moors.

Garvin lost his battle on the Lords, but won it for the doctors. Social insurance had long been his goal. To see it brought about by his opponents must have been bitter sweet. He must have been tempted, like his party, to fasten on the Bill's weak points and trounce the Chancellor for doing his work badly. But that was not Garvin's way. He was the least Laodicean of men. The *Observer* described the Bill as 'the greatest scheme of social reconstruction ever yet attempted'. It transcended all partisanship. Mr Lloyd George would need the utmost help that the Opposition could give. 'Let him have it. Let us do it together.' This was not at all what Garvin's party either expected or wished to read, but it did not come as a surprise to his undercover friends in the Liberal government. Garvin had had a long talk with the Master of Elibank two days before the debate, and had been to breakfast with Lloyd George before writing his article.

When it came to the Third Reading the Conservatives tried to get the Bill postponed till another session. Waldorf abstained. He was one of nine Conservatives who voted against their party on the final division. These were bold acts for a new and ambitious member to take. He became a marked man, worth courting by the government side, needing watching by his own party whips. Garvin's initial fears disappeared. Waldorf and he were thinking alike in politics.

The new Act required new institutions, among others a new expert committee on tuberculosis, which in time developed into the Medical Research Council. Sir Robert Morant, the ablest civil servant of his time, picked Waldorf to be its lay chairman. The fact that he was a Conservative MP helped to allay the fears of wary specialists. A greater problem was to persuade enough general practitioners to take part in the service. Morant kept Garvin closely informed — 'came to a scratch dinner . . . we are upon perfectly safe ground', as Garvin reported to Waldorf. The *Observer* carried weight with the recalcitrant doctors just because it was not a government paper. Gradually they came round. In the end they realised that they would get their money whether their patients were well or ill. That settled the matter. The first benefits were paid on 15 January 1913, as the Act provided.

## III

The National Insurance Act was the last great social reform before the war. There were three and a half years left, but they were given up to Home Rule for Ireland and Disestablishment for Wales. There was no time for anything else. No time, but great need. Garvin stressed the need when he talked to the Unionist Social Reform Committee in

October 1911. This was a small pressure group of young MPs led by
F. E. Smith and greatly feared by Walter Long and the old guard.
Most of Garvin's friends in the Commons, including Waldorf and
Goldman, belonged to it. Its members worked hard to get their facts
right; and to quote Christopher Sykes, were almost 'an unofficial and
self-constituted Royal Commission'.

Garvin's speech was delivered against the recent experience of 'a
sudden and desperate attempt to paralyse the whole national system
of transport', of 'pitched battles in the streets', and of 'social war
waged in the temper of war'. But now 'the shut fist must give way to
the open mind', a quality for which Tory MPs were not conspicuous.
And so Garvin attacked the party backwoodsmen, who hid themselves
in a cocoon so dense that 'they pass from town to country house and
from country house to town and, unless they are candidates in industrial constituencies, they never come within sight or sound much less
within whiff of a slum'. He reminded his hosts that they could still
hear fellow Unionists talk of a bread-winner earning twenty-five
shillings a week as 'an industrial incubus, a public nuisance, or even a
selfish beast ... almost rolling in unlimited drink and a gross kind of
barbarous luxury'. No wonder working-class voters were alienated.
Somehow the party must regain 'the fervour and the force and the
concentrated sympathy which burned in Carlyle's "Past and Present"
and in Disraeli's "Sybil" and by which Mr. Chamberlain won all the
power of his prime'. Garvin, like Chamberlain, was a Tory now, but he
was talking like 'Radical Joe' of old.

He and his friends would have been willing to help the government
get rid of the workhouse as it had flourished 'in all its expensive stupidity and general repulsiveness since Mr. Bumble's day'. He would have
been willing; but his party would not as long as Mr Balfour led it.


## IV

For months there had been a strong BMG (Balfour Must Go) movement
in which Leo Maxse had been especially prominent. Garvin shared
Maxse's frustration but felt bound to the man with whom he had been
so intimately associated. Ten days after Garvin's speech, however,
the situation changed. Balfour made up his mind to go. Sandars gave
Garvin the news and asked him to write the *Telegraph* leader, which
he did.[2] His words rang true. 'My dear friend,' Sandars wrote, 'Your
tribute today was the best of all, and it touched me much. To one

whose borrowed light has now gone out it was just what I wanted in its full appreciation.'

The struggle for the succession was keen. The party was equally divided between Austen Chamberlain and Walter Long. Long was the favourite of the Church of England and of the country squires — 'owns about 15,500 acres' as his entry in *Who's Who* put it. 'A man who carries no weight outside the market ordinary and not much there' was Leo Maxse's opinion. Garvin, remembering Long's part in the loss of the *Outlook*, thought he needed watching like a horse-thief. Garvin knew in his bones that Austen, though he might become leader of the party, would never be a leader of men. Nevertheless he became Austen's man because he would always be Joe's man. In a straight fight Austen might just win. If the tariff reform vote was split, Long was bound to succeed.

At this point a new MP, Max Aitken, took a hand. He was as strong an Empire man as any of Chamberlain's lieutenants, but as a newcomer to Britain he felt no sentimental attachment to the Chamberlain family. His allegiance was rather to his fellow Canadian, Andrew Bonar Law. It was natural that Aitken should think that Law would make a better leader than Austen Chamberlain. He persuaded Law to stand and Goulding to support him. Goulding failed to recruit Garvin. Honour forbade it, and besides it would let Long in.

Balfour's resignation was announced on 8 November. Next day Garvin went to see Law. He asked him not to split the tariff reform vote. He came sadly away and told Austen that Law was 'inflexible, quite determined to get the position if he could'. Although Garvin did not realise it, he had in fact shaken Law's resolution. In the morning Law wrote a letter, saying he would not run if that 'would damage C. and help L'. Garvin appeared to have won, but Law showed the letter to Aitken who threw it on the fire. Garvin had lost after all.

Meanwhile Austen had asked Garvin to come round to Egerton Terrace. There Austen told him that he had decided to stand down and had persuaded Long to do the same so that Law was in. 'Now comes the hard part,' Austen said. 'I am just going to write to my father, who has always been more ambitious for me than he ever was for himself.' When Garvin passed the news on to Waldorf, he added, 'it has been for me the saddest day I have known in politics'.

He told Goulding that every cheer for Joe at Unionist meetings in future would sound like hollow mockery. Garvin was upset that his closest friend should have been on the other side in a matter in which fidelity and honour were involved. He could not write without touching on the matter delicately, obscurely, understandingly: 'Law is irrevocably my leader ... But neither to him nor to you can I lie about my feelings and judgement. To others I hold my tongue. Even Austen admits that you were not in my position and holds you blameless.'

I

Garvin took over the *Pall Mall Gazette* in January 1912. In an attic he found the table at which his first predecessors had worked. It became his table with a brass plate and a resounding inscription:

> This is the old Editorial Table of the *Pall Mall Gazette*, and the lineal descendant of Captain Shandon's, the first editor of that famous journal, whose beginnings are faithfully recorded by Thackeray in the chronicles of 'Pendennis.' Upon this plain piece of furniture much history has been made. It was used daily from the year 1865 onwards by Frederick Greenwood, John Morley, W. T. Stead, Alfred Milner, E. T. Cook, F. E. Garrett and J. Alfred Spender until the year 1892 when it was found unworthy and with revolutionary ruthlessness was kicked out into the cold, a scarred and war-worn veteran to be sure, but still in robust health . . .

Captain Shandon, of course, was a legendary figure, but why should not a newspaper have its own creation myth? There is always a point in Genesis stories. The point of the *Pall Mall Gazette*'s was to show that Greenwood intended his paper, like Thackeray's to be written 'by gentlemen for gentlemen'.

Greenwood, the first mortal editor, suggested to Disraeli the purchase of the Suez Canal shares. He fell victim to a Liberal take-over. Stead quarrelled with his proprietor and was sacked. Astor's take-over sent Cook and his assistant editor, J. A. Spender, into the street and the table to the lumber room. Six of the seven, Liberals and Tories alike, were Empire men with whom Garvin would have felt at home. With the seventh, Morley, Garvin used to talk books with great content-ment. The inscription was in a double sense a roll of honour. Journalism is a dangerous trade.

Harry Cust, Astor's first editor, was a man of wayward genius. Alas, his three successors, and the papers they produced, were 'decorous, reasonable and also a little dull'. The paper continued to lose money. The appointment of Garvin, or a man like him for fire and drive, was good business for Astor as well as good politics. One may guess that this time Adams acquiesced rather than advised the step.

The London evening paper world was an over-populated jungle in which some tigers grew fat but more starved. In 1912 there were three halfpenny and four penny or 'clubland papers'. The name defined the radius of their circulation and the standing of their readers. Only one, J. A. Spender's *Westminster Gazette*, was Liberal in politics. Those Tories who insisted on quality read it for lack of an equally good paper of the right until Garvin made the *PMG* once more a civilised paper edited by a bookman for bookmen.

Readers could count on finding the *Pall Mall* a paper which invited the eye to read. During the autumn of 1911 Garvin had spent infinite pains on lay-out and typography. He corresponded frequently with Coode Adams. Sometimes they got on; sometimes they fought. The *Evening News*, Garvin once reminded Adams, cost only a halfpenny but was one of the best evenings: 'If the *Pall Mall Gazette* is to look as much as possible like a halfpenny paper, with narrow crowded columns like a halfpenny paper, why should people not buy the *Evening News*?' Garvin got his way. The new *Pall Mall Gazette* was an even better looking paper than the *Observer*. Its faded files are still a delight to the eye of a journalist or book-lover. Garvin was an artist in type as well as words.

F. S. Oliver wrote:

> Dear Brother-in-the-Lord, Why will you let your Celtic blood run away with you and start off before the flag is down? Here was I waiting with my benediction till January 22 and there were you anticipating events with better arrangements, better articles, better paper, and better ink.

Charles Whibley, Garvin's star contributor in *Outlook* days, was delighted to write again in the *Pall Mall Gazette* as he had done in Harry Cust's time. 'Everything must be changed in it — make-up and all,' he had written on hearing the news of Garvin's appointment. When he saw the new-style paper he was satisfied. Two of Garvin's Liberal predecessors agreed. E. T. Cook liked the make-up and sent his good wishes, 'though of course in some things — confound your politics'. Stead recognised Garvin as being in the apostolic succession: 'I give you my blessing. May I also give you lunch?'

Others were less friendly. *Punch* indeed missed few opportunities to be sour. Thus, a month after Garvin had taken over the *PMG*, C. L. Graves wrote:

His predecessors plied the pen
Of gentlemen for gentlemen;
Now other times bring other ways,
And peacocks pontify to jays.


## II


A London editor once told Robertson Scott:

> To the public [Garvin] was known as a political writer of outstanding gifts. Journalists who worked with him in his *Pall Mall* days . . . recognised that he was also a first-class editor, fertile in ideas, masterful, energising every part of the paper. Readers felt the new life that throbbed in its pages.

Garvin had edited the *Outlook* from Bromley and the *Observer* more often from St John's Wood than Fleet Street. The *Pall Mall* demanded more frequent attendance at its white elephant office. There he busied himself with everything that was happening.

His day started early: 'I now have to get up at 5.30 every morning for the *Pall Mall Gazette*, and must turn in before 10 at night to get proper sleep . . . I have stopped going out . . .' It sounds too good to be wholly true. Indeed it is clear that his social engagements lasted well beyond ten on many evenings. Of course there were fits of exhaustion when he had to pack up and retire to bed, but he had great powers of quick recuperation and could usually rise magnificently to an opportunity.

It sounds heartless to write of the loss of the *Titanic* in 1912[1] as an opportunity, but of course to an editor it was both opportunity and obligation. Before radio and television there was no other way in which people could find out what was happening. They were totally unprepared for the sinking of the *Titanic*, but the 'unsinkable ship' went down. Their faith in technology, their confidence in human ability, were shaken. They were frightened. Garvin rose to the occasion both in dignity and capability. The day the first news came the net sale of the *Pall Mall Gazette* was up by 63 per cent; three days later, when details were available, he ran a special early morning edition. The sale that day was 160 per cent above the daily average. The following year at the Derby a suffragette threw herself in front of the King's horse and was fatally injured. A predictably good sporting and social 'story' took on political and human overtones that still make it memorable. The *Pall Mall Gazette*'s sale went up by 72 per cent. In Garvin's first two and a half years there were seven occasions when over 40,000 copies were sold: only two of them were political. A good news story with strong human interest caught Clubland readers as surely as those who bought the halfpenny evenings.

Close attention to news in all its varieties, a good woman's page, serious political articles and brilliantly sympathetic literary pages were good reasons for the *Pall Mall Gazette*'s progress. Garvin's own writing was an added incentive to buy the paper. Men wished to see which way the prophet who refused to be type-cast would turn. Occasionally it was possible, or so Garvin thought, to measure the specific effect on circulation of a series of his signed articles. In May 1913 he wrote daily on the Marconi report in the week before the Commons debate. The average sale for the whole month was 26,633. For those five days it was 32,666.

## III

Garvin had a double business goal — to earn Astor the 8 per cent on his investment in the *Observer*, which Coode Adams had promised, and to make the *Pall Mall* pay for the first time in many years. In the first he succeeded. Coode Adams' 8 per cent was in fact the profit for 1910, the last Northcliffe year. In 1912 the rate was down to 4 per cent, but rose in 1913 to 15. The *Observer* net sale for 1910 had averaged 57,000 a week. An undated note in Garvin's handwriting, probably made in September or October 1914, put it then at about 100,000. The actual current figure was 170,000, but Garvin discounted this as a passing peak.

Making the *PMG* pay was more difficult. The *Observer* had had the backing of Carmelite House and only one serious rival. The *Pall Mall* had the incubus of Coode Adams and was beset by many rivals. It had been losing about £20,000 a year. Its net sale was under 10,000 a day, about a sixth of the *Evening Standard*'s and perhaps half that of the *Westminster*. That at least was Garvin's reckoning. From the beginning there was a tug-of-war between manager and editor. Adams thought first of cutting expenditure, Garvin of increasing revenue. It looks as if old Astor was inclined to back Garvin in 1912 and Adams in 1913. For the latter year economies were planned to save £16,000 of which nearly a third was to come from the editorial budget. Garvin met his target; the other departments failed. The paper's revenue was twice what it had been before Garvin, but the deficit had gone up from £20,000 to £23,000. That looked bad, but was good. Revenue, which had covered only 64 per cent of expenditure, now covered 73 per cent. In January 1914 Astor gave Garvin full power over all departments. Garvin reckoned that in 1914, 85 per cent of expenditure would be covered and the deficit reduced to £12,000, the best that could be expected from reduced operating costs. He hoped, however, to save a further £6,000 by moving out of the expensive premises in Newton Street, Holborn. He believed that improved revenue would cover the remaining £6,000.

Did Garvin make the paper pay? He thought so. A triumphant pencilled note reads: 'The Unique Struggle (quite a little epic in its way) of reorganizing the *Pall Mall Gazette* and making it pay for the first time in 25 years as a result of the absolute powers entrusted to me by W. W. Astor.' But was it really so? Waldorf thought not. The truth seems to be this. The first eight months of 1914 probably did show a profit on ordinary operating costs. Garvin may have left out of account the excessive fixed charges involved in the Newton Street premises. Waldorf would have included them.

The draconian economies had remarkably little effect on the popularity of the paper. People seemed willing to pay as much for a sixteen-page paper as they had for a twenty. In spite of labour troubles the paper sold twice as many copies in the first half of 1914 as it had in 1911, and only 5 per cent less than in the peak of 1913. It takes a resourceful editor to hold his readers by quality while giving them markedly less in quantity.

## IV

The glorious summer of 1914 seemed to be reflected in the fortunes of the *Observer* and the *Pall Mall Gazette* until suddenly out of a cloudless sky a severe storm threatened to destroy the effective partnership of Garvin and Waldorf. Waldorf had only been 'lent' his father's papers. Now his father decided to sell, as he had every right to do. His decision was made because he resented trade union interference in his works as much as trespassers in Hever Castle.

At first Astor thought of selling only the *Pall Mall Gazette* which was where the trouble was. He found, however, that, while he could sell both papers together, he could not find a purchaser for the *Pall Mall*

*Gazette* alone. So both had to go, and the Waldorf-Garvin alliance would be disarmed. Gardner Sinclair, an Edinburgh printer, secured an option, but it was doubtful whether he would be able to raise the money Astor wanted. The two papers as they stood in June 1914 were so much Garvin's creation and so stamped with his personality that it was impossible to say what the goodwill would be worth if he left. Could he and Sinclair work together? It was certain that Garvin's willingness to try depended on Sinclair's willingness to give him a free editorial hand. Would Sinclair do this? It was not so much a matter of politics as of temperament. Garvin had made enquiries and was fairly satisfied.

'Fairly' was not good enough. At the last moment Garvin asked Lord Roberts to find an alternative purchaser. Roberts was hopeful, but needed time. Sinclair would not wait and, rather reluctantly, Garvin settled with him. Waldorf lost his 'loan'; Garvin kept his job.

I

Although Garvin hated the way by which Law had become leader, he had great hopes of his leadership. They seemed justified when twelve months later Law publicly reaffirmed Joe's whole policy, including food taxes offset by imperial preference. He even went further than Garvin thought wise. He withdrew Balfour's promise to hold a referendum or an election before imposing food taxes. Lord Derby and the Lancashire free trade conservatives rose up in arms. Northcliffe and his papers were furious. Manufacturers feared that they would never get protection for themselves if food taxes had to form part of the package. Law thought again. In Ashton-under-Lyne, Aiken's constituency just over the border from rebellious Lancashire, he promised that as Prime Minister he would propose food taxes only if a Colonial Conference asked for preference in the mother country. And even then he would go to the country again before imposing them.

Garvin believed that Law would now stand and fight. He was wrong. The Conservative free traders scented surrender. Garvin did his best to strengthen Law both privately when they dined alone together just after Christmas 1912 and publicly in the *Observer*. His New Year article was a speech by 'Mr. Greatheart, M.P.' Bunyan's hero had slain Giant Despair, but Garvin could not make a Greatheart out of the man Fred Oliver christened Faintheart. Garvin's influence with Bonar Law was virtually at an end.

Law threw in his hand and decided to resign the leadership. The leading tariff reformers dined together to decide their line. Garvin was resting at Waldorf's house at Sandwich, but Waldorf and Goulding told him what happened. The majority felt that food taxes would have to go because the party must be kept together to prevent, if possible, Ulster being put under a Dublin Parliament. Waldorf, Amery, Hewins and Goulding disagreed, but in the end they gave way. Reluctantly Goulding organised a round robin asking Law to remain leader but drop food taxes. 'I felt that would be your wish,' he wrote pathetically to Garvin. At any rate there was really no alternative. Only six MPs refused to sign. Aitken was one of them. Law remained leader; food taxes were dropped.

Aitken always denied that he had had anything to do with Law's decision to drop food taxes, but Garvin and his friends were convinced that in fact it was he who had made up Law's mind for him. Garvin forgave him; the Astors never did.

Joe's plan for achieving Empire unity was dead, though it was some time before Garvin admitted it. It was that alone that had brought him into the Conservative Party. To it he had devoted ten years of his life. There was nothing to take its place; nothing in the party programme to which his naturally radical mind could respond. He might as well, perhaps better, have been a Liberal. He put it to Waldorf: 'If there is to be no effective policy on food duties, then the present Cabinet is in a better position to realise Imperial unity than we are.' It was. And Garvin put the Empire first.


II


The safety of Britain mattered even more to Garvin than social reform and imperial preference. Turkey's defeat in the Balkan war in 1912 and the consequent carving up of its European provinces made the European situation fluid. That year Garvin and Waldorf were seeing a great deal of Lloyd George. All threee were worried about Germany. They feared a deadlock between the Triple Alliance of Germany, Austria and Italy and the Triple Entente of Britain, France and Russia, a deadlock 'which only Armageddon can resolve'. The words come from a desperately serious, non-partisan article in the *Observer* of 10 November 1912. It followed a day of hastily arranged consultation. Garvin and Lloyd George met over lunch at Waldorf's. They met again at 11 Downing Street the same evening as a pencilled note by Garvin recalls. It is significant that it was the Radical Chancellor of the Exchequer and not the Liberal Imperialist Foreign Secretary who sought Garvin out.

The fear of Armageddon turned Garvin's mind back to the idea of a political truce. He wrote a secret memorandum for Lloyd George on the possibility of a coalition. Nothing came of it. It must have been apparent to Lloyd George that Garvin's standing with Bonar Law was very different from his position with Balfour two years before. Soon the worsening Irish situation and the Marconi scandal which touched Lloyd George produced a new ferocity of party welfare.

A strong and definite foreign policy required a strong defence capacity. Churchill's appointment to the Admiralty at first worried

Garvin — he had been against the famous eight dreadnoughts in 1909 — but, reassured by Fisher, Garvin soon found that he got on very well with Churchill who, like MacKenna before him, was having trouble with the pacifists in the Liberal Party. 'If only he were the Unionist Leader,' Garvin reflected one day when they had been together. 'Listening to him one thought it, and read in his face that he thought it too.'

Fisher and MacKenna had left the navy in a strong position to deal with a threat from Germany; Haldane had left the army structurally sound, but numerically inadequate. Throughout 1912 Roberts and Garvin hoped that the new Territorial Army would become a staging post on the road to national service — this had, after all, been part of the Lloyd George package in 1910. Roberts was a far sounder Tory than Garvin, but he too saw that conscription would come more acceptably from a Liberal government than a Tory one. In the autumn of 1913, however, Churchill bluntly told him that the government would not bring in national service; and Roberts, as he told Garvin, had 'let the King know that Protestant soldiers could not be ordered to fire upon Protestant citizens fighting for their religion and the Union Jack'. Even in defence a bi-partisan policy had broken down over the Irish problem.

## III

All the things that Garvin longed to see — the Empire knit together by imperial preference, the end of the old Poor Law, an army strong enough to help our allies — were stymied by Ireland.

By 1912 the sticking point was not so much the principle of Home Rule as the fate of Ulster. Garvin was having to re-think his position. In 1910 he had discounted Ulster as a separate political entity, warning the Colvins against having 'Ulsterics'. He saw deeper now as he stood in Belfast City Hall to witness the signing of the Ulster Covenant. Beside him was the *Manchester Guardian* representative, the great romantic journalist, H. W. Nevinson. Nevinson had eyes only for 'King Carson', making 'a shameless travesty of royalty'. Garvin's mind went further back to the distant days when he had fought for Parnell against the tide in Newcastle, and followed his body to its grave in Dublin. 'He kept telling me', Nevinson recalled, 'that he loved Carson, and had always loved Parnell too.' It was true, but incomprehensible to Nevinson.

Garvin realised that he was not watching make-believe, as Nevinson thought, but the making manifest of another Ireland with loyalties as

strong, as binding and as valid as those which had fired his own youth.
Federation as he had envisaged it in 1910 would have given Ireland a
place of its own among the other nations of the United Kingdom. He
saw now that Ulster too needed a place of its own. He looked hard at
the Ulstermen, then warned his readers:

> We may think the causes for which the Scottish Covenanters or the
> French revolutionaries bound themselves together right or wrong.
> But the results of the Solemn League and Covenant and the Oath
> of the Tennis Court are written across the pages of history in letters
> of blood.

A week later A. G. Gardiner in the *Daily News* gave Garvin the same
working over by ridicule that Nevinson had used against Carson. He
pictured Garvin as the man always in search of a hero, any hero, one
after another, however incompatible — Parnell, Joe, and now — 'Ah,
there is Sir Edward Carson ... [who] "will blaze at the whites of his
enemies' eyes", and, though the enemies are Mr. Garvin's old friends,
that cannot be helped.'

The 'blazing' came out of Jeremiah MacVeagh's 'Garvin dossier'
which had enabled him to fill three columns of Hansard with Garvin's
youthful bombast. Then, he had held that 'The first duty of an Irishman is to fight, his second duty is to fight, and his third is still to fight.'
He held it still. He incited the Unionists to play the same rough parliamentary tricks that the Nationalists had invented. They did. Garvin was
delighted; Oliver was not: 'I dislike and distrust more than I can say all
this talk about ballyragging in the House of Commons.' Worse still in
Oliver's opinion and in Waldorf's, though not in old Mr Astor's, was
Garvin's plan to force a general election by persuading the Lords not to
renew the Army Annual Act without which a standing army in time of
peace was illegal.

Garvin's bludgeon was for public use. In private he was a different
man. Contrast his two faces in March 1914, the month of the 'Curragh
Mutiny'. On the one hand he signed (a fortnight after his son) Milner's
British Covenant of support for Ulster. On the other hand, he spoke to
a private meeting of the United Empire Club. Its members expected a
rousing tirade. They got a sober, even tragic, plea for understanding.
He brushed aside the possibility of leaving things as they were:

> The very means by which you have been fighting for Ulster have
> so changed the principles to which you are committed that if you

win ... your difficulty with the rest of Ireland will be increased a thousandfold ... Do you think that ... beaten by Ulster volunteers they will raise no volunteers of their own? ... I beg you to think even now that the Nationalist part of Ireland may be worth winning and can be won.

If the Nationalists realised that their kind of Home Rule must end in the partition of Ireland, they might come to see that Ireland's unity could be maintained on federal lines by some form of Home Rule within Home Rule.

At a time when the Tory and Liberal leaders of Society refused to meet even on such neutral ground as a reception at the German Embassy, Garvin was corresponding affectionately with the journalistic leader of the other side, C. P. Scott of the *Manchester Guardian*. He wrote:

Ireland is not made yet. It will never be made unless it becomes like Scotland composite rather than Celtic. The inclusion policy in any shape would be felt as a triumph for the Nationalists. Why, why should they force an arrangement as distasteful to the Ulster community as the present British government is to them? ... I think they [the Ulstermen] will fight and I must help them, though much desiring to create (by ways not constraining either a large majority or a great minority) a real Ireland as there is a real Scotland.

Six months later, when the situation was desperate, Garvin was relieved to find that Scott believed that something might still be done 'with the *idea* of federation'. Garvin replied:

At least it avoids Civil War and keeps open the ideal and possibilities of Irish reunion ... Redmond is, of course, bound to speak as he does though the necessity does not make the next six weeks less awkward for all concerned.

It was 13 May 1914. Twelve weeks later Britain was at war.

# BOOK FIVE: THE FIRST WORLD WAR, FATHER AND SON, 1914-1918

---

'We meant to live for the safety of Britain and her friends during the war and for the cause of peace afterwards. As for that, one must try to live for two.'

J. L. Garvin, *The Economic Foundations of Peace* (1919)

I

On the last Sunday in June 1914, Garvin lectured on Francis Thompson and 'the mysterious, necessary process of creation by failure'. As he got back to Greville Place the telephone was ringing. His face was grave as he replaced the receiver. The heir to the Habsburg Empire had been murdered by a Serbian. A third, and possibly fatal, confrontation between the Triple Entente and the Triple Alliance was likely.

Four days later, while official London was at the memorial service for the Archduke, newsboys were crying the death of Joseph Chamberlain. The man in the street had almost forgotten Joe. Politicians had longer memories. Garvin himself would always bear Joe's imprint. He was anxious that his largely Tory readers should feel the hold that, in spite of everything, 'Radical Joe' still had on Liberals who once reverenced him next to God and Mr Gladstone. He turned naturally to John Morley, who had edited the *Pall Mall Gazette* before the great disruption. Sadly Morley excused himself. He could not do it. Words failed him. It is as good a measure of Joe's stature as any tribute he might have written.

Thinking about Francis Thompson and Joseph Chamberlain had sent Garvin on a retrospective journey to happier days. Reluctantly he turned back to a bleak present. His wife was on the brink of a complete breakdown. There was no doubt that Greville Place was a difficult household to run at the best of times. There was always friction between Tina and her mother-in-law. In this summer of 1914 there was the added burden of a visit from Jim's brother with whom she had recently had a quarrel only grudgingly made up. Perhaps she hoped that things would be better when Michael returned to South Africa in the autumn.[1] At any rate she refused to take the long rest cure that a nerve specialist advised. It was a pity that Tina's physical symptoms looked so like causes, so little like consequences. Neither her husband nor her doctors seem to have looked deeper. There were good days as well as bad, but she became increasingly dependent on alcohol. The children were not supposed to know but, of course, the elder ones did.

## II

As July turned into August Europe was added to Ireland in men's anxieties. The greatest difficulty in peace-keeping, as Garvin saw it, was to convince the Triple Alliance that the Triple Entente would stand together if challenged. There was no public commitment by Britain, no secret treaty, hardly even a gentlemen's agreement, only an assumption, rejected by many in the Cabinet. The imminence of civil war in Ireland made it seem plausible that Britain would leave France to her fate. Besides, many had moral objections to a war in support of Serbia. Garvin tried day after day to disentangle the issues for his readers:

> There are two questions, separate but interlocked ... The immediate and narrower is that between Austria and Servia. Here the balance of right and justice is with Austria ... But ... if the Servian question is to be made the basis of an attempt to break up the Triple Entente ... we must stand by the side of our friends to the last and whatever betides ...

Otherwise, and this was Garvin's agony, Britain would be left friendless, exposed to an enemy become more powerful than herself.

Nearly fourteen years had passed since Courtney gave Garvin the pen-name of Calchas, who prophesied 'Nine is the number of years that we shall have to fight at Troy.' Now, before battle was even joined, it looked as if Achilles would sulk in his tent, deserting his comrades. On Sunday Lord Roberts added a despairing paragraph to a business letter: 'So there is to be no mobilization. France is to be betrayed, and Belgium left to its fate.' But on Monday the Cabinet decided to mobilise. On Tuesday Britain declared war. Germany had done what had seemed impossible. She had united the United Kingdom.

## III

Gerard Garvin, or Ged as he preferred to be called, was eighteen. He was due to go up in October to Christ Church, Oxford, with a Westminster history scholarship, but he brushed that impatiently to one side. First things first. He was tall, handsome, fair-haired, blue-eyed, intensely musical, deeply reserved. We can picture him thus clearly because he had adopted Bess O'Sullivan, the mother of one of his

Westminster friends, as 'Step-mother', or 'Step' for short, his cold
name for an especially warm relationship. To her

> he seemed at first typically English as one associates that race
> with uncommunicative cold withdrawal, but underneath there
> was a tenderness that became, when one found it out, inexpres-
> sibly touching ... apparently destined to silence; yet when he
> talked there was an ease, a vividness that pertains to genius.

This is recognisably the same boy whom Hume Chidson, his closest
Westminster friend, described as climbing over the Abbey roof, ragging
masters, enjoying free fights in the house, but always with something
held back. It was only, he recalled, as they walked in the cloisters
or talked among the tombs that Ged would throw off the reserve
that he habitually wore.

Inevitably Ged and Chidson became two of 'the first hundred
thousand', the volunteers who formed the new armies. Garvin did his
best to enable them to serve together. The war was less than a fortnight
old when Lord Kitchener's private secretary asked Eddie Marsh,
Churchill's private secretary, to tell F. E. Smith to let Garvin know
that 'The Military Secretary has made a special note of Pylades and
Orestes, but the time for a decision has not yet come. Please reassure
Garvin that their wishes have not been and will not be forgotten.' They
would not have been the stuff of which good officers are made if
they had been content to let such devious currents float them to their
heart's desire. They had struck out for themselves. Hume was already
an officer in the East Surreys before Eddie Marsh wrote his letter;
Ged received his commission in the South Lancashire Regiment before
Lord Roberts could get him before an Officer Selection Board.

The ease with which Ged and his friends became officers was not
the result of backstairs favouritism, but the consequence of the social
system which refused to give, in Garvin's phrase, 'Every Child a Chance'.
There was just not enough educated young men. All the same, the
choice need not have been so socially restricted as it was in 1914.
When Garvin enquired about a commission for Sergeant Melican,
who had coached Ged when he won the Public Schools Fencing Championship, he soon found out that 'they don't want to make officers
of men like Melican no matter how highly qualified'.

For nine months Ged's battalion trained in England. Winter brought
rain and mud. The lines became 'a sliding swamp'. Ged thought 'the
wind howled and blustered like a German staff officer'. The men slept

on the earth on straw palliasses: small wonder that they 'seem rather down in the mouth and get fits of disgusting slackness'. After five months, however, he felt sure of their fighting quality, though the intelligence of neither officers nor men had 'yet climbed Mont Blanc'.

Gradually a handful of names became familiar in Ged's letters. Stuart McClinton, who had played full back for Ulster against Leinster, was the only one Ged called by his Christian name. The whole family at Greville Place took him to their hearts. Ged wrote little about the senior officers; what he did fell short of idolatry.

And so the winter and spring of preparation wore away. Gradually the battalion got its equipment. All was not well.

> Our machine guns are turning out frightfully shoddy. Some vital spring had been made of the very worst material, and apparently snaps like a dry twig. The gun was made in Belgium by an American firm, 'the Lewis'. Of course, you won't tell anyone about that, or that I told you. I fancy it's an offence under the Army Act.

Interesting information for an editor; disturbing for a father.

## IV

Garvin's inward eye moved unceasingly backwards and forwards between the subalterns at Tidworth and their masters in Whitehall. Fisher, Churchill, Lloyd George – these were men whom he knew, men who he believed could lead the country to victory if only they could be driven troika-fashion. Churchill had lastingly endeared himself to Garvin by 'the one initial act, historic and imperishable' which got the fleet into its battle station and the reservists mobilised before war came. Prince Louis of Battenberg, the First Sea Lord, was in thorough agreement, but these were political acts, taken on the First Lord's authority, 'a responsibility which no sailor could share', as Garvin reminded his son.

The triumphant mobilisation was followed by reverses. Three British cruisers were sunk. Antwerp fell. Years later Churchill wrote:

> The loss of the three cruisers had been freely attributed to my personal interference ... Antwerp became a cause of fierce reproach. One might almost have thought I had brought about the fall of the city by my meddling ... These were the only subjects with which my name was connected in the newspapers.

Less than a month before Garvin had told him, 'Everybody almost is your friend now; but, whether it be all fair weather or there comes a bit of the foul, you will find me always to be, Yours faithfully, J. L. Garvin.' It was a typical theatrical flourish to a promise that Garvin kept.

Churchill was not the only victim of public fickleness and malice. The gossip of the clubs, the pens of anonymous letter-writers turned against the First Sea Lord because of his German birth. Prince Louis resigned. Churchill brought back Fisher as his successor. When Ged came home on short leave his father was full of Fisher's first days back at the Admiralty – how he was to see the King once a week ('Isn't it a joke? It was reported that he would abdicate sooner than see me'); and how he could finish the war 'by Guy Fawkes Day if the "d–d" fools would send a quarter of a million men to France at once instead of keeping them at home in case of invasion'.

## V

The autumn of 1914 was a paradoxical time for Garvin as an editor. Never had his papers sold so well. The *PMG*'s net sale rose from 27,000 a day in July to 67,000 in August. The *Observer* bounded forward from 50,000 to 200,000 a week. But not for a long time had his position as editor been so insecure. Gardner Sinclair, the prospective purchaser, was an unknown quantity. Garvin had always sat loose to party. Now that his work was war work he forgot all about it. He told Bonar Law, 'Sinclair has accepted my proposal to leave me a free hand ... about policy.' The very idea horrified the Unionist machine. Steel-Maitland, the chairman of the party organisation, warned Law, 'We might at any time have difficulty with Garvin having full political control.' He suggested that Law should give Sinclair lunch and gently hint that Garvin's politics were a little suspect, but 'of course any conversation ... would have to be such that you could talk to Garvin with a clear conscience afterwards'.

In the same cautious spirit Steel-Maitland warned Sinclair to ride Garvin 'on the snaffle, not the curb'. Sound advice, but wasted. Sinclair complained about the paper's contents bills. The row that followed thundered on from the Battle of the Marne to the Battle of the Yser. How Sinclair, who was not the owner but only the holder of an option, came to interfere in trivial details is obscure. But interfere he did, and drew down a rebuke in Garvin's most exalted manner: 'Sinclair, [no prefactory "Dear" in this communication] your letter . . . surprised and vexed me very much indeed . . .' Garvin wrote again the following day:

> I told you from the first that nothing would induce me to work with you except as a partner, with full editorial control. Your verbal agreement with me on that basis is well known to Mr. Bonar Law, Earl Grey, Mr. J. F. Remnant M.P., and others.

By October Garvin feared he would lose the *Observer*.

In November a mysterious financier, Mr F. J. Benson, appeared on the scene. He praised Garvin's writing, but informed him that the friend for whom he was acting had no intention of continuing his editorship. December came and with it Garvin's fears increased. He confided in C. P. Scott. Scott had been through a similar agonising period of suspended sentence of death a few years before. He knew what Garvin must be suffering:

> What you tell me of your business anxieties and uncertainties distress me . . . It is the curse of journalism that it is a trade as well as a profession and just now it isn't even a good trade . . . I should feel it so great a loss if in the days that are coming your voice were silenced − it would be a kind of spiritual murder . . . But it won't come to that. They can't do without you.

On New Year's Day Garvin was told that Sinclair would take over at the end of the month. His relations with Sinclair had become so sour that it seemed certain that the new owner would drop the old pilot. Besides Garvin suspected what we know − that the Unionist Central Office was determined 'to get a muzzle on the papers somehow'. The *Manchester Guardian* felt sufficiently sure of its ground − probably on a word from Garvin himself − to announce that 'to the regret of all journalists' Mr Garvin would be leaving both papers. Garvin had already written a sad leave-taking letter to Waldorf Astor about 'the miserable ending to our fellowship which we hoped might long endure and achieve much'.

The following day there was a break in the clouds. For a moment the sun shone again. Garvin was to have a seat on the new board, a five-year agreement, and, if his policy was not approved, the right to retire from the editorships with £5,000 compensation. All seemed well.

All was not well. With one week to go nothing was settled. The deadline passed. Garvin put on a brave face: 'I don't care a brass farthing how it goes and hardly think of it . . . To be six or even twelve months out of things would perhaps be the best chance that could ever come.' Tina's anxiety stands out in a letter she wrote to Ged in the middle of February: 'The paper question is still unsettled and nothing at all has transpired so that Dad is worried — very.' In fact Sinclair was hoping to sell the *Observer* to Rothermere, Northcliffe's brother, for £70,000, to sell off the *PMG* white elephant office, and make a good profit. They were still haggling over the terms, though Rothermere thought he had clinched the deal, when Sinclair fell ill. He decided to give up the whole affair, and asked old Mr Astor to release him from his contract.

Astor for his part was heartily sick of newspapers and wrote at once to his son offering him both papers as his birthday present. He made one condition: 'All connection of every kind of a business nature between the publications and this office [the Astor Estate Office] is to cease.' Waldorf and Garvin resumed their collaboration, but on a different footing. They were now employer and employed. It made a difference. One immediate decision had to be made. Up to this point the Astor Estate Office had supplied the working capital and made good deficits. Now Waldorf was on his own. On Wednesday, 2 March Garvin spent the night at Cliveden. It was decided that the *Pall Mall Gazette* would have to be sold.

A week later Garvin resumed his editorship which had been in abeyance since the end of January. It was high time. When C. P. Scott sent his congratulations, he added: 'But really the *Observer* after you left it, and to a large extent the *Pall Mall Gazette*, was almost laughable — a sort of simulacrum or squeaking ghost of itself.'

Garvin had to ward off a threatened strike and set to work to make the *Pall Mall Gazette* once more a saleable property, not for his own good but for Waldorf's and the staff's. At last, in August, the paper was sold to Sir Henry Dalziell. There followed a week of 'final decencies'. Waldorf left Garvin to pay the staff and say goodbye. 'One felt at the end as an American President must do when he has shaken hands with a free and equal democracy for an hour.'

Garvin was a happier but poorer man. There were grave doubts about whether he would get the severance pay which he and Charles Russell thought was due from the *Pall Mall Gazette*. In the end he did, partly at least through a new acquaintance who soon became a close friend. Lady Sackville told him Mr Astor 'is so just and so fair and seemed horrified. I said very little really; but enough to make him think. And he must have thought!'

## VI

Tina was in a happy mood when Jim came back from Cliveden on 3 March:

> The Astors want Dad for Sunday again, but as he can't flirt and won't fall in love with the fascinating Nancy, I doubt there'll be trouble. She called across Paddington yesterday to 'get yer 'air cut.' He did and then spent 3/6d on a bottle of tonic to make it grow a bit on the temples.

Garvin had gone straight on to lunch with Churchill. He arrived in a relieved mood; he left in an elated one. This is what he told Ged: 'The Dardanelles business delights me ... I lunched with Winston yesterday — he asked about you as always — but we talked more about the spirit of things than the detail ... At any cost whatever we must get through. Winston has fibre.'

Soon Garvin realised 'It's Winston's game chiefly. I don't think Jacky likes it much.' For two and a half months Garvin watched the rift between his two friends widen as one disaster followed another at the Dardanelles. The climax came when Fisher suddenly walked out of the Admiralty without warning or leave. The *Pall Mall Gazette* had the first hard news with details of the fall of the government, but Garvin was a sad and frustrated man as he wrote to his son:

> Last week was like nothing ever before — living in taxis or at the end of a telephone or over the writing pad. The Government came down after nearly ten years of power that seemed unshakable, and of good luck that would never end. The Coalition was formed that I had worked for more steadily than any man ... but either what you want hardly ever comes or hardly ever in the way you wanted. Winston and Jacky are both out of the Admiralty — Jacky dead wrong this time ... Winston has been very nearly heartbroken after all his splendid work and the bitter injustice of villainous attacks which he has borne in silence; but his career is only beginning. I am determined to have the truth out when it can be said without hurting the country.[2]

I

On 16 July 1915 Tina and Jim said goodbye to their son before his unit went to France. There followed an almost daily shuttle of letters between Greville Place and 'somewhere in France', where Garvin's heart was. What happened there was his touchstone to measure the worth of what was happening in Whitehall.

Ged savoured letters from home 'like Jim Hawkins trickling the doubloons through his fingers'. They opened to his trench-bound vision the great world of Whitehall. His own letters were reticent except about the books he read. He was a private person, and besides he wished to shield his parents from the worst realities of life in the front line.

When fate first struck it hid Ged hard. One Sunday morning in September his soldier servant was wounded. 'I want the blood of that sniper,' Ged wrote. It is the only expression of individual hatred in all his letters. Next day his anger had cooled though his desolation remained. Two days later Ged sent his parents a warning that he might not be able to write for several days. He enclosed a short bleak note marked 'Don't open. Keep secret till I say.' It was, of course, a farewell letter. With it he sent a dirty bundle of much corrected pages of hand-writing. It was the draft of a long essay on Marshal Turenne which he had started at Tidworth.

Garvin spent Sunday, 26 September with the O'Sullivans. He arrived, as a friend noticed, 'in placid ignorance of "the great advance" ... Your father's first question was Where? but behind it one heard Gerard.' By Thursday the Battle of Loos was over, a success so partial as to be a failure. Ged's unit had not been engaged; Chidson had been in the thick of it.

II

There can have been few better informed subalterns than Ged. The central figures in his father's letters are Churchill, Fisher and after them C. P. Scott. It is difficult for a generation that thinks of Churchill as a great Tory to remember that in 1915 the Radical Scott was Churchill's natural ally and the Tory Garvin officially an opponent. For that reason Garvin's support had a special value for Churchill.

One day in the middle of October Churchill came unexpectedly to Greville Place. Tina knew very well that something momentous was in the wind. Nothing less would have persuaded Jim to break even for an instant his Saturday concentration on The Article. Nothing less would have brought Churchill out unexpectedly to suburban St John's Wood. Garvin confided to Ged that the reason for the visit was Churchill's idea of going to the front and commanding a brigade. It was a tremendous temptation to the frustrated man of action who suddenly found himself a belittled politician and everybody's favourite scapegoat for the failure at the Dardanelles. Churchill, however, was still a member of the Cabinet and the War Council. He had a voice in affairs and leverage. For that reason 'in a dishevelled talk in the hurry of a Saturday evening' Garvin tried to persuade Churchill not to resign.

On Wednesday Carson resigned from the government. Garvin apologised for leaving his son a day without a letter, but 'the political troubles here sucked me under like a whirlpool'. He felt Carson 'ought to have got others to join him or stayed, any other principle only weakens the actual Cabinet without getting a thorough change'. Carson and Churchill, working together in the Cabinet or resigning together from it, might have achieved something which neither could do alone. That opportunity had gone.

Thursday was Trafalgar Day. Garvin spent two hours with 'Jacky and his tutelary Duchess' talking politics and the strategy of Balkan warfare. 'I have never been in the Balkans, I warn them, but I carry large scale maps of it in my head and this they all seem to find interesting,' he assured Ged. 'Of course we quarrelled in a friendly way about Winston ... I will get them to make it up yet. It was very refreshing to find the old man more placable in that way.'

Next day Garvin lunched with Lloyd George and Churchill, then walked across with the latter to the Duchy of Lancaster office:

two rooms, a back and a front, ... tin boxes, bare walls, maps, papers. All neat, but good Heavens after the mighty and majestic Admiralty ... this sort of small lodgings is an incredible comedown and I realised more than before how Winston feels it. Besides he has no real executive work to do and I can no longer be surprised that he would rather go back to the army ... nor shall I again advise him to stay.

Ten days later Asquith dropped Churchill from the War Council. That settled the matter. On Sunday Garvin dined with Lady Randolph Churchill —

the usual family bevy of beautiful women there, really beautiful, but only one other man, Winston, and with him I had the best talk I ever had. As prompt and warm as ever to learn about you ... I think he means to join the army somehow and see service somewhere, but instead of going to Flanders and losing himself in the crowd of brigadiers he means to do a brilliantly adventurous and unexpected thing. Let that pique your curiosity.

Twice more that week Garvin and Churchill dined together. Once Garvin made his way in a steady deluge through the London black-out to a family dinner where Churchill showed him his 'irrevocable letter of resignation'; the next day they met at Edward Goulding's. Garvin was due to dine with Churchill again at Lady Randolph's but went instead to meet C. P. Scott 'for a talk chiefly in Winston's interests'. On Wednesday he said goodbye to Churchill, bound for Flanders after all. Garvin brought him a parting gift of Thucydides as he had done for Ged. It must be admitted that, while Ged and his father corresponded eagerly about Thucydides all that winter, Churchill confessed he had made small progress with the Peloponnesian War.

## III

On 1 December the War Council decided to restrict Kitchener to the purely civilian role of Secretary of State. That evening, as the Garvins and their guests were sitting down to dinner, Captain Solano was announced. Garvin reported his entry in the style of Alfred Jingle: 'very important — dead secret — the State in danger — only I could — would I? — of course'. Solano carried Garvin off to see Sir Archibald Murray, the Chief of the Imperial General Staff. The two men talked about finding men for the Balkans. They agreed that six divisions could be spared from France, but the French would want them back for a summer offensive. Murray said replacements could be found by withdrawing men from home defence. It was ridiculous to keep trained men at home because the Cabinet still feared a German invasion. Most of Sunday's Article was already written but next morning Garvin added a final section:

It is certain that for the present we could with absolute safety spare more Divisions from the Western Front, though we would have to make them up again afterwards ... We ought to take our resolution in both hands and fling every man we can muster into the Balkan attack.

No doubt many of Garvin's Articles had a similar pedigree, but rarely is it so clear.

## IV

By this time Garvin was absolutely convinced that there was no hope of winning the war with a government under Asquith − 'pig or Nero ... only he can't fiddle and can only swill', he told Ged. Garvin could do nothing to remove him on his own, but possibly something with Liberal allies. He sent C. P. Scott an urgent appeal:

We are still called a Unionist organ though in truth we are as little party as any newspaper could possibly be, and we feel great difficulty in moving unless some powerful Liberal journal agrees with us as to men and measures.

Scott did agree and came to London. While he was in the train Waldorf and Garvin talked late into Friday night with Lloyd George and Carson. They tried to persuade Lloyd George to resign. The piecemeal resignations of Carson and Churchill had been fruitless; Lloyd George's going would be decisive. On Saturday Scott saw Lloyd George. In the evening he took a taxi to Greville Place, arriving about 11 p.m. just as Garvin was having dinner. They talked politics till well past midnight while Scott's taxi ticked up twopences.

After lunch with Waldorf on Monday Scott and Garvin had further talk on their own. They had to admit failure. Garvin reported to Churchill that Asquith would be able to hang on because 'the worst disasters threatened won't come from all I hear'.[1] 'Of course', Garvin continued, 'without L.G. there can be no sufficient change, but he is still singularly isolated on the one hand, while on the other resolved not to jump until he is certain to land on sound ground.' Garvin's assessment was sound enough; what was wrong was his time scale. He gave Asquith 'until February or later'; the Germans 'at least nine months'. Asquith lasted a year; the Germans three.

Churchill came home at Christmas for forty-eight hours' leave. At dinner with Clementine he and Garvin argued about Salonika, 'not differing except in opinion ... Then I returned to my old aim — to make it up between Winston and Fisher. I'm glad to say Winston declared himself ready to bury the hatchet.' On Christmas Day Garvin passed the message on to Fisher, 'the best and most affectionate Christmas card that could be sent by, Yours ever, J. L. Garvin'. A letter from Churchill himself would have been even better.


# V


Winter in Flanders was cruel. 'I guess you'd like to know what the firing line really is like now. Anyway I want to tell you,' Ged wrote home. His men had been standing in water for two days and nights. When he took the rum round at daybreak his knees broke the ice on the water, but he survived the cold like any polar bear. It was the mud he hated. Once coming out of the trenches a man stuck. It took three officers twenty minutes to free him. '"Exasperation" hardly does my feelings justice; the man whined all the time.' Ged no doubt suffered 'exasperation' many times, but made no other complaint of his men and few indeed of the conditions. Instead he referred his parents to Bruce Bairnsfather's famous 'Old Bill' cartoons in the *Bystander*: 'Nothing else comes anywhere near life out here, and they for all their quaintness are truth absolutely.'

Truth absolutely, perhaps; but less than the whole truth about Ged. He wrote on New Year's Day:

I'm pencilling a note in a very cramped dug-out, horribly draughty ... Last night ... I went a bit out along one road just about midnight, walking in the sedge at the side. I just missed several ditches and went into one. I found nothing and only heard a distant word or two of German. This morning I read Catullus a bit, and I'm just reading about Brasidas, a magnificent Spartan general whom Dad will tell you about.

Catullus and Thucydides — here were inner springs on which Ged drew freely. Besides his books he had a flageolet his grandmother gave him and sheets of flute music among which he discovered 'an exquisite saraband' by Leclair. All the time his mind turned over and over a writer's problems. How should he end his essay on Turenne, 'wrestling to embody him intimately and honestly in a few phrases?'

Thus Ged survived the winter in good heart. Then on 13 March came

> the first indubitable breath of spring ... a wafted fragrance of sunned grass, fresh and sweet. One shudders retrospectively at the past winter. I've been musing lately at the attitude of one's mind to the desolution and roughness of life out here. One only shrinks from the memory of it. The actual experience comes as a normal life at the moment. When one is actually in the rifle-zone or there-abouts — one passes into another existence, with trench conditions as the standard. What bosh! Bye-bye.

## VI

Meanwhile in England Garvin, the 'obstinate reconciler', was rewarded in spectacular fashion when the navy Estimates were debated. Churchill was again home on leave. From the Gallery Garvin heard him advocate Fisher's recall:[2] The moment Churchill rose

> the House became a living, vivid thing with a man of mind and force at the centre of it ... Jacky heard the speech and was delighted as a child. As he came out in the Lobby with the Duchess of Hamilton I met them both; he walked with the step of a young man, and he knows well that but for me yesterday's scene in parliament and the great reconciliation never would have taken place.

C. P. Scott had been with Garvin in the Gallery and noted, 'frequent interruptions from Balfour ... who writhed visibly with irritation. The close, calling for Fisher's return, was dramatic, but ... the House was unprepared and puzzled.'

Next day Churchill asked Garvin whether he should return to France. Garvin advised him to stay if he could face 'the poison gas of mean imputation'. They talked from half past ten till long after midnight. Winston could not make up his mind. They met again on Thursday at the Duchess of Hamilton's, 'Jacky ruthlessly booming "Stay"', Winston very legitimately torn'. On Friday Garvin was once again with Fisher and Churchill, who was 'torn to shreds by his emotion and nerves'. He obviously wanted to stay at least long enough to speak on the army Estimates. He treated his two friends to a rehearsal of his speech, but in the end he accepted his wife's advice and returned to France. Sadly Garvin reflected, 'His political hand was out last week, too hurried. He should resign his commission or his seat. But of course his first duty is his parliamentary duty.'

'A masterly article that on the Navy. I'm sure you'll like it,' Tina wrote. Ged did. Waldorf disagreed: 'Quite honestly I regret (especially after our talk) that you put in that special article about Winston.' There followed smooth words about Waldorf's personal liking for Churchill and his willingness that the *Observer* should defend him 'when the world is unfair or ignorant'. The message, however, was clear: 'When and after he has acquired the judgment which his age and experience ought to give him will be time enough to push him.'

What was there in Garvin's 'turnover' to justify Waldorf's warning? Nothing, if Waldorf's protestations meant what they said. Garvin admitted in the article that Churchill had got his timing wrong – not for the first time.

How often have the lobbies been alternately swayed at short intervals by the successive assertions that 'Winston will be prime minister' and that 'Winston is done.' Now, as before, he is neither enthroned nor extinguished. He is forty and in some ways younger than his years. What he most needs is to become ten years older suddenly.

That was just what Waldorf had been saying, but there was no satisfying the Astors where Churchill was concerned. Sadly, Garvin wrote to Mrs Churchill:

Waldorf Astor, though personally friendly to Winston, does not want the *Observer* to 'run him' politically just now. It would be useless to enlarge on how acutely painful that is to me. It means that until Winston does or says something accepted as successful, I shall have to remember that the *Observer* is not my paper.

That was prudent, but Garvin was never prudent long.

## VII

On Easter Day Ged sent his father a long letter about La Bruyère, his latest literary discovery, only casually remarking, 'we went to Mass this morning and I went to Communion'. He can have had no idea what floodgates this would open in his father's psyche, sweeping into almost total oblivion all that he would normally have said about the Easter Rising in Dublin. Instead he wrote in a rambling, tumultuous letter what he had longed but failed to say. The language is embarrassing — 'May the Divine Lord strengthen your pure heart in all things, my Galahad' — but it provides a convincing self-portrait of a fugitive from the Hound of Heaven:

> The surprise was utter . . . and to feel that I had not known this, of so profound a concern to me, made me feel a stranger in the world. For an instant I had a passionate wish that I could have remained orthodox; with what rendings and tearings I ceased to be you cannot guess. To a Maundy Thursday of 41 years ago my mind turns back. I was seven years old then when I made my first communion and trod air. Let us go to Mass together sometimes: we can at least do that, for to be parted from you altogether when you are of the Church that I have so infinitely loved would be more than I could bear.

The next day Garvin wrote again, hoping that he 'had not upset' Ged. Ged briefly acknowledged his father's two letters, telling him that he had received communion twice before.

A week or so later a letter from Tina, venting her habitual spite against her mother-in-law, upset Ged. This letter has not been found. Ged wrote at once to his father:

> A letter from Mummy to-night tells me that Granny has told you that I have been preparing for some time secretly to enter the Catholic Church.[3] If I do I shall tell you and Mummy. Meantime there is not a scrap of truth in anything whatever you may have been told by anyone but me about such things . . . If I think or do anything further, I'll tell you both at once.

Garvin rushed to defend his mother:

> Never, never did your Granny say you had been 'secretly preparing' or anything like that. She said she was not surprised, as I was, because she had gathered from some remarks you made openly at table . . . that your mind was moving that way.

**VIII**

In London on the day set for the opening of the Somme offensive Garvin was dining with The Other Club. Lloyd George was there; Winston came in after dinner. 'We did not talk in very much detail about the prospects, but it was assumed that our affairs had been baulked a bit owing to the weather.' Garvin was surprisingly relaxed for a father with a son in the battle area. The reason was simple. Ged had been posted to Divisional Headquarters. Tina was overjoyed. 'It would do you good to see her,' Jim wrote. 'She has not been so entirely her dear self for three years at least.'

In France on the day before the assault Ged revisited his battalion. He shook hands with Stuart McClinton as on a formal leave-taking. In his diary he noted, 'Day quiet. Wind dries ground. Afternoon warm and light. Fine evening. Sunset of gold flame fading through rose and grey-violet to darkness. Night dark but clear with bright starlight.'

Next morning he wrote, 'Delicious summer morning. Thick mist. Shattering bombardment on waking. See very little from hill . . . News comes slowly. Tense expectation.' Throughout the day he jotted down news as it reached him. At first it was good, then not so good. He noted that his own battalion and the brigade of which it formed part had been transferred to the 8th Division which was in trouble at La Boiselle. Then comes a laconic entry: 'Sunday, July 2nd 2 a.m. 8th DIV evidently badly cut up and demoralised. Talk to officers coming back at night.'

For Ged's father there was the anodyne of work and the false comfort of communiqués.

It was a nuisance for me having to begin on Saturday morning . . . and use 'perhaps' and 'if' and as many subjunctives as in the Zummerzetshire conjugation of the 'varb' to be: 'mebbe suppoasing I be'. Then about three o'clock the newsboys came shouting through the streets . . . our advance in concert with the French had begun that morning . . . and was doing well! It sent an extraordinary thrill through the town and newspapers in the streets disappeared, I believe,like leaves before locusts . . . I have been in many tight places as an editor but never in a worse one. But here I go dragging in these infinitesimal personalities when all one is really thinking about is the historic stroke and the price – less no doubt than the cost of the old Neuve Chapelle and Loos methods but certain to be heavy just the same.

Ged knew how much greater the cost had been. The 7 S. Lancs. had been mauled in the fighting for La Boiselle on Monday and Tuesday. Colonel Winser, who won the DSO there, had had his first experience of walking on corpses. 'One had to use them as duck-boards,' he recalled. 'It was a beastly and never-to-be forgotten experience.' Ged was anxious to reassure his parents: 'You won't have been worrying, or I hope not,' he wrote, 'knowing I'm doing office work at Divisional Headquarters.' There was one thing, however, they had to be told 'which will bring grief to all of you. Stuart has been killed.'

'Poor, poor lad — and worse, poor Mother', Tina wrote when she heard the news. 'Of course you feel restless, knowing what's going on — and I suppose I'm selfish, but I pray God all the time he keeps you there and safe a bit.' Edward Goulding had constantly urged Jim to get his son a staff appointment; but, knowing that Ged would not wish it, 'I never spoke a word nor lifted a finger, but inexpressible was our relief.'

## IX

On 12 July Ged went back to his unit. The colonel wanted him, and he wished to return. Colonel Winser applied for his promotion to captain and gave him D company. 'To our great surprise and delight Garvin turned up again and took command,' on of his subalterns wrote. Half the men were a new draft, very few of whom had been in action before. The battalion went into the line again on Wednesday the 19th. Each step on the long night march was heavy, raising clouds of dust. It was dawn on Thursday before they reached the reserve trenches. Ged wrote a letter:

> Dearest Ones, This is just a short note for you. We go into action in a day or two and I'm leaving this in case I don't come back. It brings you both, and to the girls and Granny, my very deepest love. Try not to grieve too much for me.
>
> I hope my death will have been worthy of your trust and I couldn't die for a better cause.
>
> Please give one of my books or something else of mine to Chidson and each of the O'Sullivans.
>
> Everything else, and of course any money, belongs to you to handle as you will. Bye-bye. Heart's love and kisses.
>
> Ged XXX

A few snatches of conversation among the officers of D company during the long wait for zero hour have survived. Thus:

Gerard said, very shrewdly, 'Isn't it extraordinary that these gunners should spend the whole of a pleasant summer afternoon shooting at one another in this way?' and then he added 'and enjoy it too ... Unless you are very near the front line it is amazingly easy to forget all about the human element. Those gunners never think of it; and one never thinks of it in studying the tactics of the past. In fact, even in these front trenches, I sometimes become so absorbed in the tactics of the thing that the human element fades out altogether; and when army commanders make their plans they have to forget about the human element. Any one of them would gladly sacrifice a division for the good of the whole.' I said that I was glad that I was only a platoon commander, and that the work of sacrificing divisions was not at all to my taste. He laughed, and answered: 'Nor to mine'. And we fall to wondering whether the human element came back to army commanders when they thought they had banished it completely; whether, for example, it ever kept them awake at night.

The plan was for a night attack. Ged found himself in command of another company as well as his own. Just before zero hour he was visited by the adjutant, Captain Vellacott: 'What struck me most was his perfect coolness and collectedness ... He was in splendid form ... and I knew that his company was singularly influenced by his cheerfulness, confidence, and courage.'

Night operations are notoriously difficult. Ged had his work cut out to keep his men moving forward in reasonable order. He and his orderly were in front trying to straighten the line and prevent bunching. Then came a message 'From Captain Garvin to Mr. Porter, Carry on with the company.' He had been hit by machine-gun fire some thirty-five yards from the German line.

On Tuesday word reached Waldorf privately that Ged had been killed. He broke the news to Garvin. Two days later came the official confirmation and, during the week, a letter from Colonel Winser:

Personally his loss has affected me more than any of the other good fellows I have seen for the last time ... I thought he would live and become a great man. It has been willed otherwise. I cannot write more. Of the original lot who joined at Tidworth and

Tidworth Pennings, Vellacott and I alone remain with the battalion.

Ged's obituary filled a column and a half of the *Observer*, which also carried his 'Turenne and the Graver Genius of France' as a turnover. He would have smiled wryly, but with affection, at his father's pride so lavishly displayed. Seven months before he had made a mild protest: 'I am sorry Mrs. Colefax saw Turenne; I only wrote it for you two. Still it doesn't much matter.'

I

As Jim walked through the valley of the shadow of Ged's death his despair was apparent to all his friends. With most he was tongue-tied, and they with him. With Churchill it was different. 'Poor Garvin comes to see me sometimes to talk about his boy,' he wrote compassionately to a friend at the front. Churchill had been in France and understood.

Edward Goulding was another to whom Jim could open his grief. They crossed to France together on Midsummer Day 1917, a year after Ged fell. Next day as they ate their sandwiches in a Nissen hut near Mametz Wood, Jim quoted lines from Wordsworth:

Not for a moment could I now behold
    A smiling sea and be what I have been;
The feeling of my loss will ne'er be old;
    This, which I know, I speak with mind serene.

Then, at his friend's request, he recited the whole poem.

After lunch Jim walked on ahead, hoping to find his son's grave or where he fell. When he got home he compressed pages of his notebook into one short passage in an *Observer* article:

Here are bold poppies, deep cornflower, wild mustard, thyme and the rest ... The spirit of earth is weaving patterns of bright wonders and robing our dead as kings. In this wilderness, half dreadful and half gay, whether we find one spot we search for, or find it not — but it must be hard by — they who rest here, rest well. They were above all that was ever dreamed of, uttermost courage, honour, truth to something above self:—
    This way have men come out of brutishness
    To spell the letters of the sky and read
    A reflex upon earth else meaningless.

Ged's parents lacked the consolation of a laying to rest; but here on the battlefield, with words of Wordsworth spoken in a Nissen hut and with Meredith in his heart as he stood alone, the father performed funeral rites for his son.

There was not even that comfort for Tina. Two letters written during Jim's visit to France have survived. They speak of her own physical suffering in a mood of acceptance; of her love for her husband, 'my deepest and truest love, and no one but you have had that'; but of her love for her son there is not a word. While Jim stood by Mametz Wood, chance had brought to Greville Place the two officers who had been nearest to Ged when he fell. She gave them a good weekend. It was her way, Martha's way.

## II

On the Somme Garvin saw the inevitable result of hard fought battles. The devastation was caused as much by our soldiers as by theirs. Pride and pity marked his mood. Later, on the French front, he passed through areas that had been in German occupation. He saw rows of fruit trees cut down in 'deliberate, prosaic, wanton, jeering pain-lust'. He noted in his diary, 'The things that I have been describing put a kink in my brain and fill me with a desire to bruise Germany.' In a terrible passage on German war cemeteries he wrote: 'These Boche monuments ought all to be abolished. They pollute the soil where the enemy has disgraced himself by the most wanton and malicious destruction ever known in war.' This is a plain demand for vengeance.

Back at Compiègne Garvin dined with Sir William Robertson, the Chief of the Imperial General Staff. Another, and a more characteristic, side of Garvin showed itself. He had been talking of the confidence that he had felt existed between Plumer and his troops at Messines. Robertson broke in, 'Why can't we get along as well at home? Why is there not more union?' Garvin enlarged on the employers' lack of imaginative sympathy with the workers, and the unions' fear that their wartime relaxation of union agreements would be used against them after the war. Robertson agreed.

Garvin had crossed to France in the same boat that brought General Pershing to command the still tiny American expeditionary force, fewer in numbers than the Old Contemptibles had been. This Fourth of July, which Garvin spent in Paris, was a special occasion marked by a lavish display of Stars and Stripes and Tricolours but, as he wryly noticed, hardly a Union Jack. It was, he saw, 'a turning point, perhaps committing America to more far-reaching responsibilities than even the more thoughtful citizens of the United States had imagined'. A few days later he came across some of the difficulties Americans had in reconciling the ideas of the Declaration of Independence with the facts of European history.

From Paris he went to the liberated corner of Alsace with Grasty of the *New York Times*: 'It would be hard to imagine a more abysmal ignorance of European conditions than his, or a more dogmatic conviction that American feeling is inspired by something morally and mentally superior to European knowledge.' The two journalists came as near to a quarrel as does not matter because their eyes told them different things. Garvin saw 'ghosts by daylight'. Some of them were a thousand years old and still potent in the disputed borderland. Grasty saw only what was in front of him and took it at face value. He believed that the future of Alsace could well be settled by the counting of heads. But which heads? Garvin wondered. Those who had come into Alsace from across the Rhine sine 1871? Those who had left for France since 1871? Two brothers were serving, one in the German, one in the French army. Should both have votes? The journalists visited a village school. Garvin thought it 'absurd to have a sergeant in uniform as a class master in French. The paradox looks too German.' Grasty on the other hand was delighted at the time, but on the way back he suddenly said that Americans and Canadians would not die to make Alsace French again. 'Never in my life,' Garvin wrote, 'was I more amazed and disgusted. It seemed like a betrayal. It was a relief to get back to Paris and part company.'

## III

Garvin returned to find that Lloyd George, who had been Prime Minister since the end of 1916, was reshuffling his government. Churchill was back after eighteen months of political exile. This had been a time of close intimacy with Garvin to whom he turned frequently for advice and still more for sympathy and support. Now that Churchill was a busy Minister again, he had little need of Garvin. Their meetings became infrequent. They wrote less often to each other. Winston remained Jim's good friend but when he wrote, he slipped back, more often than not, to the 'Dear Garvin' of earlier days.

Garvin, of course, welcomed without reserve Churchill's appointment as Minister of Munitions; 'The fittest for the job, born for it; in executive power and in his grasp of technique a genius.' The same reshuffle had brought Waldorf into 'the Garden Suburb' as a very junior member of the administration, one of Lloyd George's parliamentary private secretaries, working in the huts at the back of 10 Downing Street. No doubt he thought Garvin's praise of Churchill excessive; but, whereas he had twice in the past twelve months told him to stop, this time he could hardly object. After all, Lloyd George had appointed Churchill; and Lloyd George was Waldorf's master now.

## IV

Garvin's visit to France had taken place on the eve of the third Battle of Ypres. He had heard and discounted the optimism of high-ranking officers in a hurry to win the war before the Americans made their weight felt. Passchendaele became a name of glorious ill omen comparable to the Somme. In the autumn war-weary minds thought of stalemate. Lord Lansdowne, the great Whig who led the Tory peers, wrote a Peace Letter to the *Daily Telegraph*. Garvin, 'though no Haigite, never was', would have none of it: 'Many times have we warned our readers that the real danger to Britain and the English-speaking world would come not from labour but from part of that which is called "Society".' If the old gang in Britain patched up a peace with the old gang in Germany the hope of a Britain in which 'every child would have a chance' would once again be deferred. The kind of peace Garvin wanted was incompatible with the kind of peace, virtually the *status quo*, which Lansdowne had in mind. Garvin wanted a radically different Europe. His mind, however, was still split between the mood of his talk with General Robertson and the shock he experienced among 'the murdered trees'. And so he wrote both of Germany's 'enormity of guilt surpassing every former iniquity' and of the need to 'purge ourselves utterly of hatred and vindictiveness'. Contradictory emotions tore him apart in a conflict not resolved until the fighting ceased.

## V

New Year's Day 1918 found Garvin near despair, physically and mentally exhausted. Sir Bertram Dawson ordered him a complete rest, but he could not afford it until he received his share of the *Observer* profits. On Friday the 4th he wrote to Waldorf, 'Settle it in your own way, only settle it.' When Monday brought neither cheque nor answer, he turned unhappily to Goulding, who sent a cheque for £300, saying, 'I feel it a privilege and one of the few things that really give me pleasure is to be your friend.' Three days later the *Observer* paid up.

Only desperation would have driven Jim to ask a friend, even Edward, to lend him money, but his fear of debt was stronger than his pride. Neither he nor Tina found it easy to economise. The need was obvious. Income tax was more than four times what it had been at the outbreak of war, while prices were double. Garvin's expenses were growing and his income contracting. His eldest daughter was at Oxford; his second about to start her medical training. His salary had gone down from £3,500 to £2,000 when the *Pall Mall Gazette* was sold. For a time this had been partially offset by £1,000 a year from the *New York Tribune* for a weekly column, but his contract had not been renewed, probably because of his criticism of American policy during the last months of her neutrality. He faced a probable deficit of £750.

Before the end of January 1918, Garvin was off to Lynton with the *Observer* cheque safely banked. Dawson had ordered him to rest, but his mind was ill at ease. What sort of an editor did Waldorf want? Did he really want Garvin? Would he pay enough? Garvin wondered whether to look for another job. He went backwards and forwards in his mind over these questions for six weeks as he walked long and hard over the uplands of Exmoor and along the high cliffs that repel the sea.

In London Waldorf told Edward Goulding his plan for the *Observer*. He wanted its policy to be decided by a committee. He himself would be chairman and would nominate the members. Garvin should be one. He went on to suggest that Garvin should give up the editorship in the ordinary meaning of the word, leaving all the running of the paper to an assistant editor who would in time succeed him. Garvin would write his weekly Article for which he would be paid £2,500. In effect he would be reduced to the status of a columnist. Goulding told Waldorf he could not conceive Garvin or any other man doing as he suggested.

Of course Garvin was furious. He wrote to Edward who laconically replied: 'Thanks for yours of the 18th with which I quite concur and have destroyed same.' Fortunately the last few sides survive:

for me, who have four daughters to educate, what beautiful phrases to cover the confiscation of the results of my lifework. So this is the reward of what I have done and suffered in the war ... and this is the way of the world; and Waldorf is a philanthropist ... Let him know that I am clear, calm and resolved about the two indispensable conditions ...

They were that Garvin should be editor in fact as well as name, and that he should be guaranteed something like £4,000 a year. He was prepared to swallow 'Council, consultation, under-study and all the rest', probably because he knew himself to possess the capacity for necessary insubordination.

Goulding pressed Garvin's two essential points, and Waldorf accepted them in principle. There were still five months of hard haggling, bitter reproaches, near break-ups and affectionate reconciliations before an agreement was signed on 13 August and back-dated to 1 March, the day on which Garvin had told Waldorf, 'If we are to be reconciled, let our reconciliation be thorough . . . We have been united by all the greater things.'

True; but the things that divided them had been laid aside, not buried. As Garvin said, 'But for the war and all its difficulties, and but for what had happened in the war to my family I never would have made this agreement or gone on except in full partnership – never.'

The stumbling block in the last five months had been money. Garvin needed £4,000 and was determined to get it. He succeeded. Fred Oliver smoothed the way. The agreement gave Garvin a salary of £3,500 plus a tenth share of the profits up to £500. At the end of five years he was to receive one-fifth of the total profits of those years up to a maximum of £5,000. In return Waldorf got his Council, which seems to have sunk without trace, and an assistant editor to be groomed for the succession which never came his way. Garvin had to promise to write exclusively for the *Observer*. Both men were to be protected against each other by a three-man tribunal. Waldorf nominated Philip Kerr; Garvin and Edward Goulding. They co-opted Lionel Hichens.


## VI


The absence of an effective parliamentary Opposition during the war made it important that newspapers should be independent and seen to be so. Neither was possible when their proprietors were members of the administration. Lord Rothermere (*Daily Mirror* and *Sunday Pictorial*) was Air Minister, Lord Beaverbrook[1] (*Daily Express*) Minister of Information, and Lord Northcliffe (*The Times*, *Daily Mail* and *Evening News*) Director of Propaganda in Enemy Countries, directly responsible to the Prime Minister. Waldorf Astor's job in Lloyd George's 'Garden Suburb' was much less important than theirs but his conscience much more sensitive. Twice during Garvin's absence on Exmoor the question of the propriety of Waldorf's dual position came up. He consulted Goulding about his proposed *Observer* council. Goulding bluntly told him that for him to be chairman would be inconsistent with his duty as parliamentary private secretary to Lloyd George. Waldorf was ambitious, the Prime Minister's friend as well as his assistant, a probable future Cabinet Minister. Goulding's intention was plain. He expected that Waldorf would give up his tiresome *Observer* scheme and leave Jim free.

Then two things happened which made Waldorf react in the opposite way. In the Commons, Austen Chamberlain told the Prime Minister, 'As long as you have the owner of a newspaper as a member of your Administration you will be held responsible for what he writes in his newspaper.' The doctrine of Cabinet responsibility must apply to their newspapers as well as their speeches. In Austen's opinion, then, as long as Waldorf was in Lloyd George's administration the *Observer* was not free to criticise government policy. Waldorf took Austen's view to heart. Besides he himself was under attack. The *Observer* had criticised Sir William Robertson, the Chief of the Imperial General Staff. Admiral Sir Hedworth Meux alleged that this was part of Lloyd George's plan to replace Robertson by Sir Henry Wilson. Waldorf protested; Meux retorted:

The day you, a very wealthy temporary major on the active list of the Army, accepted the post of Parliamentary Secretary to the Prime Minister, that same day the *Observer*, your personal property, *ipso facto* ceased to be an independent newspaper. I sincerely trust Lloyd George will next week take the opportunity of explaining his subservience to wealthy newspaper proprietors.

Once again Waldorf consulted Goulding though he did not tell him that he had already sent in a letter of resignation, a fact which Goulding had learned from Lloyd George's political secretary. The Prime Minister, however, had not yet seen the letter. Goulding persuaded Waldorf to think again. This was the opposite of the advice he had given only ten days before, but it had the same meaning: leave Garvin to get on with his job. Waldorf withdrew his letter. Five months later he became a junior Minister at the Ministry of Food. Strange are the forces that in practice determine the freedom of the press.

**VII**

Soon after his return from Exmoor Garvin was involved in a controversy where the *Observer*'s action was open to the criticism that Hedworth Meux had made. Lord Milner, the Minister of War, asked Waldorf to expose Colonel Repington. To that extent the astonishing *Observer* of 12 May was directly inspired by the War Office, though the public were not in a position to know it.

Repington had been *The Times*' military correspondent from 1905 to January 1918 and a contributor to the *Outlook* and the *Observer* during Garvin's early years. In those days he had been described as 'the first military writer in Europe' and the 'twenty-third member of the Cabinet'. Now his judgement had gone, but his love of intrigue remained.

Garvin's attack had been suggested by the War Office, but its manner was his own. His pen stuttered with bad taste: 'The mad maenad in uniform is no pleasant type, and that is what Colonel Repington, disordered by passion and private enmity, has been for six months . . . spreading mutiny in the exploited name of General Robertson.' To Garvin it seemed sinister that Repington was 'working in ill-omened association both through the *Morning Post* and that dubious sheet the *Naturalised News*, the one High Tory, the other well of the Left'. There was no such paper as the *Naturalised News*. The name was Garvin's silly, schoolboy nickname to draw attention to the fact that the *National News* was edited by a former Austrian and financed by a former Dutchman. Ernest Newman, Mrs Humphry Ward, J. H. Thomas and Robertson Nicoll wrote for it. The *National News*, only a year old, was the kind of Liberal Sunday newspaper that Garvin would normally have respected, even though he might have regretted that it cost a penny compared to the *Observer*'s new price of twopence. In fact, he and Waldorf had tried and failed to get it suppressed. He now publicly savaged it because it was 'carried on at a heavy loss for no easily intelligible reason', except perhaps to attack 'the British Government in ambiguous circumstances such as are not tolerated in any other belligerent country'. Garvin thus came near to denying freedom of the press in time of war. This is both astonishing and alarming, a measure partly of Garvin's own state of mind and partly of the general anxiety that the German breakthrough in France and the collapse of Russia had produced.

There was another and more important news story on which Garvin had to comment that week. Sir Frederick Maurice, who had been

Robertson's right-hand man at the War Office, knew that Lloyd George's figures on the strength of the British army were wrong. He believed they were deliberately wrong. He wrote to *The Times*, knowing it would wreck his career, but believing that 'his duty as a citizen overrode his duty as an officer'. Asquith demanded a Select Committee. Lloyd George convinced the House that his figures had been supplied by Maurice's own department. Nevertheless, for the only time during the war, the official Opposition forced a division. 'I have never seen such a collapse as Asquith's yesterday,' Waldorf told Garvin. 'You couldn't find him with a magnifying glass, although Gulland [the Liberal Whip] was seen supporting and pushing him into the division lobby.' Lloyd George's was a damning indictment, unless one knew that the figures he gave the House had been corrected by the War Office before he spoke.

Clearly General Maurice was more important than Colonel Repington, but Garvin insisted that he was 'neither here nor there', 'a cypher', 'a mere means to Repington's ends'. This is hardly consistent with the treatment Garvin gave him. Maurice's letter to *The Times* would, he wrote, 'justify any citizen in the new armies impugning his officers or leaving the trenches. The private would be shot. There must be no mild indulgence for the General.' Presumably Garvin did not want Maurice shot. Did he want him imprisoned or fined? He did not say. Nor did he comment on the responsibility of the editor of *The Times* for publishing the letter. He seems, too, to have forgotten that not long before he had urged Churchill, then a serving officer, to do something like Maurice had done.

## VIII

A week after the Repington exposure came Germany's heaviest air raid on London. The windows of 9 Greville Place were broken; Garvin's youngest child was unable to sleep for night fears. Jim moved his family to Otford, about an hour from London. It seemed prudent. It was not. The Garvins' troubles were far more internal and personal than the result of enemy action. They could not be left behind with the furniture.

While Ged was alive, his parents had used him as a lightning conductor. From Tina's letters to him one learns of Jim's epic rages. There was the occasion, for instance, when seventeen-year-old Viola had been neglecting her piano practice:

Dad (overworked, overwrought, over-worried, over-smoked [12 a day], over-stouted) gave her one of those awful scenes that, as a rule, is reserved for me ... We got him to bed at 1.15, and he came down again to me at 5.40 and started again. As he had to breakfast at 7, I stayed up and looked after him. I spoke to Blaber [the family doctor] and told him I thought he was going mad, but after he got home last night he asked me to read 'The Legend of Montrose' for an hour.

Two days later Tina reported, 'Dad and Vi are better friends than ever.'

Garvin's temper was not confined to the family circle. There was, for instance, wild rage in a letter he wrote to Lady Lee of Fareham in 1918. Garvin's old friend, Arthur Lee, had given Chequers to the nation. He received a peerage. The *Observer* associated the two things in a paragraph which drew an angry, bitter letter from Lady Lee. Garvin, who was personally blameless, worked himself up into a counter-attack of unpardonable ferocity:

At the moment of attaining your new position contrasting with what this war has meant for others, many memories, many decencies ought to have restrained you ... I must return the Turenne picture for how could I keep it; I will frame your letter instead, and I desire to forget that our friendship ever existed ...

The danger period of the anniversary of Ged's death was approaching. Lord Lee with insight and compassion managed to restore a relation which one would have thought irretrievably damaged.

Neither Tina's ill health nor her dependence on alcohol was left behind in Greville Place; what was necessarily abandoned were the familiar activities she enjoyed, her Thursday 'At Homes' where one might meet Sybil Colefax or Mrs Robert Grosvenor, her visits to the theatre and her shopping expeditions. She had to give up her war work in a canteen for soldiers. Jim's mother had died in November 1916, a blow for him, a relief for Tina. For eighteen months she had had her own home with all its treasures to herself. But now at Otford she could only brood. She wondered whether she still held Jim's undivided love. She was jealous by nature and she probably guessed that she had cause for alarm. Compulsively, against her will, she was repelling him. Her tongue was tart.

Jim poured out his troubles to the Colvins:

My helpless wife didn't want to leave London and there has been a bad return of the worst of miseries. On Tuesday night last I packed my bags to leave even the children who are all I have left, and to go away to become a homeless, lonely man for good. But the evident intention brought some return to sanity and promises of amendment so I am staying. There may be a more tolerable period. I can't tell. The horror of the cat and dog life I can't endure, and if it returns I must go.

A tolerable period quickly came: 'My dear, dear friends,' he wrote to the Colvins only six days later. 'There is a marvellous change since the danger of the irrevocable breach became so plain. She has emerged as so often before like one coming out of a possessed state and changing personality . . . Heaven send it last.' Of course it did not.

# IX

The Garvins moved back to Greville Place at the beginning of November. The war was all but won. On the 11th the Armistice was signed. On the 25th Parliament was dissolved. The last *Observer* before polling day was a strange blend of longing for revenge and hoping for Utopia. Garvin, resilient as ever, was writing a book which would provide a blue-print for a better world. By Christmas Eve he reckoned it was five-sevenths done.

Tina, like so many others, was suffering from influenza, but she was making a good recovery. Then she insisted on going out to do her Christmas shopping on 23 December. That evening she and Jim had an affectionate talk; they saw for a moment their ugly present in the light of the happy past so that it briefly dissolved into a future of promise. Tina was over-tired next day and stayed in bed. On Christmas Day Jim wrote to Waldorf:

There's disaster here. My wife died suddenly at six last night of heart failure following relapse of influenza. She had been weakening her heart. At four the doctor said no danger at all, but about six she went as if fainting in bed. She's lying cold upstairs. The children and I are amongst the Christmas things — all she bought for us, she would go out on Monday, and all we bought for her. You know this was her birthday. Though life had become so frightful, and worst these last seven or eight months, I clung and clung to her to the last. The children adored her, but I had to tell them [of their mother's death]. The two youngest were playing down-stairs; the two elder came romping home to the front door. Everything in me is rather smashed for the moment except holding on for whatever is not me . . . Excuse this scrawl. I can scarce see and can't write today. God bless you all there. Say it to your wife for me. How happy we too were altogether once when Christmas came.

Tina was buried at Golders Green in a high open place chosen by her eldest daughter. That night Jim slept in Tina's room. Next day he confided to Frances Colvin: 'I put a love-knot on her pillow.'

**Part Two:**
**'GARVE', 1919-1947**

# BOOK SIX: A SECOND SPRING, 1919-1927

---

'You are rapidly becoming one of the younger generation.'
Arthur Greenwood to J. L. Garvin, 1919

**I**

His wife's death hardly interrupted by a day Garvin's work on *The Economic Foundations of Peace*. He had begun to write as soon as the Armistice was signed; he was determined to finish in time to influence the peace. He thought he had completed five-sevenths of it by Christmas Day, the day Tina died. On New Year's Day he hoped to start proof-reading in a week's time. Of course it did not work out like that. In the end he reckoned that it had taken him three months working eighteen or nineteen hours a day.

There was always intensity in Garvin's writing; this time more than usual because his book was a plea that his son's death should not have been in vain. Many wanted revenge; Garvin refused to regard the Germans as 'irredeemable'. With Ged in mind he wrote:

We had a common taste for German studies, and owed much to them, but were under no illusions about the approach of what we regretted. We meant to live for the safety of Britain and her friends in the war and for the cause of peace afterwards. As for that, one must try to live for two.

*The Economic Foundations of Peace* is not a great book, hardly even a good one; but it is important – something for the historian as well as the biographer. Once again, as when Edward VII died and Garvin proclaimed a Truce of God; he perceived before most others the need and the possibility of an about-turn in public opinion. His quick action helped to bring it about. He not only put forward an agenda for peace which most liberal-minded English people, irrespective of party, came to accept in the twenties, but he provided an explicit warning of what must, and did, follow a failure to carry it out.

**II**

In 1919 Garvin was fifty, a battered man looking at a battered world, but as he wrote he felt the throb of new life. As he put it, 'When Columbus set out, it was not America that he meant to discover. It met him on the way.' To Garvin the world's sole hope was American involvement:

> Both the English speaking peoples have been led through the war towards quite other results and trends, as towards even greater opportunities, than they imagined when they entered it. Their choice is either to accept the mission they have found — or rather which has found them — or to turn back and make all civilisation turn back with them.

The mission was to establish a League of Nations. In America they called it 'The League to enforce peace', a definition 'partly inadequate and partly contradictory'. The need was rather to organise peace. Prospects seemed a little brighter when Garvin finished his book than they had looked when he started. The complete breakdown in Central Europe had forced the reluctant allies to form a Supreme Council for Supply and Relief.

On the other hand the argument about paying for the war was going badly. The popular idea was 'Make the Germans pay.' Garvin saw its stupidity and impossibility. The German race could not be kept for decades as 'international serfs. It could not be done.' The problem too was wider than reparations. The war had made America the world's creditor. She was inexperienced in that role. She wanted to receive money but keep out goods. Garvin saw the contradiction. Calvin Coolidge had a simpler view: 'They hired the money, didn't they?'

Then there was the question of whose League it was to be. Garvin saw that, unless Germany and Russia were allowed to join, it would become 'an entangling alliance'. Unless — or else. The alternative was sombre. Germany's economic resilience might be as spectacular as her present collapse. She had raw materials and good communications. Her people excelled in technical skills and hard work:

> In twenty years, then, the German race might possibly again be the strongest on this side of the world. Its chance might come to get back what it has forfeited, and to acquire much of what it failed to gain in the recent struggle.

So what about disarmament? To Garvin it was not a panacea, but at least it would 'dull and diminish the war habit'. It would have to start in Germany, but

> eighty millions of people cannot be subjected indefinitely as regards armaments to exceptional laws not applying to other peoples. The kind of medicine which the Allies and America prescribe, they themselves must swallow in a given time, or there will be no peace.

In any event disarmament on the scale expected before the October revolution in Russia was now impossible. Garvin detested Communism. He loved Russia and rated highly her potential power. He wanted a strong Russia; he did not want a Communist Russia. Could there in 1919 be one without the other? Communists might be 'insane fanatics, cruel dogmatists, blood-smeared despots, merciless persecutors', but they had in Lenin 'the most formidable single person thrown up anywhere by the war'. In fact 'the question is not . . . whether the League will allow peace with the Bolshevists. The question may be much more whether the Bolshevists will allow peace with the League.'

With realistic pessimism Garvin examined various courses. The first he called 'localisation' — a defensive line from Finland to Romania. It would be as hopeless as 'drawing up a sanitary cordon against germs of pestilence in the atmosphere'. The second was 'limited intervention'. It was like 'proposing to subject a hippopotamus to a converging fire of pop-guns'. A third suggestion was that Communist and non-Communist Russians should compromise — 'Like proposing a calm meeting between flame and sulphur'. The fourth option was 'decisive intervention' followed by free elections and admission to the League. That was Garvin's prescription when he wrote his book. It was already as impracticable as the others. It would have meant sending Marshal Foch in Napoleon's footsteps to Moscow — and back again, as Garvin would have said if he had seen more clearly. He soon did — far sooner than most. When he did, he gracefully accepted Hobson's choice.

Garvin had made his name by writing about the British Empire. He always meant by it a free association of the British democracies throughout the world. He now called it the British Commonwealth, a better name for the same thing; but also, he hoped, a stepping stone to something new, a League of Nations united in the same way as the nations of the Commonwealth. He had learnt from wartime talks with the Dominion statesmen in London — with Smuts, W. M. Hughes and Robert Borden for instance — to take a less London-centred view of the Empire, to depend less in his thinking on a fixed network of tariffs and preferences and more on a community of purpose. It was this free association of like-minded British nations in cooperation with the United States that he saw as the 'activating force' to establish the League.

Anglo-American concord was still for him 'a feeling like the twin of patriotism'; but he now realised that most Americans could not share this feeling. They came from every nation in Europe; each had a feeling for the country from which his people came. Britain was only one of many. A League of Nations would have a stronger appeal than an English-speaking Union. It was the only cause likely to bring England and America lastingly together.

Garvin had not only changed his name for the Empire, he had changed his ideas about world economic organisation. He now accepted the doctrine that lies behind our talk of 'developing countries', recognising that no nation would be content to remain a land of primary producers only: 'Every people wanted not only an economic development broader in degree, but the additional kind of creativeness and employment which technical industry brought with it.' India would be next in the queue. Garvin welcomed it. Others feared the competition which must follow; but, as Garvin saw, 'nothing could be more destructive of peace and cohesion in the world than any attempt to veto the industrial growth which other societies desire'. It was for the United States and the United Kingdom to see that this did not happen.

Wise words, but unheeded. The strongly Protectionist Republicans won control of Congress.


## III


*The Economic Foundations of Peace*, though finished on 19 February, was not published until 19 March. The first edition was sold out that day. Six weeks later the *Observer* accurately foreshadowed the peace terms. Garvin's hopes had been frustrated; his fears realised. He called his next article 'Peace and Dragon's Teeth'. In the name of reparations Germany was 'expected to keep working for others decade after decade'. It would lead to 'international agitation and intrigue'. It did. Germany west of the Rhine was to be occupied by France for fifteen years – 'sheer militarism'. The proposals for Eastern Europe were even worse. Overgrown Poland was already alienating every neighbouring state and every minority inside her frontiers – Germans, Lithuanians,

White Russians, Ruthenians, Czechs and Jews. Sooner or later Germany and Russia would be able to change that. Twenty years later they did.

If the Germans were wise, they would sign the treaty, but use every opportunity to get rid of it. There were bound to be plenty of chances. Meanwhile:

> If conscription is suppressed ... they can develop, as after Jena, gymnastics and athletic exercises throughout the country ... The terrible lesson of Armageddon is the facility with which armaments and armies can be improvised in emergency by any race with a highly scientific and manufacturing equipment.

Garvin was right. On the other hand he felt sure the English-speaking democracies would never fight to enforce the treaty. In 1919 Garvin saw that as a hopeful factor making for a peaceful revision of unjust terms. He did not foresee – who could? – that the Brown Terror inside Germany would make treaty revision the imposition of a hateful tyranny on men who had escaped it.

The only good thing Garvin could bring himself to say about the treaty, apart from its negative quality of being unenforceable, was that it included 'the saving Covenant of the League'. Two days before the treaty was signed Smuts thanked Garvin 'for the magnificent courage and ability with which you have fought many of its reactionary provisions. ... This Treaty is *not* the Peace: it is simply the last echo of the war.' But both Smuts and Wilson found in the League a sufficient justification for signing. Four months later, almost a year to a day after the Armistice, the United States Senate removed that justification. America never joined the League. Garvin's dream dissolved. In the spring he had hoped that he was helping to lay *The Economic Foundations of Peace*; by autumn Keynes was mourning *The Economic Consequences of the Peace*.

## IV

In January Lloyd George had reshuffled his government. Waldorf Astor had worked happily for six months with J. R. Clynes, the President of the Local Government Board under which Food Control, Waldorf's concern, came. Now he was moved to the new Ministry of Health under Christopher Addison. In both his ministerial appointments Waldorf served under Labour, or future Labour, Ministers. For Garvin this meant continued good contacts with the left.

He continued to press vigorously for bold social reform and a broadly based government reflecting the real majority in the country — Labour, Liberals and progressive Unionists. The company Garvin was keeping, the thoughts he was exchanging are well reflected in a letter from one of his regular contributors, Arthur Greenwood, yet another future Labour Minister: 'Congratulations on your article again to-day. You are rapidly becoming one of the younger generation — which is the highest compliment I can pay you. All good people are trying to become one of the younger generation. I am trying myself.'[1]


## V

Two days after Garvin finished *The Economic Foundations of Peace* C. P. Scott dined with him. Scott's usual interview notes were written simply to remind himself and inform a few others of what he had learnt about the political situation. This time, although he started with politics, he became so interested in an unexpected turn their talk took that he went on to speculate about the man. There is hardly another passage like it in Scott's interview notes:

> In the evening dined with Garvin. Found he had cooled a good deal in regard to Lloyd George. Said he had been injured by power — not in the sense of being puffed up and thrown off his balance, but he had become entranced by the handling of great affairs and by the great game of politics. He had lost his ideals and forgotten that little thing, his soul.
>
> Said he had ... been making an elaborate study of Labour conditions — also of 'The Language of Keats.' Had just finished a book to be published in two or three weeks giving a connected statement of his political faith and was about shortly to issue the Keats study. Mentioned incidentally that he had been going right through the old classics — all Shakespere, all Molière, and I don't know what besides. An extraordinary person. I only hope that Keats will be pretty good. He would care more perhaps about that than about the other.

'The Language of Keats' remains a mystery, but there is no doubt that Garvin, like General Wolfe, would rather have written Gray's 'Elegy' than take Quebec.

I

For many weeks after his wife's death Garvin had been sunk in gloom and wistful longing for the good days long since gone. On New Year's Eve he turned to Lady Sackville for consolation. He was fifty, she fifty-six. 'I do understand so well what you tell me', she replied, 'about "Death sweeping away all accidents" in your own case. I don't think it could happen to me, as I have been too unhappy and hurt and bruised morally.' On Twelfth Night he dined alone with her. She recorded in her diary,

> He has had a great shock over his wife's death, but he will get over it in time. It is the first time he had been out since she died and so I must excuse him if I found him full of contradictions ... He worries so much as to what he can do for the best for his four girls who he loves.

In March Garvin had a reassuring medical check-up, though for a time his 'cramps, aches, cripplings, flus' persisted. He sat 'for hours motionless almost glorying in self-pity [for his] years of public strain and private crucifixion ... No Christ because not taken down from the cross where I have hung for seven years'. (Jim did not seem to understand that perhaps Tina and he had crucified one another.) He finished his letter to the Colvins and then began an oddly similar yet strangely different one to Mrs Lee-Mathews whom he had just begun to call Allegra – 'I don't know why the Beethoven trio suggests such a name for you but it does – Milton and music joining in the mind of this Penseroso – or would it be tolerable Italian to call him Penserosissimo!' He complained to Allegra, as he had done to the Colvins, of 'cramps, flu, snapped nerves, clouded mind for everything but work', 'remorseless overwork' and 'private crucifixion'. His conclusion, however, was quite different: 'Whenever I see you I am always cheerful immediately whatever the background of life ... Bless you. And so till Monday Café Royal 1.30.' The letter to the Colvins is pure winter; there is a hint of spring in Allegra's. Both were written on the same day. It was 21 March. It was spring. That evening Viola Woods pledged

Garvin her 'everlasting troth'.

## II

Garvin's love for Viola, who was seperated from her husband, had started before his wife's death. Tina had been both perceptive and jealous. Suspicion had driven her to drink more, provoking the scenes which made Jim turn away and turn elsewhere. At the very end, however, Jim assured her in a long intimate talk that he still loved her, though he did not deny that he was in love with Viola Woods. That is how his youngest daughter put it when she told me what her father said not long before he died.

Viola Taylor and Maurice Woods had been twenty-six when they married in 1908. Maurice was beginning what promised to be a brilliant political career. At Oxford he had been President of the Union. He had also fallen through a skylight into the bedroom of Warden Spooner's daughter while on a night climbing expedition. Spooner lost his head and called the police. Oxford rocked with laughter. So no doubt did F. E. Smith, a former President of the Union and rising Tory politician. A combination of brilliant undergraduate politics and dare-devil undergraduate escapades was just the thing to take his fancy. At any rate he took Woods under his wing and put him in charge of the Unionist Social Reform Committee. Woods and Garvin were inevitably thrown together. They became friends. By 1911 Woods knew Garvin well enough to try to borrow money, and Viola felt able to write confidentially:

> I'm having such a thin time with [Maurice] these last three weeks that I felt it was the last straw that there should be any possible sort of misunderstanding between you and him ... I deserve any snub under the sun if I ask you to treat him as the child he is and make him happy again.

But of course she was not snubbed. Viola was young and beautiful and in distress. Garvin was chivalrous and impressionable.

Soon it became apparent to the Garvins that all was not well with the Woods' marriage. They took Viola's side when Maurice hung about Nancy Astor as his wife was approaching her confinement. Worse was the result of Maurice's association with F. E. Smith and his harddrinking friends who lived at a pace Maurice could not afford. His mother left an unfinished autobiography. In a chapter on Maurice she wrote: 'As soon as a man has lost control over himself in respect to drink or drugs, he is practically insane and it should be permissible to exercise control over him as it is exercised over other mental patients.' Strong words for a mother to apply, even obliquely, to her son.

They explain the situation as Garvin knew it in 1916. By then Tina and Jim were fiercely on Viola's side. Maurice, according to Tina, was 'a brute', 'that awful creature'; to Jim he was 'indescribable ... one of the job lot officers we sometimes get in the army of today'. Jim interviewed Maurice at the *Observer* office; Tina comforted the 'dear, tired, weary one' at Greville Place. Viola was always sure of a welcome. The fact that she was not only in distress, but a beauty in distress was a danger that Tina did not at first recognise.

## III

By the summer of 1918 Maurice had deserted Viola. A week or so after Tina's death Viola asked him to return to her. He refused. Whether at that time she really wanted him back is not clear. There was no doubt, however, what she wanted when at the end of May she formally repeated her request. Once again he refused. She filed a petition for restitution of conjugal rights which was then the necessary first step towards divorce and the freedom to re-marry. Garvin hurried to tell his intimate friends about his hopes of happiness. Edward Goulding was the first to know. Lady Sackville, Allegra and the Colvins soon followed.

From this time on Jim Garvin became 'Garve'. It was Viola's name for him, and it was thus that he was known to all and sundry in Fleet Street and Whitehall during the rest of his life. Jim dropped out of use. It belonged to his mother and Michael and Tina. It was buried with them.

Garvin now took to dining out a good deal. He went frequently to the Russian ballet; when Nigel Playfair put on *The Beggar's Opera*, he was there night after night. He spent one or two days in most weeks at Brighton. 'It does me a world of good,' he told Frances Colvin. Of course it did, for Viola was living there —

tolerably tall, well-walking, bright head, blue Irish eyes that see, wayward nose that doesn't quite curl right up but can't quite get itself straight at all, firm-chinned, not sentimentally amorous (for the humour is incorrigible) but capable of deeper attachment and tenderness than she easily avows, even of utter devotion ... and while she will often be wilful she will never be insipid in this world. No deity — very woman.

Such was the advance publicity that Garvin sent Lady Colvin. Viola herself recalled their August visit.

I was sweating from the heat, but still more from my terror of the step-friends and Garve was like a cat on hot bricks ... Lady Colvin must have been well over eighty and of a terrifying youthfulness of emotion ... Hers was the head of a Sibyl that might well, with the furnishings of the house, have come out of the British Museum .. She always fingered a feather boa which had a way of moulting and making a chicken house of the hearth, and she smelled strongly of lavender.

All went well. Sidney and Frances included Viola in the love they felt for Garve.

Poverty condemned Viola to sordid lodgings in a back street in Brighton. One night a fellow lodger came home drunk, bawled down the house and struck his wife. Next morning she apologised to Viola;

I could not but be extra kind: I did not add that I had known it all — the covering up of last night's noise, the bluffing over unpaid bills and worse ... Such degradations and humiliations ... leave their mark and one does not escape one's environment. Yet without them, one is not equipped to deal with humanity. Remember this, Garve, what I say goes very deep.

In November Viola got her decree for restitution of conjugal rights. Maurice of course did not obey it. Desertion was established, but Viola still required proof of his adultery. It was hard to get. Maurice was not forthcoming. Garvin turned for help to his old friend F. E. Smith, now Earl of Birkenhead and Lord Chancellor. Viola's was a common enough predicament and one which evoked Birkenhead's sympathy. Indeed he had before Parliament a Bill to make desertion a sufficient ground by itself for divorce.[1] It was, however, only a Bill and not an Act of Parliament. The law still demanded proof of adultery as well as desertion. Garvin hoped that Birkenhead would be able to persuade Maurice not to make things difficult for Viola.

A few days later Edward Goulding discovered over luncheon with Beaverbrook that he was 'much disturbed at the L.C. being consulted' about Maurice, who was his political secretary. Garvin interpreted Beaverbrook's annoyance in conspiratorial terms. He thought, perhaps rightly, that Beaverbrook saw in Viola's predicament the opportunity for striking a bargain with Garvin. Beaverbrook, the rising newspaper proprietor, would have liked to recruit Garvin, the famous Empire-crusading editor. Garvin for his part wanted evidence from Maurice Woods, Beaverbrook's man, which would enable him to marry Viola. Very well, Garvin should have the evidence if he agreed to join Beaverbrook; if not, he would find great difficulty in obtaining it. As the weeks went by and Maurice failed to provide evidence and private detectives to find any, Garvin was more and more convinced that his interpretation was correct. It was a bargain he would not stoop to make. In despair at the end of May he turned again to Birkenhead. Birkenhead used the opportunity of a casual meeting with Maurice at the Oxford Union to tell him that he owed Viola reparation. Maurice agreed. Viola got her evidence. Her petition for divorce was presented on 8 July.

During 1920 Garvin's fury with Beaverbrook knew no bounds. To read what he wrote that year one would say that the lava from his volcanic pen had buried for ever any hope of restoring even moderately amicable relations. Yet within a few months Goulding was busy building bridges between his two friends. He drew Garvin's attention to 'one or two very friendly notes [that] Max has written to you in the *Express*: he is a curious man. I wish you never had that row with him. He will always be a man with great friends and enemies.' Ten days later Garvin's engagement diary records a meeting with Beaverbrook. The rest of this book provides much evidence of their renewed friendship. On Garvin's side it was often affectionate, but always wary. We have Garvin's story of the first half of 1920; one would like to have first-hand accounts from Birkenhead, Beaverbrook and Woods of what passed between them during that time.

## IV

While Viola was waiting for her divorce petition to be heard her sister, Una Troubridge, was involved in a slander action, Radclyffe Hall *v*. Fox Pitt. Fox Pitt, a leading member of the Society for Psychical Research, had threatened to expose Radclyffe Hall if her nomination to the

Council of the Society was not withdrawn. His objection had two grounds — scientific, because she was involved with a fraudulent medium to the discredit of the Society; and moral, because she had broken up the marriage between Admiral Troubridge and his wife by her lesbian affair with Una. The case was bound to be the talk of London. Not only was spiritualism a specially sensitive subject in the aftermath of the slaughter of the war, but Admiral Troubridge was remembered as the man who let the German cruiser *Goeben* escape in 1914. In fact The *Times* report ran to eight columns. Viola was deeply worried about the effect of the exposure on Garvin. Had that been in Lady Colvin's mind when she warned Viola, 'Remember, Darling, he will always be a little old-fashioned and never a man of the world'?

The jury awarded Radclyffe Hall £500 damages. Fox Pitt appealed. Viola continued to worry. She told Garvin:

> It would be very terrible for me if ever Una had a smash and wanted to come back and you forbid it . . . When I have once really loved, I forgive everything to a culpable extent. She is not wrongly but rightly called 'the wicked Lady Troubridge'. My little Garve,[2] this is the truth — the tragedy is greater than the scandal, but the tragedies of individuals form the jokes of the world.

The appeal was heard in the middle of March 1921. A new trial was ordered, but fortunately Radclyffe Hall was persuaded to drop her claim. Viola need not have worried. Garvin was understanding and besides he was in love.

## V

At the end of January Viola had been granted a decree *nisi*. Maurice did not contest the case. For the six months' waiting period Viola took her son, Oliver, to Boulogne where living was cheaper than in Brighton. Besides she had an old liking for this corner of France. Mrs Woods, Maurice's mother, came as chaperone, but Viola believed that her indiscretion nearly brought the King's Proctor in to stop the divorce. Mrs Woods had been totally cut off from her son. At the end of March he tried to reopen communications through an Oxford friend. Viola complained to Garvin, 'I have explained before and I explained again the gravity of such a move while she is with me during these six months. Of course it is a very clever move of X,' the pseudonym which she and Garvin gave to Beaverbrook in their letters. Were Viola's fears justified? This indirect contact with Maurice might just conceivably be construed as collusion by a suspicious mind. Moreover the judge in granting Viola custody of Oliver had stipulated that he was to remain within the jurisdiction of the Court. Had she obtained permission to take him to France? All was well, however, and the decree was duly made absolute on 10 August 1921.

## VI

While Viola was in Boulogne, Garvin spent a month with Northcliffe on the Riviera. Perhaps he went there with some idea at the back of his mind that they might once again become business associates. Northcliffe was known to be considering changes in *The Times*. Viola warned Garvin: 'Be personal friends with N, but never let want of money rob you of your independence'; and again, 'I don't worry at all about the N question. I do not at all want to be rich, but for you to be utterly independent in action and expression – and to be a man of letters as well.' It was over books that their minds came most naturally together, though their tastes were often wide apart. Viola was no Wordsworthian but kept quiet about it; Garve thought she admired the wrong French authors and told her so.

Garvin's friendship with Northcliffe was one thing – 'After me, you love him best,' she wrote understandingly; but his friendship with Lady Northcliffe was another matter. Innocently he confided to Viola how 'noble' she had been about the divorce and about Una's lesbianism. Viola was furious:

> No man who has ever loved me has ever humiliated me to the extent you have done, or denigrated me. Maurice humiliated my body – that was pallid and minor. I am weary of your letters breathing the great disadvantage this marriage is to you, full of a desire to run away and marry me in some corner as if I were a tart. [Garvin wanted their marriage to be on the Continent] ... Why should Lady Northcliffe be noble over me? To be crude – in the eyes of the world she is a woman who was once a typist and has now a lover and a *mari complaisant* ... To have Una always dragged in – well, no woman would stand it.

Next day they made it up, but Viola admitted, 'Lady Northcliffe came nearer to splitting our marriage than anything has ever done.'

## VII

The rebound from this quarrel led them to put prudence aside. On Sunday Viola wrote invitingly: 'Do you love Viola? Because you shall, if you like, but there is La Police? By Saturday she was wondering 'what sort of a man you will be — what sort of a way with you'. The following Wednesday she was

> more than happy because you have forgiven me, because you are coming, because it has turned warm . . . Nannie and I will meet you. I don't think I had better come alone as there is often a good handful of British night passengers on that boat.

A month later Viola sent a warning: 'One thing. You must not anticipate again. It must be the solitary time.' Three days later she asked him to make provision so that she should not again be thrown on the world with a child to be at the mercy of relations.

## VIII

Garvin was too shy, too embarrassed perhaps by memories of Tina, to tell his children that he hoped to marry Viola Woods. She saw the danger and pressed him to break the news, but it was the end of March before he told the elder ones. It was another two months before the youngest, then aged thirteen, found out through a family friend who thought she knew. Ursula decided that it was rather a good thing. That had not been the eldest's reaction. Viola Woods advised Garvin to 'break the awful unnatural silence about the primary thing in your mind. If she goes elsewhere for consolation, it will be fatal, fatal for us, fatal for her.' In fact she turned to Muriel Lee-Mathews, Garvin's Allegra, for comfort, and got it. 'Of all the crowd of women you are the one', Garvin told Allegra, 'that knew how I care for the children, and how to lighten the load, and did.'

Garvin's second daughter accepted her father's re-marriage with less apparent difficulty. As Viola Woods put it:

> Una will of course marry. You must remember everything is relative.

In the milieu of medical students — apart from her beauty and her brains — she is considered a very good catch as your daughter. In the world in which you move, the young men expect to marry princesses! She is not likely to do anything foolish, or she would have done it already. But, my darling, they have to go their own way.

There was still Viola's nine-year-old Oliver to be told. Back in Brighton he began to notice a new visitor to their lodgings:

a large man in eye-glasses, attached by a black ribbon. He wore butterfly collars, a grey Homburg hat, and carried a gold-topped cane. He always conversed with me gravely, as with a contemporary, and would on occasion take me to luncheon at the Royal Albion, when he used to stuff me with oysters . . .

One evening my mother came into my room and sat on my bed. She appeared to me intense and took some time coming to the point. Eventually she asked me what I should feel if Garve were to join the family and become my father. Next day I had another lunch with Garve at the Royal Albion. Afterwards we walked along the front for a while, and he told me that he very much loved my mother and would like to be a father to me if I approved. By this time I had thought it over and decided that I did.

## IX

A civil marriage was of course inevitable. Viola disliked the idea so much that she even entertained the impossible dream that Garvin could persuade Father Bernard Vaughan, the fashionable priest of the 1920s, to marry them. She seems to have closed her eyes to the fact that, although she was now free to marry Garvin according to the law of England, she could never do so according to the Church of Rome as long as Maurice lived. Viola was not troubled by philosophic or scientific uncertainties as Garvin was. She was sure of the psychological wisdom of her Church and asked no questions. She loved the ritual and romance of the religion in which she felt completely at home. Brought up as an Anglican, she had become a convert to Rome like most of her Taylor relations. Now, reluctantly, she set her will against its will, but neither her heart nor her mind turned aside.

Garve and Viola were married in Hampstead Registry Office on

21 August 1921. The witnesses were Waldorf Astor, Edward Goulding, Oliver Locker-Lampson and Mrs Mackail. The marriage remained childless.

I

The nineteen-twenties were harvest years. Not only did Garvin find happiness with Viola, but almost at the same time there came into his life a young man whom he quickly began to hope would in time take over from him. It might have been difficult to find anyone whom both Waldorf and Garvin would welcome as a present deputy and future editor, but Edward Grigg was a good talent scout, trusted by both. He knew Astor through the Round Table group; he had been Garvin's assistant editor on the *Outlook*. 'It seems yesterday', Garvin recalled, 'since you opened a door and I liked you like anything at first glance.' First impressions were always important to Garvin. Fortunately Grigg's candidate, Barrington-Ward, B-W to one and all, had made a similar good impression on Garvin in a fleeting meeting before the war. Garvin had told him then, 'People I don't like, I don't want to see. I like you. Come and see me whenever you like. I mean that.' B-W's battle was therefore half won before he came for interview in February 1919.

Astor was not so impulsively impressionable as Garvin. He asked the young man to supper and found him 'very nice — straight, intelligent, modest'. Geoffrey Dawson, whose editorial secretary he had been at *The Times*, had given him a good chit, but Astor was noncommittal and suggested to Garvin that B-W should have a trial for a year or six months 'till we could tell about him — and he about us!' B-W therefore joined the *Observer* with undisclosed prospects, wondering whether Grigg's suggestion of 'an assistant editorship straightaway and the prospect of succeeding Garvin might not after all prove a mirage'.

He need not have worried. When Garvin sent him to Paris during the Peace Conference, he met Lionel Curtis who offered him the editorship of the *Round Table*. B-W hoped to double the two jobs, but Garvin told him that he could not be in the counsels of two political journals at once, even if they were as like-minded as the *Observer* and the *Round Table*. After many consultations, B-W told his diary, 'I ended by plumping for the *Observer*.'

His probation ended on 20 November. B-W told his father about

191

a long, friendly, and intimate talk with J.L.G. The upshot is this. He has offered me a contract of three years, or five years, whichever I please. The first three years at £1,000 a year, with not less than £1,200 for the next two. This for four days a week, Wednesday to Saturday. I am to be Garvin's complete deputy and take his place and responsibilities when he is away . . . I hope you will agree with me that this is highly satisfactory.

Garvin found in B-W one who became to him, as it were, Ged's elder brother. After five years together, Garvin told him,

I dare say you know I have come to love you like a son, which perhaps is natural in the circumstances. There's no other young man I care for half as much . . . I'm the last male of my race, and when the stock has been strong that is humanly a hard thought, though philosophically a very foolish one. All I can say is, your coming has made it easy to bear.

B-W had been Captain of the School at Westminster the year Ged went there. Both joined the army as soon as war broke out. Ged was killed; B-W came back with the DSO and the MC. Later, after reading Siegfried Sassoon's *Memoirs of an Infantry Officer* he wrote: 'The war, with all the crudities it threw up, was essentially fine in spirit. The peace was essentially vindictive and vulgar. The peace has put many honest people wrong about the war.' Garvin and B-W at least did all they could, and with a fair measure of success, to put honest people right.

## II

One immediate advantage to Garvin from B-W's appointment was that it deflected some of the more tiresome consequences of the Astor ownership. Garvin was prepared to pay the price Astor demanded in the shape of articles denouncing brewers and premium bonds but praising Christian Scientists. He now gladly passed them over to B-W.

B-W's diary shows that at times he felt the load was more than he could bear and that the Astors did not properly appreciate the hard work the *Observer* staff put in. 'The *O* is a happy and therefore all the more efficient family. It's a pity the Astors don't realise how much work is done there and in what spirit.' Or, again, 'W. A.' doesn't know how inconsiderate he is.' Inconsiderate he may have been, but it was only through ignorance of newspaper work. He was certainly not ungrateful.

In fact the Astors had taken a great liking to B-W. He was a bachelor, a rising young man of the kind Nancy liked to collect. At her house he made contacts invaluable to him and useful to the *Observer*. Even so, there was a price to pay. Thus, one evening he recorded a last-minute invitation from Lady Astor.

> Found a large party. The Queen of Rumania, her sister Princess Beatrice and her husband the Infante Alfonso of Spain, the Neville Chamberlains, the Samuel Hoares, the Ormsby-Gores, Brands, Garvins, Geoffrey Dawsons, Sir Leslie Scott, Miss Maxse, Mrs. Phillips, Miss Christian (Richmond, Virginia), Philip Kerr.

Clearly Nancy Astor was one man short, and that mattered; she did not realise that it mattered more for the *Observer* to be one man short, and that man the duty editor and the day Saturday.

Still, B-W found Nancy fascinating: 'She has the pluck and vitality of twelve men, great charm and wit, a very good heart and a very quick feminine intelligence – not the blue-stocking kind, man-made at Somerville and Girton.' All the same he felt that there was something wrong, or at least unseemly, in being sent to Plymouth to work for Lady Astor's election. He felt that a member of the *Observer* staff had no business 'to figure as anyone's political lackey'.

The by-election was the consequence of what had happened in the Astor family during the war. Old Mr Astor had accepted a peerage in 1916. He had not consulted Waldorf, who was furious, partly at least because it automatically put a ceiling to his political ambitions. When his father died he would have to go to the House of Lords where he would have much less chance of high Cabinet office. There was then no way of renouncing a title. Lord Astor died soon after B-W joined the *Observer*. Nancy fought and won Waldorf's vacant seat.

Waldorf remained a junior Minister, but of course the Lords took less of his time than the Commons had so that there was more for the paper. Eighteen months later Waldorf's chief was forced out of office and Waldorf went with him. He never held office again. Fortunately, by this time B-W was so well established that Garvin was happy for him to deal directly with Waldorf. On all major questions the three men agreed. They disagreed on matters that were marginal to Garvin and B-W, but very near Waldorf's heart. B-W was by nature discreet and kept his exasperation to himself and his diary; Garvin was easily provoked into telling Waldorf just what he thought, and more than he intended. The danger of an explosion was always present, but there was less risk now that B-W was on the *Observer*.

I

Since early 1919 Garvin had been estranged from Lloyd George over
the Treaty of Versailles and the Black and Tans in Ireland, but they
had continued to meet. After all, Waldorf was a member of Lloyd
George's government and Cliveden was a hospitable house. One Sunday
in February 1920, for instance, Garvin found Lady Astor's house
party gathered in the big hall round the great hearth arguing about
that morning's *Observer* in which Garvin had urged L.G. to retire
for a short time. He described the scene to Viola:

> The PM was sunk in an arm chair, his hair all wispy and now coming
> to be nearer white than grey. I was thrust up at once and the talk
> was between me and him, the others pressing closer and closer,
> standing behind sofas and chairs ... It was a big talk − a battle
> foot to foot − about faiths and facts, principles and expedients,
> vision and short sight. It was continued in a private room and
> ended not unfriendly. No one dares to stand up to him as I do −
> no one − and of course all opposition chafes him now when he's
> tired ... and wants to believe only what he wishes to be true; but
> he knows I am an honest and seeing person, and in the end good
> comes out of the encounter.

By the end of 1921 things were better. The Irish Treaty was followed by the news that at last there was to be a conference at which
the victors, the vanquished and the neutrals of the World War would
sit down together. There were to be no pariah nations. At Genoa in
1922 Lloyd George tried to do what ought to have been done at
Versailles in 1919. That spring Garvin saw more of him than at any
time since the Truce of God first brought them together.

For the only time between the wars Germany and Russia were
present together as full members of a major international conference.
All the European neutrals were represented. The United States had an
observer who did more than observe: 'We were conscious of being
overlooked.' There were thirty national delegations; six hundred
journalists. Garvin dared to hope that this just might be the real

Peace Conference.

Leaving B-W in Tudor Street, he spent the whole six weeks in Genoa. He had given his Rome correspondent less than a week in which to rent a villa. There was, of course, no villa to be had. All the hotels were full; the delegations were spread over thirty miles of coastline. Nevertheless she managed to borrow a friend's flat only a few yards from the conference hall. She brought a cook and a man-servant from her castle in the Apennines. The cook just happened to have a nephew in the special conference telegraphic service so that Garvin's outrageously long telegrams got priority. What more could any editor expect from an old hand?

Lina Waterfield, however, was a beginner. She had met Garvin for the first time, apart from a fleeting encounter in 1910,[1] during his honeymoon in Florence the previous autumn. Viola had known Lina at the turn of the century, a radiant beauty whom Charles Furse painted in *The Return from the Ride*. Now she was

> not the less beautiful because the corn-coloured hair had turned chestnut . . . her head and shoulders folded in a shawl that made her look as if she had escaped from a Greek frieze and was protecting herself from the cold of the British Museum.

Over lunch Garvin tackled her about Italian politics. She kept up with his barrage of questions, but was very surprised when he followed it up by a letter asking her to become the *Observer*'s Italian correspondent. Garvin's impulsive decision was justified. Seven weeks later at Genoa she carried out with deft mastery the role of 'housekeeper, journalist, secretary to Garvin, accountant (!!), Master of the Ceremonies for the *Observer*, lady-in-waiting to Mrs. Garvin, and interviewer of P.M.s and delegates'.

For the first fortnight Lina was on her own as hostess for Garvin and his twenty-two-year-old daughter, Una. Small wonder that, as Viola put it:

> All the Italians had concluded that Lina was Garve's wife, and when I appeared on the scene that I was his amusement. The only thing that baffled them was that Lina and I were on such good terms . . .
>
> It was my first experience of a conference and, as waiters poured red wine into my glass of white wine, I marvelled at how any work got done in such an endless round of luncheons and dinners and gaiety of every description . . .

Lloyd George was outside the town in a villa smothered in small white roses. At dinner we talked of Boulogne and one would have thought the Haute Ville were the ramparts of the world for him and I the solitary inhabitant. He had that inestimably valuable quality of making everyone feel this satisfaction with themselves and him.

After dinner a crowd gathered below in the garden under the rose-curtained window to listen to the music. I watched his leonine head as he sang *Will ye no come back again?* and I asked myself, 'Will he?'

Then Garve, not to be outdone, challenged heaven with the *Veni Creator* and told how the crusaders had set out to sea to those strains, the Bishop's ship starting and the following ones taking it up as the people knelt on the beach.

Garvin enjoyed the conviviality and made it useful. He had come to work, and work he did like a mountain torrent. There were breakfasts with Lloyd George, who would sometimes also call at Garvin's flat. There Garvin gave many working luncheons to men like Stambuliski, the Bulgarian Premier; Vanderlip, the American banker; and Gustav Cassel, the Swedish economist. Lina Waterfield described for her son how Garvin got his messages done:

He used to start writing his long cables at about six and finished at 2 or 3 in the morning. Mrs. Garvin and I used to sit curled up on the low divan, dozing and watching in turn for him to cast off a sufficient number of sheets for us to take to be type-written at the International Press Bureau – the *Stampa* ... After 11 p.m. we could take no more as the young lady had to go to bed, and then I finished the job. Gasperini [the friend in the telegraph office] used to wander in at 1 a.m. and wait for the cable to be ready to send off.

At the opening session of the Conference Garvin, sitting among the 'personaggi', watched 'the delegates come in by their companies. It was like the Noah's Ark of Nations.' He felt relaxed; things were going better than he had expected. Next day English and Italian journalists met the German Chancellor and the Foreign Minister, Walter Rathenau:[2]

A fountain played high in the air [Garvin wrote]. It was like politics in Paradise. Herr Rathenau addressed us, standing on the steps, with the white facade of the villa behind him. His speech was a wonderful effort of lucid and persuasive English ... Most of his auditors ... were entirely sympathetic to the idea of a full reconciliation and co-operation with Germany. But Herr Rathenau had managed to leave ... an indefinite, strange, haunting impression of mental reservation. We felt he was speaking incomparably well, yet vainly well — that the thing on his tongue was not the main thing in his mind. We wondered what was at the back of his mind. We augured something disquieting. We were right.

While Rathenau had been speaking, one of his staff was negotiating with the Russians. Shortly before midnight they had a treaty ready for signature next morning, Easter Day. The treaty was in itself good. Had it been made, as it might have been, before the Conference opened there could have been no complaint. To sign it during a meeting whose purpose was to arrive at a pan-European settlement of the same questions seemed to Garvin 'one of the crassest political blunders made in Europe since August, 1914'. No doubt the Germans feared the 'result of those conclaves in Mr. Lloyd George's villa, where Germany was not even a keyhole participant'. 'In pique and panic' they had rushed to make their own peace with the Russians. 'They confronted the Allies with an accomplished fact. It was a small affair, yet in temperament and psychology it was like Kiao-Chau, Tangiers, the Bosnian squeeze, Agadir, the ultimatum to Serbia, the violation of Belgian neutrality, the submarine campaign.' Calchas was guiding Garvin's pen. When the terms of the treaty became known, the first impulse of the French was to break up the Conference and march into the Ruhr valley: 'Could Mr. Lloyd George — could Britain and Italy together — save Germany from herself?'

Garvin, writing for a Sunday paper, had time to brief himself thoroughly. He dined with the Russian delegates. He could not, of course, quote what they said, though his readers could infer it. Instead he described the strangely assorted company in the closely guarded villa:

We were five. Mr. Tchitcherin is, of course, an aristocrat of a certain, quiet, attenuated distinction, whom we could not help calling a Cecil of Russian democracy.[3] Next to me, on the other hand, was Mr. Litvinoff, like an exaggerated cherub, so round, florid, smiling and astute. Opposite, the tall worn man with the intent, taking face and the narrow head was Mr. Vorowsky, the able Soviet agent in Rome. Finally, there was Mr. Krassin, with the pointed, twinkling, cogent countenance which would make a cheerful and practical impression in any company.

This one episode must stand for Garvin's doings throughout the Conference where crisis succeeded crisis. The hope of a united Europe was in danger from Poincaré, the French Prime Minister, who 'with his utterly enclosed mentality is the Kaiser of the Peace, and may be fatal for Europe'. There was danger, too, from Lloyd George's enemies in England. Garvin rarely referred to them in his messages, but in his last article about Genoa he turned savagely on *The Times* and the whole Northcliffe press for its spiteful attacks – 'what is it but the voice of one mortal and fallacious man full of personal kinks and political hallucinations, charming by fits in personal intercourse, hopeless and menancing in his method of dealing with public affairs'.

Meanwhile Garvin had given his readers a memorable picture of Lloyd George as a great man facing an already impossible task:

In the early phases he bore himself magnificently – better than one had ever known. It was conspicuous genius in happiest play – he seemed all compact of pluck, fun and mastery ... We of the British lot were rather full of tribal satisfaction. We were proud. The Italians were carried away. He became a demigod and a legend ... What matters, however, is not how a man begins a fight of this magnitude, but how he ends it ... We are all wondering what he is going to do. The *dénouement* cannot be the weakest page in his biography. It ought to be the strongest. But how is he to make it the strongest when individualist France and Soviet Russia insist with equal obstinacy on their incompatible principles?

There was no answer, and Garvin knew it. The Conference was a failure. The best that could be hoped for was to avoid an open breakdown. 'Yet the sequel', he wrote, 'will not be in the least what the wreckers imagine. Genoa is not so much the end of an episode as the beginning of a campaign. This case is like the body and soul of John Brown.' At any rate it was to Garvin.

## II

A few days before the end Garvin fell ill and had to return to England.

In London he wrote a last word on Genoa, tidied his desk, and took Lord Dawson's advice to retire to Duff House, Banff, for a four-month cure. His breakdown seems to have been comparable in severity to his illness in 1905. Overwork, over-excitement and disappointment had taken their toll. He gave his grief over the failure at Genoa a characteristic personal twist. 'Amidst the seething virulence of the old hates at Genoa', he told Muriel Lee-Mathews, 'I almost felt at last as though my dedicated life's fight for Ged was in vain, and that's really what nearly destroyed me.'

By the middle of July he was 'down from 13 stone nearly to twelve and a quarter, very thin and fit. Incredibly hungry. Stupid beyond example.' Accordingly after a bare two months he defied his doctors and broke off his cure when it was only half done. He came back partly because Northcliffe's complete mental and physical collapse made anything else unthinkable: 'The tragedy is grievous and wipes out all bitterness though not all judgment.' The news had moved Garvin as few events had power to do. There was between the two men an affinity of temperament deeper than their differences of opinion. Both were visionaries, though they looked in different directions; both were risk-taking men who fought to make their pioneering dreams come true. Garvin owed his great chance to Northcliffe. Some men find gratitude difficult; Garvin never did. He quickly jotted down the thoughts that tumbled into his mind as it roamed backwards and forwards through the twenty years they had known each other, regretting perhaps that the last thing of his that Northcliffe could have read was his vituperative counter-attack in defence of Lloyd George at Genoa. From his haphazard jottings Garvin fashioned a worthy memorial article when Northcliffe died in August. Perceptively he wrote of his old Chief as 'the Rousseau of our time who, like the other Rousseau, brought into the play of public affairs whole classes whose lives had previously been untouched by political interests'. That was a side of Northcliffe, and of the *Daily Mail*, to which many people were blind. Perhaps the fact that Garvin saw it was the reason Cecil Harmsworth asked him to write his brother's biography. It was an invitation he had to refuse. We are the poorer.


## III


At Duff House Garvin had felt as cut off from the world as though he had been on the Arctic Circle. He came back to find the world had changed and Lloyd George with it. In Anatolia, Kemal Ataturk (to give him the name he was soon to take) was making a vigorous nation state out of the remains of a ramshackle empire. He had turned the Greeks out of Ionia, massacred the population of Smyrna (Ismir), and was ready to cross into Europe and repeat his exploits in Thrace. Italy and France hastily withdrew their troops to the European shore. At Chanak on the Asiatic coast a small British force was isolated.

'It's a longer way from Genoa to Chanak than ever it was to Tipperary.' In these words Garvin contrasted the peace-making Lloyd George of May with the the sabre-rattling Lloyd George of September. The British government issued a bellicose manifesto, asked the Dominions for military help, ordered the British commander to stand firm, and encouraged him to give the Turks an ultimatum. Harington stood firm. Fortunately he did not issue an ultimatum. If he had, Britain would have been on the brink of war with both Russia and Turkey, without allies and with the certainty of antagonising the whole Muslim population of the Empire.

Garvin was in Paris, supposedly convalescing, when the news broke on Monday, 17 September. He spent three or four days in busy lobbying, then on Thursday he sent Barrington-Ward a telegram, telling him to back Curzon and Grey, which meant opposing his two friends, Lloyd George and Churchill: 'France nearest right on Eastern policy . . . We cannot have war.' Early in the following week, still in Paris, he sent B-W one of the longest letters he ever wrote. It was rambling, repetitive, bare of the plums that tempt one to play Jack Horner. The most significant passage was in brackets and clearly not for publication: 'I wish this Government was out at any price but we must think that out more. They are stale, stale, stale — L.G. stalest of all except for the spasms of dramatic demonstrations.'


## IV

Devoted though Garvin was to the idea of National government, he saw that the Coalition was no longer capable of formulating or carrying out a coherent policy.

A Unionist Government in the spirit of Lord Beaconsfield would at least — like France and Italy — have settled with Turkey. A Liberal Government would at least in the spirit of Mr. Gladstone have settled definitely with Russia ... The Coalition Cabinet could agree on nothing.

It was no longer working, could not be made to work again, and ought to be broken up.

There was bound to be a general election within twelve months. The question was whether Lloyd George should go to the country as Prime Minister, or let the Conservatives, the largest party in the House, form a government on their own. Garvin thought he should resign. He would soon find himself 'Kingmaker in politics until the time came to resume the crown himself ... It may possibly be later than sooner, but at some time Mr. Lloyd George will be once again the most powerful politician in the world.' Lloyd George, however, wanted to fight the election as Prime Minister. He persuaded all but one of the Unionist Ministers to support him; but that one objector, the unconsidered Stanley Baldwin, carried the day at a party meeting. Before the next *Observer* appeared Lloyd George was out. Friends bringing wholesome but unwanted advice are apt to be remembered as enemies. Twelve years later Frances Stevenson[4] had not forgiven Garvin: she wrote in her diary: 'The wolves were howling, headed, strangely enough by Garvin, who loved D but hated the Versailles Treaty.'

In the general election Churchill lost his seat. It might be, the *Observer* thought, 'the very best thing that ever happened to him'; if, that is, he took to heart the rather schoolmasterly advice that Garvin (or B-W) gave him:

Whether he comes to the very top, or not, will depend upon the answer to one old question. The tendency to rush into warlike enterprises ... has been the very bane of his life, and unless he corrects this bias all else will be in vain.

Yet Churchill came to 'the very top' only because he had the power to carry through a seemingly hopeless warlike enterprise.

The world of party politics after Lloyd George's premiership and before Churchill's was one in which Garvin's role gradually changed. From being an eager, active player, he became a touch-line commentator. No party programme was sufficiently to his liking to command his whole-hearted support; no party leader big enough to win his entire allegiance. He was as much a political animal as ever, but he had become the cat that walked by itself.

I

There had never been a chance that the second Mrs Garvin would take over the first Mrs Garvin's house: 'Whatever happens that has to go.' Garvin procrastinated; Viola spurred him on: 'Are you going to keep four servants there for no one at all next winter?' In fact it was two winters and a spring before Greville Place was given up. Meanwhile Viola wisely left her namesake, Garvin's eldest daughter, to run the house as she had been doing since her mother's death.

Garvin thought that the editor of the *Observer* ought to live in town and entertain in style. The Berrys did; so should he. Waldorf should help him since it was for the good of his paper. He asked Waldorf to put up half the cost of a house in Lancaster Gate Terrace. Waldorf was not forthcoming, and Garvin had to settle for Marble Arch where the Cumberland Hotel now is. Plaintively he complained that the house was so dark that the strain on his eyes was 'unending and severe'.

The Garvins left Greville Place at midsummer 1923, two months after what Garvin boastfully called 'one of the greatest journalistic strokes of the *Observer*'. He had announced that Bonar Law, who had been Prime Minister since Lloyd George's fall the year before, would resign. That same evening Downing Street retorted, 'The Prime Minister has no intention whatever of resigning.' Most people and most newspapers believed Law and not Garvin; but in six weeks Law went; in six months he was dead. In retrospect, the *Observer*'s foreknowledge seems of trifling importance; more to the point is the change in Garvin's life that followed. The two men had been friends since the stirring days of Joseph Chamberlain's imperial preference campaign. They had been estranged by the struggle over the Unionist leadership, but the war had brought them together again. Law's successor was Baldwin with whom Garvin had no shared memories and of whom he had but small expectations. Among his own particular political friends only Leo Amery was in office. Austen Chamberlain, Birkenhead and Churchill did not come back until the end of 1924. Lloyd George never did. There was little in Whitehall to tempt Garvin to stay in London in a house he did not like.

Besides he already had another house that he loved. In the months

203

of waiting for her divorce Viola had pestered Garvin to find a house near Weybridge. He stalled, and suggested instead somewhere near Slough. Viola would not hear of it because Maurice had been 'notorious for drink and debts for miles around'. Just after Easter 1921 they found a house that pleased them both. 'Gregories' at Beaconsfield was the dream house of the verses they had exchanged in 1919. Garvin's ran:

> Give me a house, well-ordered, gracious, fair,
>   A trellised garden rich with scent and hue
>   Sunned fruits, good wine, few servers, children few,
> Faithful to my sole love, one woman rare.
>
> \* \* \* \* \* \* \* \*
>
> Still with broad mind, firm judgment and calm breath,
> To tell my beads and tend my orchard ways,
>   And wait at home the gentlest hand of death.[1]

Of course at 53 Garvin was far from ready for 'the gentlest hand of death'. He was still tempestuous, unquiet, in search of new worlds to win; but, when death should come, he had no doubt that it was at Gregories he would like it to find him. There he put down roots. He would not again stand transplanting.

At Gregories Garvin soon found that he could do all that he had to do, and on the seventh day rest from his labours when he had made the week's *Observer* and seen that it was very good. After that, Great Cumberland Place never had a chance. In 1925 Garvin turned the outbuildings of Gregories — it had been Edmund Burke's farm bailiff's house — into a home for his books. That settled the matter. Where his books were, there he must be. He could edit the *Observer* from nowhere else.

The house in Great Cumberland Place was given up at Christmas 1925 after only two and a half years. At first the consequences were partly veiled by the fact that he took a small house in Ebury Street, largely for the sake of his young people. He made litte use of it himself, and in 1928 he gave up the tenancy. For the rest of his life he lived wholly at Gregories. 'I suppose you do come up to London for the day occasionally?' Leo Amery once protested, half in admiration of Garvin's abstention and half in disbelief. As time went on, it became all but the whole truth.

## II

Of course Garvin had not buried himself in a remote village. Edward Goulding was nearby at Wargrave — he became Lord Wargrave the year after Garvin bought Gregories. The Astors were even nearer at Cliveden. Chequers was within reasonable distance, and Garvin was welcome there when Ramsay MacDonald or Churchill was Prime Minister. It was easy to lunch at Gregories on the way to or from dinner in Oxford or London. The main difference Gregories made in Garvin's life was that people now had to come and see him. He no longer went willingly to them, the very great excepted.

Prominent people had to make the journey when they wanted his help. Sir John Simon, for instance, was glad to lunch at Gregories in order to brief Garvin about his report on the government of India. This particular visit proved doubly useful. Garvin's stepson was at home, preparing for an Oxford scholarship. When he looked at the examination paper a week later, he read: 'Explain the Indian Question and give your ideas about its solution.'

Others came simply because they loved Garvin's company. Thus, Brendan Bracken was a regular visitor from the time he was twenty-one, and Garvin fifty-eight. Oliver Woods retained a boyish 'vision of his arrivals, all glistening red hair, glittering spectacles, and shiny blue Rolls Royce coupé'. He was soon completely at home with the Garvins; a privileged visitor indeed, but there were certain things nobody was allowed to do. One was to break into a Beethoven evening. He found a way round. He put on the next record. The gramophone broke down. They talked politics as Bracken had intended.

Their friendship was based on a similarity of temperament, style and taste. They loved books and politics; both tastes were satisfied by their fellow Irishman, Edmund Burke, whose name was never forgotten at Gregories. Garvin and Bracken were both shrewd, exuberant, eloquent, nonconforming. Bracken's letters have the infectious hilarity that had marked Fred Oliver's before the war. They are happy even when they are gloomy. He listened avidly to Garvin's political talk as Garvin had once listened to Joseph Cowen. Gregories was in a way his university. He made contacts there and turned them to good account. He met W. B. Yeats at Gregories, and Yeats found himself contributing to *English Life*, the magazine Bracken was running. And so did Mrs Garvin. Another encounter at Garvin's dinner table changed Bracken's life. Churchill, out of office and even out of Parliament, was Garvin's guest. When Bracken left, Churchill asked Garvin point-blank: 'Who's this extraordinary young friend you've been hiding away?' Garvin told him what he knew (nobody knew very much about the mysterious young man), and Churchill commented: 'Well, he strikes me as very bright indeed and I would like to see him again.' Bracken for his part had fallen under Churchill's spell. Garvin in the role of Prospero had turned his very English home into an enchanted island for the meeting of a shipwrecked politician with a young castaway returning from Down Under.

## III

Greogories itself and the pattern of life there have been described by Garvin's daughter, Katharine, and his stepson, Oliver Woods. The house was long, rambling, L-shaped. Oliver thought that seldom could so much wall have enclosed so little utilisable space. There were seven acres of grounds and two ponds, one almost big enough to be called a lake.

At one end of the L was Garvin's study, the Shepherd's Kitchen of the old farm house. Garvin once described its state after a spell on his *Life of Joseph Chamberlain*: 'A piggery littered – floor, long sofa, chairs, shelf-top – with letters, old Cabinet memoranda, old despatches, books, maps, and the huge dull worthless records that the family compiled.' And his own condition? 'The whole body cramped like an Indian fakir's to the figure of a chair, arms and legs even in bed seemed stuck into the chair shape.'

At the other end of the house was the drawing room where Oliver's mother, her friends and his stepsisters were based, the *selamlik* and the *harem*, so to speak. Oliver, because he was both young and male, had the run of both ends and so had an early training in domestic politics. Between the Shepherd's Kitchen and the drawing room was the dining room with its woodcut of Turenne and his autographed requisition for corn and cattle. It had been Lady Lee of Fareham's gift to Ged whose memory lived on in his father's bedroom. Ged's books were kept there. On the wall was the photograph taken the day he won the fencing championship; on a canvas screen there was a drawing of him as a young boy. Their presence showed that Garvin had at last come to terms with his grief. As late as 1922 he had been unable to look at Ged's portrait.

**IV**

Garvin had been able to edit the *Observer* largely from Greville Place because his house was under four miles from the office. Gregories was twenty-three. To edit at that distance with the poor communications of the time was a much more adventurous undertaking. It was only practicable because he had absolute confidence in Barrington-Ward. The main link between what Oliver called the *Observer*'s battle headquarters at Gregories and its main headquarters in Tudor Street was a direct telephone line:

> It required a lot of cranking before it raised 'the office'. In the small room where the telephone was kept, one could hear the rattle of Garvin's instructions, interspersed with long pauses. 'Quiet, I'm thinking,' he would say. The man at the receiving end would then, so we were told, turn round to his colleagues and request in reverent tones, 'Quiet, Mr. Garvin is thinking.'

There was also a car, provided by the paper. Garvin's first car had been a Daimler, but his chauffeur, Morison, hankered for a Rolls. Lord Wargrave was a director of Rolls Royce. Between them they persuaded Garvin, so Oliver held, that 'there was something unpatriotic about *not* having a Rolls'. On Saturdays Morison needed all his wartime experience as Allenby's driver in Palestine to rush page proofs back and forth from the office.

Secretaries and messengers shuttled between London and Beaconsfield, and once a week there was an expedition to London when business could be transacted in Tudor Street before or after an editorial lunch on the top floor. Its purpose was not to plan the paper but to develop a corporate sense, a feeling of belonging to the *Observer* and of knowing not only what was in the editor's mind, but of knowing the man. It was this intimacy of association which Ivor Brown, Garvin's colleague and successor, picked out as one thing at least which the *Observer* had in fuller measure than the *Sunday Times*.

**V**

Sunday lunch at Gregories, however, was the highlight of the week. First, the host as Oliver remembered him:

A large rather shambling man, given to wearing loose tweed suits. If one classified human beings by their animal resemblance. Garve belonged to the elephant class. It was not only his size and the bagginess of his trousers which gave the elephantine impression – he also had a long nose, with spectacles perched half way down it, and largish ears ... But by far the most striking feature of my stepfather's face was his eyes. Unlike those of the elephant, they were extremely large, prominent, and luminous ... as expressive and changeable as the skies above us. At one moment they were almost vacant, fixed on space, the eyes of a seer; at others they could relax into a very charming expression of humour, attentive to the person he was talking to. At times they took on a look of extreme guile.

And the hostess? 'In every way a contrast to Garve. Angular, with a straight fringe, a nose slightly flared at the nostrils, and quick movements. If one hung a label round the neck of anyone so individualistic as her, she was a Pre-Raphaelite.' So Oliver; Kit pictured her as the happy mistress of a beautifully kept house whose welcome to the children's friends made those days in the twenties some of the gayest that she could remember anywhere. She realised that Gregories exactly fitted Viola, recalling how 'she used to sit cross-legged before the log fire – there was one at time time in every downstairs room – making dragons and lions and birds in red and blue cross-stitch'.

Then the occasion, as Kit remembered it:

On other days people came more or less singly and for special purposes. On Sunday anyone might bring anyone – with due warning, of course ... The guests would generally sit in the drawing room with my step-mother and any of the children who happened to be about until the food was on the table. Father was always late; probably he had some special crony for private conversation in his study. Despairing of him the hostess and her guests would take their places at the table, continuing their pre-luncheon conversation. Suddenly, the door would open and Garve would appear, enunciating some statement or theory ... All other conversation stopped for the moment, and he would continue to control the conversation in massive sentences from his end of the table. My step-mother would nobly continue the more intimate conversation at her end. Guests in the middle of the long table would turn their heads first this way, then that, keeping the see-saw going.

Two separate conversations were almost inevitable since there were few areas in which Garvin's mind met Viola's. She was devotedly fond and immensely proud of him, but she cared not at all for politics or history. She was not musical as he was, and, though she had grown up among artists, she had no great love of art. Both loved words and had skill in using them, but in literature their tastes were dissimilar. Garvin once told his daughter Ursula that, while one half of Viola's mind was as polished as a diamond, the other half simply was not there. It was not an obstacle to a happy marriage — indeed it may have made it easier.

Garvin thoroughly enjoyed Sunday lunch, but at supper he would switch on the wireless. 'Why do you want it on, Daddy?' Katharine asked. 'Because they make me talk so, and they can't make me talk when the wireless is on.' And so the day would end with a characteristic little ceremony which Oliver described:

Every evening, before he went to bed, his eyes were bathed in Optrex by Mrs. Saul, our housekeeper, while my mother and I, and anyone else who had come into the Shepherd's Kitchen to say good night, stood round. Garve's *couchée* was a sort of eighteenth century *levée*.

**I**

Mercifully, Garvin could not see what Barrington-Ward was writing in his diary while he himself was packing up before leaving Great Cumberland Place for good. It was:

*(Saturday) December 5, 1925*: I don't get reliable help, I hope I give it, but that's a different matter. Very done up at the finish. Apart from that, I now feel I am due for a change. I have done one job for nearly seven years. I ought to move.

The thought once there was bound to recur. For the moment it was masked by the absorbing excitement of planning a greatly expanded *Observer*, designed to counter the aggressive plans of the *Sunday Times*.

*(Wednesday) January 20, 1926*: J.L.G. at the office in the afternoon. We were there till nearly 7.30 p.m. dicussing the 'new' *Observer* i.e. the paper as it will be after the end of next month with its 32 page machinery. J.L.G. in excellent form, sparkling with ideas . . .

*(Sunday) February 28*: Down to Gregories, Beaconsfield to see J.L.G. . . . We sat out in the sun and talked, first, of birds, then of Austen's foreign policy.[1] Before that I had been shown the new library . . . an enviable collection. What is even more enviable is the mind that has not merely collected this host but absorbed it . . . After lunch sat with J.L.G. in his study and talked of all our problems and the future. V. interesting and useful.

*(Friday) March 12*: Worked at the office. Last preparations. J.L.G. and I dined at the Constitutional off a dozen oysters and a fried sole each . . . Then back to the office.

*(Saturday) March 13*: Had to get down earlier for the big paper. A great moment when we watched the new machines turn slowly over at the beginning of their run and start out the renewed *Observer*.

It is a very fine issue with a special poem by Thomas Hardy and a hundred other choice things.

*(Friday) April 16*: J.L.G. quoted himself as saying to Bobby Grant this week that I was 'the only right hand he ever had.' Which cheered up the day.

## II

That right hand was never more needed. There had long been a crisis in the coalfields. It came to a head after Garvin had gone to Aix-les-Bains. The owners insisted on a reduction in already low wages. The miners refused and were locked out. The TUC called a General Strike. So completely did Garvin trust B-W that he not only continued his holiday but did not attempt to dictate what the *Observer* should say.

B-W managed to arrange for a Roneo edition of 40,000 copies and another 20,000 printed on an old-fashioned flat-bed press at Finchley. When he saw the makeshift *Observer*, he wrote in his diary: 'The paper does not disgrace us (looks like the *Observer* of 150 years ago) and it keeps us on the map.' His own feelings and sympathies come out clearly in a letter to Garvin:

The Government have put us in an intolerable position. It is, as you know, a war of blunders, not of passions, though the passions will come ... The sight of our own special picket – the most reluctant and pathetic picket ever seen in an industrial dispute – would move your heart. Our strikers have addressed to the office a most appealing and disarming epistle ... I have nothing to add except to say how loathsome the business is. All its paraphernalia make a kind of mocking and distorting mirror of the war.

## III

Garvin and Waldorf had reason to be well satisfied with the way in which B-W had risen to the emergency. Others also were impressed. Two months later Geoffrey Dawson hinted to B-W about a possible opening on *The Times*:

*(Friday) July 23* [1926]: Geoffrey Dawson said to me 'Why did

you leave *The Times*?' and, implying a shortage of lieutenants, said I should have been 'high in the hierarchy now.' I reminded him that I didn't go back because he himself was parting with Northcliffe and leaving his job and advised me to go to the *Observer* — where indeed I have been very well treated. But I must have a change sometime, though not at the expense of friendship and honour.

The bait was tantalising. B-W, one must guess, was half hooked. A month later, however, another attractive prospect appeared. The new American owners of the *Encyclopaedia Britannica* had asked Garvin to become editor-in-chief of the fourteenth edition due to be published in 1929. He had already written for them *A History of Our Own Times*, published in 1924, and edited three supplementary volumes to the existing edition. The fourteenth was to be an entirely new venture. Garvin wanted to take it on. He was neither miserly nor greedy, but he was chronically short of money. He did not see why he should be. He was prepared to work hard to get it. An entry in B-W's diary reads:

*(Thursday) August 19*: Lunched at the Berkeley at 12.30 with J.L.G., Cox and his son. Cox is an American, and the business head of the *Encyclopaedia Britannica*. J.L.G. wants me to assist him with the new edition. This is a great and most timely chance. We had a long talk about plans.

Timely it was since B-W was hoping to marry and would need more money. A fortnight later he announced his engagement. He was married at the beginning of December.

The *Encyclopaedia* job would have given B-W another £1,500 a year for three years 'with almost continuous revenue afterwards from work on the supplementary volumes'. In addition, now that the enlarged *Observer* was launched and doing well, Garvin wanted to raise B-W's salary from the £1,500 fixed in January 1925 to £2,500. Unfortunately he had neither broached the matter to Waldorf nor told B-W.

At the end of March 1927 Garvin's negotiations with the *Encyclopaedia* were going badly. This hitch, and the failure to get B-W's salary increase settled, proved fatal. B-W's diary records:

*(Friday) April 1, 1927*: J.L.G. told me he had had to postpone the *Encyclopaedia Britannica*. Geoffrey Dawson rang up and asked me to see him. A strange conjunction of events.

That same day Dawson went to see Waldorf. Either Dawson was deliberately devious or Waldorf unbelievably simple or inattentive. He told Garvin that Dawson

> wants to know if we would lend him B. Ward for say a year whilst he is training some one else or at all events finding another young man who would be suitable when experienced ... it would do B.W. a great deal of good as part of his training ... but of course it would be a nuisance whilst he was away ... Let me know what you think about it. I have not mentioned it to B.W.

It is incomprehensible that a newspaper proprietor could imagine that the editor of a rival paper would be brash enough to ask to borrow − not exchange − a key man for a whole year. Waldorf, however, apparently believed just that. It is quite as difficult to see how he could have thought of agreeing. He ought to have known that both Garvin and B-W were overworked − but perhaps B-W had been right when long before he suggested that Waldorf had no idea how much work was done at the *Observer*. Garvin was undoubtedly justified in his comment: 'The astonishing proposition really means that *I* would have to do double work for a year for the convenience of *The Times*.'

He soon found out that this was not the proposition. B-W's diary records:

> *(Sunday) April 3*: Saw Geoffrey Dawson at his house. He offered me a post as assistant editor of *The Times*. He had consulted the Astors but not J.l.G.

> *(Tuesday) April 5*: Saw J.L.G. at the office. Much upset about my move to *The Times*.

If Garvin had been able to make his offer to B-W when he first thought of it, and if the *Encyclopaedia* project had not run into difficulty, B-W might have felt bound by gratitude, affection and honour − he was that sort of man − to reject Dawson's offer. In that event he might never have become editor of *The Times*, but he would almost certainly before too long have become editor of the *Observer*. It is not for a *Guardian* man, like the writer, to comment. B-W, however, had always hoped that one day he would edit *The Times*, and Garvin had encouraged the idea. 'The strange conjunction of events' on 1 April settled the matter. B-W did not consult Garvin. He accepted Dawson's offer.

That night Garvin had some kind of physical collapse. Next after-noon he told B-W:

> Last night I feared that it was going to be another long job for Lord Dawson — as after the weeks of terrific over-strain at Genoa. I kept my head in every sense by the extremest effort of will — a very singular sensation — and only got a slight knock on the knee.

He went on to take a regretful farewell:

> I thought ... that we would be happier than ever together for a few more years; and that then you would go straight to the top at *The Times*. In this other way of approach you will need the most skilful steering with an eye to right, left, and ahead, but our own navigation has not unfitted you for that, and I don't doubt the issue for you at all ... I don't think outside your family you will ever find anyone to love you more than I have done ... God bless you and may you and Adele be happy and fortunate together long after my passage from this life, but I want to live to see you at the top.

He did. B-W became editor of *The Times* in 1942.


## IV

The search for a successor began at once. Garvin's favoured candidates were either unobtainable or unacceptable. Peter Fleming preferred *The Times*; Gerald Barry, editor of the *Spectator*, did not want to move; Francis Meynell, the son of Garvin's old friend, withdrew Raymond Postgate's name when he heard that the job was political. Brendan Bracken suggested R. H. Mottram, then a bank clerk in Norwich. Garvin considered J. B. Atkins, once London editor of the *Manchester Guardian*, but Waldorf thought him too tainted by the brewers. 'By far the best' of the obtainable in Garvin's view was Douglas Woodruff, a thirty-year-old leader-writer on *The Times*; but, as he sadly added, 'he is a Catholic'. It was an appointment the Astors would never have tolerated. Barrington-Ward was irreplaceable.

# BOOK SEVEN: APPEARANCE AND REALITY, 1929-1938

---

'Mr. Garvin, the celebrated editor of the London *Observer*, perhaps the most celebrated editorial writer in the world.'

W. E. Borah, Chairman, US Senate Foreign Affairs Committee

'One hears people talking — and I note that it is beginning to affect our own internal morale and that the staff wonder when you will be able to take your full part as editor again.'

Waldorf Astor to J. L. Garvin

I

In 1929 Baldwin looked forward to a general election with complacency. For the first time women in their twenties could vote. He felt the six million would be grateful. But there were also the million unemployed whom Baldwin had not bothered much about. Garvin did. 'I am not a Conservative, but anti-Conservative,' he told his friends. 'I have spent decades of my life fighting down the Conservative old Adam in the Unionist party.' Ideas for getting men back to work were coming from J. M. Keynes and being popularised by Lloyd George. The fact that Lloyd George was the leader of an opposition party was of little consequence to Garvin. He admired the man, had worked happily with him before, and saw no reason to reject his good ideas because they came from the wrong side of the House. A political journalist need not run in the blinkers favoured by party leaders.

Garvin knew he had no influence with Baldwin, but believed that he might make some impression on Churchill, who was now Chancellor of the Exchequer. In that hope he visited Chartwell just before Budget Day. 'Six hours talk, five hours in the car, not a Sunday rest,' he told his wife. 'We shouted at each other as usual: half in affection, half in real combat. He tries to talk everyone down, and of course from me that brings thunders until he is finally daunted.'

One of Garvin's fellow guests was Harold Macmillan, a young MP on whom and his like Garvin pinned his hopes for social reform. He, too, had come to argue for a Keynesian-type Budget. Churchill, courteous to the younger man, allowed Macmillan to expound his views at length without interruption. Then it was Garvin's turn to elaborate the argument he had put forward in that morning's *Observer*: 'Empire and Employment; Work and Markets; *Something* for £1,000,000 a week instead of *nothing* for it.' He pleaded with Churchill for a large loan, half to be spent on public works in the Empire using British materials, and half on modernisation at home — road building and railway construction.

Garvin told Waldorf:

It's always worth while wrestling and battling with Winston. He

217

fights hard — a powerful intellect. But if one answers him unflinch-
ingly on facts and sense with chapter and verse, he faces the thing.
He said at last with good humour: 'Empire and Employment' — I
can't help liking it.

Like it, he may have done; but as Garvin suspected, he did nothing
about it. Instead, 'I suppose something will be done for tea to please
all the women.' It was; but the men on the dole wanted work.

Baldwin, unlike Churchill, liked neither Garvin nor his 'Empire
and Employment'. He fought the election on 'Safety First'. Macmillan
was defeated at Stockton and 170 other Conservatives lost their seats.
Against the tide, Bracken won Paddington North. 'Dearly beloved
Garvin', he wrote, 'The P.M. is, I am told, altogether unrepentant and
really believes that the wisdom of the electorate is foolishness with
God.' By the time Garvin visited Bracken the following Sunday the
political world had a strange look. No party had a majority. The Conservatives had most votes, Labour most seats, and the Liberals had
nearly doubled their vote. Baldwin had resigned and Ramsay MacDonald
was Prime Minister for the second time. Bracken was furious with
the 'stiff-necked, rubber-bottomed fools' of the Conservative Central
Office, who were campaigning against Lloyd George. He felt, like
Garvin, that 'if we establish good relations with the Liberals we can
drive the constituencies before us'. But, as Churchill had said to Garvin
that Sunday at Chartwell, the Diehards in the Cabinet hated Lloyd
George so much that they would hand over the country to Socialism
or the devil to thwart him. So they had. Garvin, on the whole, was not
displeased. He had always got on well with MacDonald.

## II

Garvin had now been editor of the *Observer* for twenty-one years. His
friends thought it a good excuse for a celebration, not of course a
farewell dinner, but rather a coming-of-age party. He thoroughly
enjoyed the luncheon which the *Spectator* gave in his honour in November 1929.

It seemed as if all, or nearly all, those who mattered most in Fleet
Street had gathered in Stationers' Hall for a family party which had
something of an improvised air. It was remarkable how many busy
men had found time to come at only five days' notice. There were
the editors of the five leading political weeklies — the *Spectator*, the

*Saturday Review*, the *Nation*, the *New Statesman* and *Time and Tide*
– and seven of the nine general London morning newspapers. Lord
Burnham, the 'Mr. Harry' of Garvin's time on the *Telegraph*, was
there as well as its current owners, the two Berry brothers and Edward
Iliffe. Rothermere sent a message and two other Harmsworths were
present. So was Beaverbrook and, of course, Waldorf Astor. His brother
John, of *The Times*, like its editor, neither came nor wrote. Garvin's
host, Evelyn Wrench of the *Spectator*, was both owner and editor, the
ultimate guarantee of editorial freedom that Garvin coveted but
lacked. There was another risk-taking editor-proprietor to whom Garvin
felt a special affinity. C. P. Scott, though he could not come, bestowed
on Garvin the supreme honour in his gift, the 'long leader' in that
morning's *Manchester Guardian*.

Arthur Henderson, the Foreign Secretary, set a nostalgic tone,
harking back to Newcastle in the eighteen-nineties. Garvin in turn
conjured up 'the young iron-moulder . . . manly, cool, clear and courteous in address, but speaking to the top-hatted not in terms of petition
but of direct labour representation as a right'. Lloyd George claimed
that Garvin had

> attracted to the *Observer* about the most influential circulation
> in the world, . . . There are no leaders of thought in this realm
> who do not take that paper in . . . not merely to read the news . . .
> but to know what Garvin's opinion about it is.

The extent to which Garvin was out of favour with his own nominal
party is reflected in the guest list. Only four members of Baldwin's
recent government were present. There were six Labour Ministers.

Lord Hewart, when trying a libel action, once remarked, 'If a man
desires to have a book reviewed, he would rather, I suppose, have it
in the *Observer* than in any other paper.' *Observer* reviewers were
there in force with Garvin's daughter, Viola, who had been assistant
literary editor since 1926. J. C. Squire had been the *New Statesman*'s
first literary editor; in 1920 Garvin had signed him up for the *Observer*
at fifteen guineas a week and allowed him as much space as he took
himself. In the age of the Squirearchy, as the ribald dubbed it, the
*Observer* profited from having the Squire himself, but it was finding
his procrastination increasingly tiresome. There was no such complaint
about Humbert Wolfe, a distinguished civil servant as well as a poet
with a considerable fame in the generation before Auden. Gerald
Gould, another poet, had been an Oxford don before he became a

journalist. 'My dear Garve', he wrote at this time, 'your letter (so signed!) warmed and lifted my heart ... I cannot tell you what it means to me to work for you – and for her! – it is a perpetual, unfailing inspiration.'

St John Ervine had been the paper's dramatic critic since soon after the end of the war. He was an Irishman after Garvin's heart, a playwright who had managed the Abbey Theatre before joining the Dublin Fusiliers and losing a leg in France. 'I would rather write for the *Observer* than any other paper in the world,' he told Garvin. One can see why. Just as Garvin would allow nobody to interfere with his political judgement, he was determined that his staff should have freedom and responsibility in their own fields. That was why people liked working for him, and why he was able to pick writers whose opinions were almost as much in demand by the readers of the *Observer* as were his own.

## III

After the *Spectator* lunch, a Beaverbrook dinner. At the beginning of June 1930 he invited delegates to the Imperial Press Conference to dinner 'to meet Mr. J. L. Garvin'. Four hundred and fifty accepted his invitation to the Queen's Hall; Nancy Astor refused. 'Much as I love you', she told Garvin, 'I cannot accept Lord Beaverbrook's invitation to meet you, and it hurts me to see your names together!!!' It was a warning that he had better be careful.

He was careful. Since the general election Beaverbrook had been engaged in his Empire Crusade. Empire free trade was a different name for the cause for which Garvin had thrown his hat into the ring in 1903. Could Max persuade Garvin to renew his crusader vow in the vastly different circumstances of 1930? It was worth a try. Max knew just how to set about it:

> It ought to be your affair. We may be defeated. But we ought to make one more attempt ... I am really disturbed at the hopeless outlook you unfold to me. In the secret places of my heart I fear you may be right, but I feel we should fight on just the same.

Garvin must have longed to respond, but his mind dictated caution. Empire unity – yes, that above all and at any cost; Empire free trade – yes, if it could be obtained, but this was doubtful. Max had to be content with that.

The day before the dinner Baldwin delivered a vicious personal attack on Garvin's host whom he accused of trying 'to dictate, to domineer, to blackmail'. It was, in A. J. P. Taylor's words, 'peculiarly crushing and peculiarly dishonest'. Garvin must have wondered whether to take up the challenge on his friend's behalf. He decided that a party that included three Labour Ministers, the recent Prime Minister of Australia and newspaper men from every part of the Empire and of every political opinion was not the place for Conservative Party in-fighting. He brushed the morning's sensation aside as 'some domestic amenities'. He did not mention Baldwin; he praised Beaverbrook, but evaded Empire free trade. Turning to his host, he said:

We both know that Rumour has been busy ... The purpose of [this dinner] in your mind and the soul of it, was to bring together people who believe in the Empire no matter how they believe ... Your way is not entirely my way, not at least as to the time-table ... *Yes*: but when you, Sir, started your crusade the whole cause of the Empire seemed in danger of becoming a sapless and a fading issue in British politics at home.

You breathed life and action into it again; you revived the interest in it of your opponents as well as of your adherents; and you brought back to the common cause the courage, the colour, the imagination and the energy, without which in democratic politics there is nothing to be done.

This was as far as Garvin thought it prudent to go. He passed into his peroration, recalling his first Imperial Press Conference twenty-one years before when Rosebery's 'solemn and thrilling oratory prophesied a storm to come'. The Empire took that warning to heart: 'The voices of the dead sound like a distant torrent's fall.' 'That sound for ever in our ears has made many a man and woman resolve to live for two.' With his son's invisible presence beside him, Garvin asked:

Is there a single man or woman amongst us who believes that the constructive sequel of the war has been worthy of our memories and our duties? I think not one. Are there any who believe that things as they stand are the best we can do? I think not one.

Garvin put his notes away and wrote on the envelope: 'The speech, chiefly owing to its compression into ten minutes, was a very great success; and confounded by avoidance all the elements which had been busy for mischief.' There is, as so often with him, a childlike quality in his self-satisfaction which makes one smile. Again, as so often, his satisfaction was justified.


## IV


Garvin refused to commit himself to Empire free trade because, on the eve of the Indian Round Table Conference, 'all else had to give way'. He had never forgotten the India, 'stranger than all the rest of the earth put together', which he had seen twenty-eight years before. He never went back. His thinking about the India of Gandhi's spinning wheel was obscured by the vividness with which his mind's eye still saw the India of Curzon's Durbar. His blindness was increased by the minority company he kept during the Round Table Conference. The delegates with whom he made friends were predominantly Muslims and representatives of the princely states. He took an immediate liking to Sir Akbar Hydari, the leader of the Hyderabad delegation, 'the wisest of the whole lot', as Lord Lothian thought. Garvin got on equally well with Sha'afat Ahmad Khan, a man twenty-five years his junior, who was secretary to the group of Muslim delegations. An historian who had studied in Dublin, Cambridge and London, and who liked country walks, had plenty in common with Garvin.

The Hindu to whom Garvin felt closest was Dr Ambedkar, another fine scholar whom Garvin found 'deeply impressive and instructive about the fifty million or more of his fellow untouchables'. The measure of Ambedkar's quality is that in the end he persuaded Garvin to endorse his cause.

Among the British members of the Round Table was Philip Kerr, Lord Lothian. Garvin had known him for a very long time, but it was at this period that he began continuously to see a great deal of him. Lothian was constantly at Cliveden so that it was easy for them to meet there and at Gregories. They enjoyed long sessions together, each influencing the other. The friendship that grew up between them helped to relieve the strain that was growing more apparent in the relations between Nancy Astor and Garvin. Philip's friend could not be as black, she felt, as his intimacy with Churchill and Beaverbrook suggested.

The 1930 session of the Round Table Conference had one consequence that affected Garvin closely. The Indian princes agreed to enter an All India federation. The Congress Party could not afford to be left out of the constitution-making. Gandhi was released to attend a second session of the Conference. This pleased Garvin; but it made Churchill a Diehard. Their ways parted. Garvin gave consistent support to Sir Samuel Hoare, the Secretary of State for India, earning his effusive thanks. Churchill carried on a violent campaign against the government's Indian policy in the Conservative Party, in the Commons and in the country.

Garvin and the Astors agreed for once on the political impossibility of Mr Churchill. This, like Garvin's friendship with Lothian, relieved the tension between Cliveden and Gregories. Garvin and Churchill, however, did not allow 'the rancour and asperity of party politics' to cloud their personal relations. Out of office and off the Front Bench, Churchill wrote the life of his ancestor, the first Duke of Marlborough. Garvin read the proofs, making suggestions which reflected his and Ged's admiration for Turenne. Their friendship was kept in good repair against the day when once more it would do the state some service.

# V

When C. P. Scott retired from the editorship of the *Manchester Guardian* in 1929, Garvin tried to get him the O.M. He made sure that Scott, who had persistently refused all honours, would accept it if offered. He replied:

> Yes, I'm sure I should value the O.M. very much. It's the only thing of the kind, I think, that one would value. But also I shouldn't miss it if it didn't come my way, and indeed I don't think the idea of it would have entered my head, but for the bouqets which you and other kind friends have thrown out. But who wouldn't be proud to be a companion to Galsworthy?

Garvin had already talked to Ramsey MacDonald and approached the King's secretary. Lord Stamfordham, however, was discouraging.

On 10 October MacDonald told Garvin that 'the authorities who guard the O.M. will not hear of Scott, and Scott will hear of nothing but a Privy Councillorship'. That in MacDonald's view would have been inappropriate while he was still a working journalist, but might be possible now. Obviously, however, MacDonald was not keen, or else was doubtful whether he could get it through. 'Will you let me know if anything new has occurred and if Scott is still firm in refusing any other form of recognition?' Garvin sent Scott a cryptic telegram and got a charming letter back:

> Forgive me if I have not acted on its advice, but I have a rooted objection which somehow I can't get over, to 'a handle to my name'. Not that I am ungrateful. Anything which brings me a letter from you is welcome!

MacDonald had gone on to ask whether Garvin would accept some distinction for himself other than a privy councillorship, which 'must wait a more aged Garvin'? Was there any other badge of honour he would like? It was an unusually handsome invitation; but, since Scott had got neither the O.M. nor a privy councillorship, Garvin refused MacDonald's offer as he had refused Lloyd George's in 1918, probably then because after Ged's death he did not wish to appear in a victory honours list. He had accepted an honorary doctorate from Durham in 1921, and was to receive another from Edinburgh in 1935; but, as far as the state was concerned, he preferred not to be honoured by those who would not honour the greatest living journalist.

I

Outwardly all was well with Garvin in 1928. Those who knew him best knew better. In January his doctor, Lord Dawson of Penn, repeated an earlier warning: 'Caring so much as you know I do about you, I am beginning to be anxious. I know that the longer you wait the bigger the price you will have to pay.' The fact that many of Garvin's troubles were of his own making did nothing to ease their burden. Heaviest and most demanding was his never-ending *Life of Joseph Chamberlain*, but that must wait till the next chapter. The others were serious enough.

Dawson asked Waldorf to give Garvin two months' complete rest. Waldorf agreed, but told Garvin: 'One hears people talking – and I note that it is beginning to affect our own internal morale and that the staff wonder when you will be able to take your full part as editor again.' That wounded Garvin's self-esteem; a second passage threatened his pocket:

> It would be only just and fair to the *Observer* that you should take steps to end the commitment of the *Encyclopaedia* as soon as possible. That really is quite different from 'Joe' and you are not under any personal obligation to them.

Garvin was furious. He dashed off an angry letter. He followed it up with what he meant to be a reasoned memorandum, but it turned out to be just as violent as his letter. Waldorf showed remarkable patience and forbearance in replying to his 'dearest Garvin', sticking to his point, but assuring him of the 'warm genuine personal affection which not even the Sunday memorandum has dimmed in the slightest degree!'

II

If Garvin had been asked why he undertook to edit an encyclopaedia when he already had two full-time jobs, he would have said that he needed the money. For the new *Encyclopaedia Britannica* he received £10,000 under an agreement finally reached three weeks after Barrington-

225

Ward had accepted the *Times* job. Margaret Bryant, one of the editorial staff, told Garvin that 'twenty-four volumes in two years is no proposition for anyone who has a real respect for the Enc. Brit.' She was right, and Garvin must have known it; but he took it on and did the job on time. The *Encyclopaedia* duly came out in 1929. This was the first edition produced under American ownership with an editorial staff in New York as well as in London. Garvin directed the English team and, as editor-in-chief, correlated their work with the American. The fourteenth edition was intended for 'Mr. Lincoln's plain people, and within the sum of $1,150,000'. It could not hope to be as scholarly as the one it replaced, but within its limits it was a good piece of work.

According to Garvin it was a negligible burden: 'I don't write a line for the Encyclopaedia and told them I could not add to my eye work or hand work ... it only takes a talk every week.' It was, he maintained, 'a refreshment and a relief'. This was true, but not entirely true. There was in fact eye work in plenty and a good deal of hand work.

The main means by which Garvin did his editing was by a weekly dinner party at Gregories. Oliver Woods found this a fascinating part of growing up: 'Thoughts and ideas flashed back and forth across the table. We always looked forward to Encyclopaedia night.' Sometimes the thoughts and ideas produced sparks as, for instance, when Basil Liddell Hart was present: 'Basil had the gift of getting under the skin of editors almost as quickly as under that of generals.'

What the work involved can be seen from the surviving volume of Garvin's *Encyclopaedia* 'bible'. This contains the minutes of the weekly meetings, and records the numerous written questions put up for consideration and his decisions on them. One Monday, for instance, Garvin read and annotated articles on Chatham, Churchill, Clemenceau, George Moore and James II. He appointed a contributor on Psychical Research; made a short entry about the long-running problem of who should write on the Vatican; and agreed to discuss at the weekly dinner the question of articles on individual commercial companies which had 'sorely troubled' the London office.

It was to trouble them still more. The last entry in the book is an eighteen-page handwritten

Memorandum by the Editor in Chief upon circumstances ending in Mr. Garvin's announcement of his immediate resignation and total severance from the *Encyclopaedia Britannica* unless supported with absolute unanimity by his colleages in the London Office on certain matters of principle and procedure.

This broadside followed an amicable discussion at Gregories. Unfortunately the minute summarising it could just possibly be read as an order from New York to include an article on Sears, Roebuck, the chain of American nation-wide department stores, of which Garvin had never heard. Garvin, always on the look-out for encroachments on his editorial freedom, perversely chose to read it that way. Only after he had extorted written apologies from the secretary and the editor-in-charge did he minute: 'October 13, Mr. Garvin receives . . . a full and hearty apology . . . This not only closes the incident but leaves Mr. Garvin grateful . . . for the confidence they express in him and for the spirit of faithful comradeship they have restored.' It was a gracious though pompous close to a testy and unnecessary encounter. The *Encyclopaedia* was not always 'a refreshment and relief'.

## III

Meanwhile Garvin had intermittently been toying with the idea of leaving the *Observer*. It was the last thing in the world he wanted to do − it was his as no other paper could ever be − but he felt driven to consider it partly because Waldorf would not give him the long sabbatical break which he needed to finish *Joe*, and partly because the negotiations for a new contract had brought into the open again his fundamental divergence from Waldorf over the relation of editor and proprietor. Besides he felt he was worth more than Waldorf was paying him.

If he decided to go, he would have no difficulty in finding another employer. Sir William Berry wanted him for the *Sunday Times* and was ready to offer him a preliminary sabbatical year as an inducement. So at least Garvin said in a letter he was writing to Waldorf on the day Geoffrey Dawson asked Barrington-Ward to join *The Times*. Perhaps he hoped it would bring a counter-offer from Waldorf; but of course Barrington-Ward's departure put paid to any such idea. Waldorf could not have spared him. Garvin would not have felt justified in leaving.

The Berrys did not give up hope of securing Garvin. They tried again a few months later to get him for the *Daily Telegraph*. A note in Garvin's hand reads:

Gomer Berry . . . called at Gregories Christmas Day, 1927 and asked apropos of the Berry-Iliffe purchase of the *Daily Telegraph*[1] whether I would not like to be associated with it. I had to explain at once that the Chamberlain biography would tie me for six months yet and I would want a long holiday after.

That was certainly not a refusal.

A year later it was Brendan Bracken, now a successful newspaper proprietor, who made encouraging suggestions to Garvin. He quoted Jack Hills, the chairman of his *Financial News*, as saying, 'if we had Garvin as our editor, he would be worth fifty thousand a year'. 'He said well,' Bracken continued, 'You must join our ark when Chamberlain is finished.' It was a tempting thought. Bracken had the reputation of not interfering with his editors, and Jack Hills, one of the Unionist social reform MPs, was the solicitor who had acted for Garvin during his *Outlook* troubles. Moreover Oliver Locker-Lampson promised to raise £3,000 for Garvin so that he could put in five months' uninterrupted work on *Joe*.

Nothing came of either the Berrys' or Bracken's suggestions. On Garvin's side the reason almost certainly was that, fight as he might with Waldorf, he was too attached to him and to the *Observer* to leave unless he was forced to go.


**IV**


The battle over Garvin's 1929 contract was as fierce as the struggle in 1918. Garvin wanted more money. Even more he wanted to be sure that Waldorf would not attempt to over-rule his editorial judgement on policy. Waldorf, however, believed that he owned the *Observer*'s views as well as its resources, and wanted to write this into the contract. A draft was ready in November 1929. Garvin wrote on his copy: 'I replied that the proposed agreement was such as no man of sense or character could sign.' He suggested shelving the problem until he had finished *Joe*. Waldorf refused: 'You will have seemingly tempting alternative offers put before you and I will feel that others are trying to draw us apart.'

Perhaps the deepest level of disagreement was reached when Garvin told Waldorf:

I do not accept your view in any particular. In the interval [till

*Joe* was finished] I will conduct the *Observer* or not just as you please ... I reserve my freedom in every respect, and for the rest I am quite through. Yours as ever, J. L. Garvin.

The he had second thoughts, at least about the signature. Waldorf accepted the tiny gesture: 'You erased the formal "J. L. Garvin" and substituted the friendly Garve. So I now sign myself genuinely, Yours as always, Waldorf.'

The problem was remitted to the three-man tribunal of Wargrave, Lothian and Lionel Hichens. In the end Garvin got less freedom than he wanted, but more money than Waldorf intended. Waldorf stipulated that, while the tribunal might mediate, it could not adjudicate between editor and owner. Failing agreement, it could only fix reasonable terms for parting. Clause 4 provided that 'the Editor will ... conform to the general lines and instructions ... laid down and given by the Chairman of Directors as to the general policy to be pursued and advocated by the *Observer*'. Garvin had protested on 3 November that for no money would he accept this clause, but in the end he signed.[2] Waldorf should have remembered that

A man convinced against his will
  Is of the same opinion still.


# V

In 1921 the business manager of the *Observer* had reported that the Court newsagent delivered to the palace six *Observer*s, one *Sunday Times*, three *Sunday Pictorial*s, one *Sunday Dispatch* and one *People*. By 1931 an order of this kind already belonged to a past age.

In 1915 the Berry brothers had bought the nearly derelict *Sunday Times* for £75,000. They could not develop it during the war because of paper restrictions; but, once these went, Waldorf and Garvin recognised that they would have a tremendous struggle to keep the *Observer* ahead. So it proved. By 1930 the *Sunday Times* was selling 153,000 copies a week to the *Observer*'s 201,000.

In the thirties the *Sunday Times* could beat the *Observer* in news thanks to the backing of the *Daily Telegraph*, and equal it in features. Some even hinted that Herbert Sidebotham, 'Scrutator', was as sound a political commentator as Garvin himself. Ernest Newman, James Agate and Desmond MacCarthy were at least as good as their opposite numbers. In 1931 Garvin got rid of Squire and put Basil de Selincourt in his place. Before long he had to admit: 'It can't go on . . . our readers do not want to read the books he chooses for review. They want to read other books' — Day Lewis, for instance, whom de Selincourt had not heard of. T. E. Lawrence complained:

> Now really, really, really, and in your paper, you who used to read yourself! Day Lewis is no beginner: after Auden, I suppose he has the best established name among all the living poets who are not so young . . . Think how all the under-forties are laughing tonight.

The greatest difference between the two papers, however, was in management. The *Sunday Times* through the nation-wide Berry organisation had resources of a nature which the *Observer* had lost when Garvin and Northcliffe parted company. Northcliffe moreover would never have allowed the *Observer* management to slide into the desperate state in which it was discovered to be in 1931.

The Wall Street crash immediately involved the Astors with their American-based fortune. After two hurried visits to New York, Waldorf came back to a miserable Christmas. He told Garvin he would have to close Cliveden for a year at least. Suddenly, too, the *Observer* was in trouble. The Hatry crash in the City of London hit company advertising. Other advertising was also heavily cut. The paper's profit was down by a third. There was worse to come.

In February 1931 Garvin tried to withdraw £3,000 from the Reserve Fund. It stood in the books at £18,500, but the sums annually voted to it had been left unidentified and unprotected in the ordinary account. When times were good, as they had been for so long, there had been cash enough. Now, when times were bad, there was nothing. According to Garvin, the principal villain was Blanch, the commercial manager, 'always tipsy by afternoon', a compulsive gambler, willing to accept suspiciously large gifts — a cabinet of cigars, for instance, 'nearly as large as a wardrobe'. This is the kind of office gossip which comes to the surface when the danger of speaking out is past; but Garvin wrote of what both he and Waldorf knew for fact when he recalled how Blanch had been caught using the firm's money to pay private debts. 'That dishonesty was forgiven when discovered because neither Lord Astor nor Mr. Garvin knew or guessed the truth about this man's ways, but treated him as an old friend who had temporarily fallen from grace.' One may think that they had only themselves to blame for the loss of the Reserve Fund, and perhaps of much more.

## VI

When MacDonald took office there were 1,200,00 men out of work; by January 1931, 2,600,000. At midsummer the figure was 2,800,000 and still rising − nearly a quarter of all those insured. Lloyd George believed he could conquer unemployment, but the electors had refused him the chance. A group of junior Ministers in the Labour government thought they could succeed, but J. H. Thomas, their overlord, and the Cabinet did not allow them to try. Was there a hope? A. J. P. Taylor's verdict is 'Only Oswald Mosley . . . rose to the height of the challenge.'

When Mosley's proposals were rejected, he resigned from the government, and later from the party, setting up one of his own. Garvin kept clear of it. He shared Mosley's frustration with the economic ineptitude of the Labour government in the face of human tragedy, but he thought the remedy was to form a National government, not to found a New Party. Meanwhile, with the future of India at stake, the existing Labour government ought to be kept in office with general support. He and Waldorf were convinced that from the beginning of 1931 MacDonald shared their view.

At the end of July, an expert committee demanded drastic economies and increased taxation as the only possible remedy, as indeed they probably were in the world economic panic. Certainly Waldorf and Garvin thought so. The Labour Cabinet met for the last time on Sunday evening, 23 August 1931. MacDonald was in favour of cuts in unemployment benefit, Henderson against. MacDonald resigned. He was then invited to form a National government. Garvin at once wrote privately to both men. Both replied the next day. Each told the story of the crisis in his own way.

MacDonald wrote:

> You will see that immediately after you wrote it [Garvin's letter of the 24th] I crossed the Rubicon . . . I have taken my life in my hands and I have no doubt at all that I shall lose it.[3] I shall always be grateful to you, however, for the very kind things you have said, and the splendid backing you have given me whenever it was possible for you to do so.

He told Garvin how he had explained to the Cabinet that the Bank of England's advice was limited to what would have to be done to secure international loans. He had convinced the majority, but 'the minority was too numerous and had made up its mind to resign; therefore unity was impossible, and the continuation of the Government equally impossible. They will go out and say: "it was a Banker's Ramp.'" They did. It was not. But the Labour Party and the TUC believed that it was.

Henderson, like MacDonald, was grateful for Garvin's letter which 'brought with it that sympathetic touch which always appeals to the human heart under such circumstances'. He told Garvin that he had persuaded a good many of his colleagues to accept a revenue tariff. Ministers separated on Friday having reached agreement. On Saturday they found that they had not gone far enough to satisfy the Opposition. It was then that a 10 per cent cut in benefit was suggested, and the Cabinet split. 'Some of us', he wrote, 'were placed in considerable difficulty ... because we had informed [Labour MPs, the General Council, and the National Executive Committee] that cuts in the unemployment benefit were not included in the proposals.' Did Henderson wish Garvin to understand that, but for this, he would have agreed to the cut?

There is a tantalising 'if'. If Lloyd George had not been in hospital, he would have played a major role in the political crisis and might have emerged as Prime Minister. Certainly no National government could have been formed without him, and one in which he held office would have had a decidedly more national look. Garvin for his part would have found time for busy breakfasts in Downing Street instead of an occasional leisurely lunch at Chequers with an ageing and captive Prime Minister.

## VII

Garvin's relation to his eldest daughter, Viola, was unusually close, almost morbidly intense. In 1931 she was deeply in love with Humbert Wolfe, one of the bright constellation of *Observer* reviewers. Her love was returned, but Humbert had a wife and there was no way by which he could become free to marry Viola. Garvin worried as any father would, but said nothing. Viola fell ill. Garvin sent her out to France to Mrs Lee-Mathews to recuperate.

One evening while she was away, Wolfe came down to Gregories. Garvin wanted to talk to him about their situation, but refrained. Instead he wrote to Viola. He began before midnight and did not finish till after three. The pith of what he had to say was:

As things are the plan of future life . . . is to put marriage out of the picture entirely and to shape just as if it could never be. Then, if the two are equal to it, an eternal steady love-friendship ... has wonderful compensations and preserves the soul's comradeship that the routine of marriage almost invariably destroys ... Bird[4] began to say that there had been something of this kind. I could not bring myself to enter into it ... You must be strong for two, or break the thing someday no matter what the devastation would mean. I hope to God not that.

One wonders what the other Viola, Garvin's wife, would have made of the letter. One sentence seems to bear on their own marriage:

> To make it [marriage] work either one of the partners must be eternally and stupidly or stoically subordinate to the other; or they must be fast friends on very temperate terms; and with money enough to enable them to go their separate ways while keeping their friendship.

Garvin and Viola kept their separate friends, and there was money enough to enable Viola to spend the worst of the winters each year in the south of France.

Money enough, but not to spare. Garvin's income was now lower than it had been for ten years since it depended in part on the *Observer*'s profits. He did not complain because that was how he wanted it. At the same time he had been forced to sell capital to pay the increased taxes. His family commitments continued unabated. Of his children, only Una, who had married her doctor and was well on the way to a fine professional reputation of her own, was financially independent. Each of his three unmarried daughters still had an allowance, and his stepson was hardly living the life of a poor student at Oxford.

Garvin had long been worried about his daughter Viola's expensive tastes and happy-go-lucky way of gratifying them. In 1927 he had had to pay off serious debts. Now creditors were everywhere chasing debtors. Viola's debts were again heavy. Garvin had to sell out more capital to put her straight. He told her:

> the proposal to make you bankrupt has been seriously discussed, only my name and action have averted it this time; and the thing is known amongst our advertisers.
>
> Four years ago I tried to explain to you what this last factor meant in making my personal situation unbearable. Again and again

I underwent the appalling humiliation of shops, some of them amongst our advertisers, writing to me saying my daughter was in debt to them; and that they understood she was employed on 'my' paper; and requesting me either to pay them or to see that you did. These things were sent to the office. Blanch and Bell got hold of some of them. The Astors were told — another way of injuring me in the struggle of that time . . .

Viola's *Observer* salary and her tax-free allowance between them gave her a net income of £1,100 a year. It was, as her father told her, 'ample'. It did not prove to be, but then nothing could. In money matters she was incorrigible.

I

In Garvin's diary for 1930 there is an entry for 7 July: '1.30 lunch 58, Rutland Gate: meeting with Austen and Neville Chamberlain about their father's biography very disagreeable'. No doubt. Eleven years had passed since they had asked him to write their father's life. They had seen nothing.

At last, early in 1932, Garvin was able to invite the Chamberlains to Gregories to see the progress he had made. Austen was delighted with what Garvin read to Mrs Carnegie, his father's widow, and himself. He waited impatiently for the first volume. His advance copy came on the day before his sixty-ninth birthday:

> I read it with absorbing interest from two o'clock to two o'clock a.m. and even then went reluctantly to bed to resume my reading at nine in the morning and to read on till I turned the last page about 11 o'clock last night. And now I shall begin again, less breathlessly, dwelling lovingly on each episode. I can as little express my deeper feelings as my father before me, but I want very simply to say I thank you for a picture every page of which helps to paint the man.

No writer could wish for more.

Neville Chamberlain had not gone to Gregories. He saw no point. As he told Goulding, 'I have never doubted he has written a great deal. My doubts have been whether he could put what he has written into a form in which it could be published.' When he received the book, he acknowledged it with a brief note: 'Somehow or other I must find time to read it.' A little later he wrote once more to Garvin: 'I hope the sales keep up. I hear nothing but praise of it.' It was perhaps the warmest congratulation he could manage. There was a deep incompatibility between the men.

Garvin planned to write two volumes on Chamberlain and Democracy and two on Chamberlain and Imperialism. Three volumes came out in successive years. They were lavishly praised and with reason. John Buchan, who had once hoped to publish the *Life*, thought it 'one of the greatest (or perhaps the greatest) biographies in English'. Harold Macmillan, who brought it out, reflected 'how different things would be today if we had such a leader' — an interesting comment to come from a member of the 'Tory YMCA' about Chamberlain in his radical days. J. L. Hammond in the *Manchester Guardian* admired Garvin's ability to deal justly and sympathetically with all his characters, Chamberlain's opponents as well as his friends: 'No higher tribute could be paid to his sense of history than to say that whenever Gladstone steps into his pages he brings a breath from Olympus.'

## II

The year before Garvin's first volume came out, Henry Harrison published an important book, *Parnell Vindicated*, in which he argued that Chamberlain probably provoked and subsidised O'Shea's divorce petition. Garvin brusquely told Harrison that he 'totally disagreed' and was 'not going to change a line of what he had written'. In his book he dismissed Harrison's case as being 'without a particle of truth'. Whatever the reason — an unwillingness to go back over ground he had already covered, or an inability to accept a flaw in his hero's character — it was a stupid line to take. An argument that convinced Hammond when he came to write *Gladstone and the Irish Nation* deserved to be taken seriously. There the matter rested until in August 1938, when the world was on the brink of war, Harrison published a book, *Joseph Chamberlain, Parnell and Mr. Garvin*. This was a personal attack on Garvin. He could reasonably either have ignored it or replied in a detailed argument. He did neither. He dismissed the Czechoslovak crisis in one column and devoted five to what one would call a review of Harrison's book if he had named either the author, the title or the publisher. Many of his readers must have wondered who it was that Garvin considered guilty of 'obsessed enmity' and 'pathological suspicion'. Twenty years before, at a similar dark hour in history, Garvin had shown a similar lack of balance in his unbridled attack on Colonel Repington.

## III

The third volume of *Joe* was finished by Easter 1934 but not published until the autumn. In the interval Garvin's doctors intervened. Lord

Dawson was peremptory. Garvin arrived at Ruthin in North Wales 'bulky and flabby, making every movement with difficulty'. Two months later he emerged 'thin as a poker and nearly as hard'. He told his stepson: 'Of course it's done strictly on cold water and small rations, and to both I shall have to stick for a long time, perhaps always — except a glass of wine on Sundays and fiestas now and then.' To Lina Waterfield he added: 'They have reduced my weight by a stone and a half and raised my spirits by a wing and a half. Barrington-Ward was told that he would not recognise Garvin or else would think that somebody you knew ten years ago had turned up again'.

It is impossible to say how ill Garvin had been ('complete exhaustion' his doctors called it), but there is no doubt that he had been frightened. When Lina Waterfield was ill the following year, he wrote to her:

What you say about feeling the mind separated from the body . . . interests me deeply. It is just what I felt when at first there seemed little hope that I should ever be myself again, even if long for this planet . . . When one is looking right into the face of the worst and finds oneself undaunted, one has seen, as it were, this world from the other side and can never forget the experience.

Garvin was taking fifteen-mile walks before he left Ruthin. He made up his mind not to lose the ground he had gained:

Every day, usually about six o'clock in the evening, I walk at least six miles and sometimes eight, with my two black dogs, tramping over rough and smooth, getting into remarkably wild places such as still exist in our chalky box and refuse to be stopped by any gate or hedge or even by barbed wire. At need, I get over the gates and under the hedges and the barbed wire. To see me doing the latter, lying quite flat on the ground like a boy and the two dogs after me, would make you laugh.

'I don't fear Joe IV,' Garvin assured his stepson when he returned from Ruthin. He expected it to take him a year. It did not work out like that, even though he must have had in hand a good many thousand words left over after he decided to stop the third volume at 1900 instead of 1902. One difficulty after another prevented him from making a start. The *Sunday Times* was becoming an increasingly powerful rival. It had passed the *Observer*'s net sale in 1933 so that Garvin had to exert himself in long abandoned ways to try to restore the position. Instead of starting work on the last volume, he had, as he told Barrington-Ward,

> a grappling time putting the office to rights and, after years and years, going down again on Saturday nights to show how we used to turn it out, and what a world's difference may lie between a first edition and a third!!

In fact he managed to increase the *Observer* circulation, but he could not prevent the *Sunday Times* drawing slowly away.[1]

Garvin had other business worries, too, that imposed a severe nervous strain. His contract was due to expire in 1937. The negotiations for a new one followed the pattern that had made 1918 and 1929 such a misery to Waldorf and Garvin. Waldorf, worried about the *Observer* and exasperated by Garvin, was in no mood to give him time off to finish *Joe*. Austen Chamberlain sympathised but could not help: 'I feel really angry with Astor ... I should have hoped that after so many years of devoted service to the *Observer* Astor would have facilitated instead of hindering your task on the book.' So a decidedly older Garvin had to go on carrying the double burden he had borne since 1921.

Apart from business troubles, Garvin was from 1933 onwards incessantly and rightly preoccupied with Hitler. A time when a man believes that he is helping, however humbly, to make history is not propitious for writing it. Nevertheless one Sunday in October 1937 Barrington-Ward noted in his diary:

> For a man just on 70 he is a miracle of suppleness in body and mind. Not noticeably grey, either ... is really at work now on the last volume of Joe. Means to go through and finish it and, if he has to choose between Joe and the paper, will choose Joe.

A month later Garvin assured Harold Macmillan that the last volume would be complete by September 1938. Of course it wasn't. A year later the Second World War ended all hope of Garvin finishing the book.

## IV

*The Life of Joseph Chamberlain* is not the portrait Garvin intended. He would have thought the proportions wrong. He planned four volumes. There are six. 'The statue he was making out of pebbles' remains a majestic torso to which another hand has added a head out of scale with the trunk.

Garvin's work ends at the point where he himself was soon to become one of his hero's principal lieutenants. In the first three volumes Garvin had been writing as a scholar and spectator; in the fourth he would himself have been a supporting actor. Biography would here and there have merged into the trickier field of autobiography. Would he have preserved the detachment that Hammond and Austen valued?

Only one thing can be said with conviction. Garvin did not see Chamberlain's life as a failure. The sole purpose of his last campaign had been to ensure the unity of the Empire. Imperial preference, his means to that end, came to nothing, but in spite of that in two world wars its countries stood together and prevailed. In a synopsis for a final chapter Garvin wrote:

The World War – The greater Rally of the Empire – Its people what he had believed and far more – ... He was the great spirit of his race in that time. By many was his name often remembered then and will for ever be.

Here perhaps are the words with which Garvin would have said farewell to Joe.

# BOOK EIGHT. A DIVERSITY OF DICTATORS, 1933-1947

'We have landed in ill times; the skies look grimly
And threaten present blusters. In my conscience
The heavens with what we have in hand are angry,
And frown upon 's.'

*The Winter's Tale*, Act 3 Scene 3

I

In 1919 the *Observer* and the *Manchester Guardian* had been foremost in warning their readers that the victorious Allies had sown dragon's teeth. In 1933 they took the lead in warning them that the dragon was alive, powerful and malevolent. Their task was made harder by their earlier success. They had – rightly as Garvin still believed – given English people a bad conscience about the unjust peace terms. The truth about Hitler's Germany was in any event so outrageous and so bizarre that it was difficult to believe.

*The Times* was as well informed as the *Observer* and the *Guardian* about the true state of affairs in Germany, but it kept too much of its knowledge to itself. Garvin was determined to let his readers know the worst. In the week that Hitler became Chancellor he wrote that, whatever the result of an election, Hitler would never surrender power. It was no longer possible to be optimistic about Germany. At the end of March he denounced 'the barbaric anti-Semitism of the Swastika superstition'. A fortnight later he gave his Article these self-explanatory headings: 'The German Enigma; Hitlerism and Mania; "Nordic" Humbug and its Origins; The Swastika Superstition'. Alfred Rosenberg, the German propagandist, asked one of the British Embassy staff why English newspapers were so down on Germany. The diplomat happened to have a copy of the *Observer* in his hand. He gave it to Rosenberg, saying this would answer his question.

In the autumn Goebbels banned the *Observer*, but told its correspondent that, if the paper changed its tone, the ban would be removed. Garvin retorted: 'If we can falsify our opinions, we shall be passed by the police. If not, there will be a further ban ... By their leave it cannot be done for any money.' The ban was the result of thirteen consecutive articles on Germany. Two had given particular offence. In the first Garvin complained of the Nazis' 'repulsive cruelty towards the Jews'. He pointed out that Milton would have been beaten with rubber tubes filled with stones or killed outright for writing *Areopagitica.* In the second he pilloried the professors who taught 'the countrymen of Bach and Goethe how to turn themselves into the Matabele of Europe'. He compared Nazi Germany with 'darkest Africa' when 'orgiastic drumming, chanting, war-dancing, such as a dusky General Goering would approve' had continued until 'the young men who had not yet "killed" went forth and fleshed their assegais in the bodies of the weaker tribes'.


## II


Garvin was determined that his countrymen should not become a weaker tribe at the mercy of the Matabele of Europe. They lacked both arms and allies. Without arms, allies could not be found. Re-armament was the first essential. But for this, Garvin's views on Nazi Germany would have made him the darling of the British left. But when Labour won a memorable by-election in East Fulham, Garvin thundered:

> Take the Socialists. Their way is the shortest of all cuts to catas-trophe. First they infuriate Hitler by their 'Brown Book'. Then they inform him that nothing on earth will induce them to fight. They might as well say 'Heil Hitler!'

In the spring of 1935, more than two years after Hitler came to power, the National government at last decided that we must look to our defences because 'Germany was . . . rearming openly on a large scale'. This White Paper on Defence was one of MacDonald's last major political acts. It recognised reality, but did too little about it. The Defence Estimates took only small, timid steps which could never over-take Hitler's quick march. Even so, they were too much for Labour members. They voted in the 'No' lobby; some because arms cause wars; some because these arms might be used against Russia.

The Labour leaders with whom Garvin had shared many hopes for a new Europe and a better Britain in the twenties had either left the party, or been expelled, or were dead. Only Arthur Greenwood was left of his friends from those days, and the two men had little com-mon ground now that defence had replaced social reform as the supreme issue. Garvin had no personal touch with the new leader-ship. Probably he did not seek it. It would have seemed pointless. Garvin and the Labour Party both spent the thirties in the political wilderness. They did not travel together because each thought the other's oasis was a mirage.

**III**

Garvin looked longingly across the Atlantic. In the spring of 1933 he wrote of Franklin Roosevelt's first Inaugural Address: 'America has found a man. In him at a later stage — and it cannot be very long deferred — the world must find a leader.' Two months later he argued that

> unless Hitlerism can be brought to its senses in time, it will lead with absolute certainty to European war, and so to parallel wars in Asia and elsewhere. Directly, instantly involved — just like other nations — America will have to fight to the death for her own sake.

So it was in the end, but for the present Europe had to look to itself. Britain's need was greater than when Calchas wrote, but his fellow countrymen were unwilling to pay attention. Garvin confessed to Leo Amery, 'This people is blinder than it was before 1914; and without treble the air-power and a solid alliance with France and Belgium will come to its doom next time.'

Austria and Italy seemed to him to hold the key to lock Hitler in. He hated Nazis and disliked Fascists, but he never mixed them up. Their ideas and their interests were often far apart. He wanted to play on that divergence.

His attitude towards Fascism and towards Italy, two separate things, comes out in the long and intimate letters he exchanged with Lina Waterfield. It is difficult to imagine any world newspaper except Garvin's *Observer* relying for its Italian news on a correspondent who lived in a remote castle in the Apennines some 250 miles from Rome. She had, however, the entrée to every one who mattered. She could, for instance, secure an interview with Mussolini when one was needed; and, though he knew very well what she thought about Fascism, her personality and position were such that he forced himself to be polite to her.

Lina would have liked the *Observer* to be outspokenly anti-Fascist. Garvin refused. He thought it wrong for an English paper to intervene in Italy's internal affairs, or to side with one Italian party against another. He showed her, however, how to get round his own prohibition 'by putting in the form of questions what the natural man and woman would be strongly tempted to put in the form of assertions. It makes all the difference.'

Garvin hated Mussolini's ban on non-Fascist parties and his special courts for political offences, but he stuck to his view on how foreign correspondents should work. At the end of an excessively long letter, written late at night after the others had gone to bed, he added:

> Put the bias a little against your desire. The more impartially you write, the more effect you have. To say from time to time the best that can be said for the things one does not agree with is an indispensable condition of sustained influence — perhaps the greatest quality of convincing journalism.

During the whole of the pre-Hitler period of Italian Fascism Garvin and Lina argued gently with one another about where the accent should fall in her correspondence and in the paper's editorial position. They were in sufficient agreement, however, to work together and enjoy an unrestricted and affectionate friendship.

There is a significant contrast between the restraint Garvin imposed on Lina Waterfield's writing about Fascists and the freedom with which he wrote about Nazis. Mussolini and his party bosses might be cruel and corrupt. Hitler and his following were evil. He wrote of them in terms he had never used about the Kaiser's Germany. He saw no objection to Britain aligning herself with Mussolini against Hitler if that could be done. He thought it possible.

## IV

The two dictators viewed each other warily. Austria was the reason. The opening words of *Mein Kampf* expressed Hitler's determination not to be a foreigner in the land of his birth. If he achieved an Austro-German union his southern frontier would be the Brenner. Below the pass was South Tyrol with its quarter of a million Austrian Germans who were now reluctant second-class Italians. Fragile and impoverished post-war Austria could not help them; a Greater Germany could and would. The integrity of post-war Italy depended upon the continued independence of a weak Austria. More than that was at stake according to Garvin:

> The incorporation of the Saar and Austria would give Greater Germany a population of nearly 75 million. The magnetic effect of that mass would tend to disintegrate Czecho-Slovakia with its large

German minority ... It is hard to see how general war could be avoided.

The struggle between Mussolini and Hitler over Austria reached a climax in 1934. In February the Austrian Conservatives, backed by Italy, established a Fascist state after a short, stubborn civil war. In July the Nazis made their bid. They planned to murder the whole Cabinet, but succeeded only in killing the Chancellor. Mussolini moved Italian troops to the Austrian border and promised to support the government. Thousands of Nazis fled into Germany. The *putsch* had miscarried. So far, so good, Garvin thought. Mussolini could be counted on. He continued to urge his readers to realise that 'If we are forced to make a choice between disagreeables, the Fascist system is saner and more civilised than the barbaric autocracy of the Nazi creed.'

In 1935 Germany's half-secret rearmament was made public. The Luftwaffe was established. Conscription was introduced. France, Italy and Britain met at Stresa to consider how they could stop further German moves. Lina Waterfield was at the station when Mussolini greeted MacDonald and Simon. She asked the Duce whether he was optimistic. 'How could I be?' he replied with a wry smile. She told Garvin:

The English are not in Mussolini's good books with regard to our policy towards Germany, which seems mild, whereas Italy would prefer ships in the Baltic (English ships, of course) and an iron ring round Germany. This is the view of most Italians even the best informed.

With a surer grasp on the situation than her editor's she added that it was doubtful whether Mussolini, the realist, would be ready to follow this line of policy. At the end of the conference the Western Powers condemned Hitler's breach of the disarmament clauses of the treaty, reaffirmed the Locarno guarantees, and again underwrote the independence of Austria. Privately they had started talks on how to defend Alsace and the Alto Adige as the Italians called South Tyrol.

## V

A few weeks later MacDonald was succeeded by Baldwin. The best Garvin could find to say about his relations with the new Prime Minister was that 'they remain civil'. It was a precarious foothold from which to attempt to influence Baldwin's Cabinet-making. He tried because he believed that in 1938, perhaps even in 1937, we should be on the brink of a world war: 'If Britain is strong enough . . . that war will be averted. If not, not.' And so, for the first time in his life, Garvin wrote a letter to Baldwin. He asked for an interview before the new Cabinet was settled. The two men met at Cliveden. Their conversation was 'humanly long and good; politically I fear null and void . . . Cunliffe Lister is given by some who ought to know as a certainty for Air and Goering's opposite number – at which every separate hair stands on end.'

The next day Garvin repeated in the *Observer* what he had said to Baldwin: 'No one can compare with him [Churchill] in the power . . . to bring executive mastery to bear on the whole problem of national and Imperial safety . . . The time has come to stop the quarrel and close the ranks.' When the new government was announced, 'those who ought to know' proved right. Cunliffe Lister was in; Churchill was out.

Garvin had to resume his advocacy of rearmament in a personally more difficult situation. For twenty-five years or more he had been accustomed to close personal contact with the leading politicians of both sides. They sought him out; he asked to see them. It was a two-way traffic. His influence had been direct and personal as well as through his writings. After 1935 it was only indirect through the *Observer*. This was only partly because he disliked leaving Gregories. After all, he had found Chequers accessible enough in MacDonald's time. But, though Ministers now rarely met Garvin, they had to know what the *Observer* said. Its sale was still rising, though slowly. Its readers were people of influence. Their opinions counted; and so, therefore, did his.

Of course, Garvin had friends and allies. The trouble was that they were as powerless as he was. Amery was excluded from the National government in all its editions, while Grigg came back from the governorship of Kenya only to linger disconsolately on the back benches. Garvin had risked a row with the Astors by urging Churchill's claim on Baldwin at a time when Nancy Astor was telling him that to put Churchill in the government would mean war at home and abroad: 'I know the depth of Winston's disloyalty,. she wrote, 'and you can't think how he is distrusted by all the electors.' Baldwin could see for himself that Churchill was a discredited politician who could safely be ignored. Garvin and his friends had become prophets without much honour and totally without power in their own party.

Very different were the conditions in which Garvin had worked before the first German war. Then, there had been a great Secretary of State for War and two outstanding First Lords of the Admiralty; now, there were far lesser men in their shoes and a 'Minister for the Coordination of (our inadequate) Defence' whose appointment was 'a ludicrous mistake'. Then, there had been Jacky Fisher and Earl Roberts; now, the Service chiefs were well-disciplined men, schooled to silence. 'Monty' had the essential quality of insubordination which Fisher praised and practised, but he was only a lieutenant-colonel commanding an infantry battalion. Then, public opinion had been pacific; now, it was almost pacifist.

Garvin himself lacked at sixty-seven some of the vigour which had been his when he was forty in 'the memorable spring of the naval awakening of 1909'. Then, he lived four miles from Whitehall; now twenty-five miles away. Then, he argued his case in the *Fortnightly* and the *National Review*, the *Daily Telegraph* and the *Daily Mail* as well as the *Observer*. Now, he wrote only in the *Observer* and that with long gaps while he struggled with *Joe*. More important, probably, was the fact that his pro-Italian foreign policy alienated many who agreed with him on defence. It distracted his readers' attention from hard and unpalatable facts to doubtful moral judgements. Garvin drove himself further and further into the wilderness.

## I

Early in 1934 Lina Waterfield had heard rumours that Mussolini was planning to invade Abyssinia. The British Embassy professed to know nothing, but the German ambassador in Rome told her it would probably be in the summer or spring of 1935. She warned Garvin. With unusual naïveté – perhaps because his wishes for Italy were often father to his thoughts – he brushed aside her information:

> There's absolutely nothing in the wild reports about what Disraeli called 'The Mountains of Rasselas'.[1] I have been familiar with Ethiopian scares for nigh forty years and they were serious in the times of Adowa and Fashoda – but there's nothing in this one.

In December, however, there were frontier incidents in Italian Somaliland.

At Stresa Lina Waterfield tried to find out what Mussolini proposed to do. She was told 'Abyssinia is not on the agenda,' and made to feel that she had asked a foolish question. The British Ministers were similarly put off. But of course Abyssinia was high on Mussolini's list. Throughout the summer there was increasing tension. War now seemed inevitable. Britain and France had to choose. They could back Abyssinia against Mussolini, or they could keep Italy as an ally against Hitler. There was no middle course, though they tried to find one.

## II

Britain in the thirties was neither a dependable ally nor a dangerous enemy. The public was bemused by the idea of 'collective security' through the League of Nations. Its supporters in England organised a Peace Ballot. Over eleven million took part. Nine out of ten thought the League should apply economic sanctions against an aggressor, but only 60 per cent thought that, if necessary, these should be backed up by military sanctions. Presumably very few indeed would have supported military action unless it was ordered by the League. That question was not asked. Outright pacifism was wide-spread. Canon Dick Sheppard had formed a Peace Pledge Union whose members promised not to fight in a war. Within two years it recruited 100,000 members. The European Powers took note. So did the British government. It was prepared to support economic sanctions, provided they did not lead to war. In practice that meant economic sanctions which did not include an embargo on oil.

This was not a theoretical debate. It was a practical discussion about what Britain should do if Italy invaded Abyssinia. Most people felt about Abyssinia as they had felt about 'brave little Belgium' in 1914. To them she seemed a small innocent country disgracefully bullied by a Great Power. Something must be done. The League must do it.

That was far from Garvin's view. Week after week throughout July and August he wrote about the deepening crisis, striving to prevent Britain 'making the League a laughing stock' by forcing it to undertake what it had no power to accomplish. America, he pointed out, had left the League; so had Japan and Germany. Its writ did not run in America, Asia or Africa. If Italy seceded, it would no longer run even in Europe – and 'the keystone of the whole European arch is Austrian independence'. That was one side of Garvin's argument. In other articles he pictured Abyssinia itself, swollen within living memory to twice its former size, a land where an Amharic minority oppressed people alien in race and religion, where tyranny and slave- trading prevailed.[2]

His articles delighted Churchill.

My dear Jim [he wrote from Paris], I cannot set out upon my holiday without writing you these few lines. I think the last eight or nine articles you have written in the *Observer* a more majestic and comprehending series than I can remember in journalism ... The range, the weight, the coolness, the fairness, and the authority all combine to produce the effect, and I doubt not has been convincing and compulsive upon many of your readers.

This is not to say that I have never dreamed of a Cromwellian Administration which would have handled the Italian Dictator in a resolute fashion. As it is, we shall see: 1. The League of Nations deeply injured; 2. Ourselves humiliated; 3. Italy estranged and 4. Abyssinia subjugated. I had hoped that some at least of these might have been avoided. But I fear HMG will achieve the lot.

It did. Ten days later in Geneva, Hoare, now Foreign Secretary, proclaimed: 'The League stands, and my country stands with it, for the collective maintenance of the Covenant in its entirety.' Britain was enchanted. Italy was not deterred. She invaded Abyssinia, not entirely unprovoked, on 3 October; the League declared her the aggressor; sanctions were imposed — but not on oil; sanctions failed. In December Hoare and Laval worked out a possible compromise by which the non-Amharic lowlands would have been ceded to Italy, while Britain would have given Abyssinia a corridor to the sea through British Somaliland. Public opinion, led by *The Times*, the two archbishops and Austen Chamberlain, was furious. Baldwin gave way. Hoare resigned. Never was canonisation turned more swiftly to excommunication.

Garvin too was isolated. He had thought sanctions a mistake; he considered the jettisoning of the Hoare-Laval peace plan a disaster. His friends were distressed. Some, like Michael Sadler, told him why:

> Your friendship means a lot to me, but I feel that if I were to fail in telling you privately how far I agree with what you gave us to read yesterday, and why I disagree, I should be guilty of what Julien Benda calls '*trahison du clerc*'.

Others preferred silence. One Sunday in 1936 Barrington-Ward noted in his diary: 'To lunch with the Garvins at Gregories. We differ, and have differed, so much on foreign policy that I haven't sought him out lately, preferring to keep personal relations intact. But I was glad today's opportunity came through Viola.' Wickham Steed, who had bombarded Garvin with appreciative letters up to and beyond Stresa, stopped writing to him in mid-August because, as he later said, 'Your espousal of the Fascist cause in the Italo-Abyssinian war made discussion seem unprofitable.' Whether Garvin knew that his daughter, Katharine, was disenchanted one does not know, but she recalled, 'Only once did he disappoint almost everybody ... I felt so keenly about it that I never discussed it with him; so I do not know what his explanation would have been.'

## III

As it happens, we have Garvin's explanation. Lina Waterfield's daughter and her husband called at Gregories at Christmas 1935 just after Hoare had been replaced by Anthony Eden as Foreign Secretary. The spontaneity of the evening's fireside oration comes freshly across in the account Jack Beevor sent his mother-in-law. Garvin enlarged, for instance, on what he called

> the Freemasonry of the non-white peoples against the white and said that the real *casus belli* was the Abyssinian-Japanese Treaty of 1932 which . . . showed that the Negus's[3] objective was to call in Asia to keep out Europe . . . a deliberate slap on the nose to Italy. The results were the natural results which a slap on the nose produces in ordinary life.

Garvin that evening was a prophet of doom. He was deeply worried about Britain's position in the Mediterranean:

> He thinks British policy for fifty years has had as its chief support, though little recognised, the friendly relations with Italy on Mediterranean matters . . . If Italy is to be hostile to us in future much energy and attention will be side-tracked to keeping the Mediterranean open and, and if our hands are full in the south, Germany will find the opening, for which it has been waiting, to reassert itself in the north.
>
> He gave a brilliant little sketch of German efforts to precipitate a crisis, not immediately because they are not ready, but soon. Dr. Goebbels summons the editors one by one. At 10 a.m. the editor of the *Deutsche Allgemeine Zeitung*: 'Good morning, good morning. I wanted to have a talk with you before I saw the rest of the press. You are doing admirably, but you may be a little more outright. England is a great nation. She stands for law and order; she will take a firm stand by her obligations. You understand?' 10.10 a.m. Herr Kirch of the *Frankfurter Zeitung*: 'Good morning, Kirch. Excellent, excellent. You were once of a liberal persuasion. You understand opinion in England and the Middle West. England will not stand for the subjection of the black races . . .' And then Herr Schmidt of the *Munchener* at 10.20: 'Herr Schmidt, you live in the South in Münich — only sixty miles from Italy. England is a great nation. Italy too is a great nation and a young nation. Her character is at stake!' And so forth, culminating in a gloomy prophecy of how Germany sees the realisation of her plans for Mittel-Europa handed to her on a silver dish — Italy leaving Austria to be *angeschlosen*, Hungary absorbing Czecho-Slovakia, and the formation of a German-Hungarian-Rumanian corridor leading to the Rumanian oilfields against the day when sanctions are applied to Germany.

Jack Beevor had been deeply impressed, but not convinced except by what Garvin said about Germany. Lina Waterfield, too, felt that Garvin was dangerously wrong, politically and morally, about Fascist Italy. Since Stresa she had been seriously ill, but even if she had been working, she would have been unable to influence Garvin. He thought her politics 'early Victorian' and had come to the conclusion that, fond as he continued to be of her, their views were now so far apart that she could not usefully continue as the *Observer*'s Italian correspondent. It was a bigger loss than perhaps Garvin realised. The editor had benefited quite as much by her confidential briefing letters as his readers from her messages.

## IV

Garvin's gloomy Christmas prophecy was well on the way to fulfilment by Whitsun. Hitler had refortified the Rhineland; Mussolini had conquered Abyssinia. His Stresa confederates had proved to be half-enemies; Hitler was at least half his friend. The prospect for Austrian independence was bleak.

The Astors and Philip Kerr were together at Biarritz that May. They brooded over the situation and came out with a diagnosis and a prescription which Waldorf set out in a long letter. Garvin took a new notebook and wrote:

> *May 21, Thursday*   Horrified though not surprised to receive from W at B another letter of great length pointing to dangerous inclination of W, N, P and others ... towards project of war by a so-called League Coalition against Italy in the summer of 1936; and generally towards policy of Icarus [Eden?] who threatens to be both a firebrand and blunderer — which is a bad combination and perhaps the worst possible.
>
> This movement on Waldorf's part might be the turning point for many things and indeed for the whole of life, public and personal.

Garvin then set out Waldorf's argument in quotations interspersed with a running commentary on his own such as a tetchy and talkative tutor might make on an undergraduate's ill-considered essay.

Waldorf's argument was that it would be better to face

the menace of Italy now when the Pacifist and Labour Party would give us their full support ... and when we can count on the help of many countries that might be neutral or hostile later. The issue is not merely peace or war, but of war at the best or worst moment for ourselves.

He argued that we could not face war with both Germany and Italy. We should therefore seek a *détente* with Germany and urge the French to do so too.

A full quotation from Garvin's notebook may give something of its flavour:

*W.A.* Hitler wants friendship with England — so do many Germans. But so do neither Musso nor the Italians.

England is ready to be pro-German but not pro-Italian. Hitler also does not want to invade France. Perhaps France is ready to realise this.

*J.L.G.* Completely wrong and truth the opposite ... Hitler's friendship for England is ... self-interest with a touch of sentiment instinctively added to make his self-interest more pleasing to the sentimental British people.

Hitler does not 'want' to invade France. He would be a fool if he did. He wants to establish by expansion eastward and south-eastward a vast Pan-German Empire or federation including the Ukraine ... The Greater Germany ... could then take Denmark, Holland, Belgium, Alsace-Lorraine or a bit more of France and probably would take these. A Britain which had become dependent on Germany in the first phase could do nothing.

*W.A.* A strong Germany would be a check on Italian ambitions particularly if it was based on a German, British and French under-standing.

*J.L.G.* ... Solicitude lest Germany should not be strong enough. 'A strong Germany'!! *Is Germany not strong enough already?* What increase of strength, Good God, are we to desire.

Two days later Waldorf explained that he did not mean that we should precipitate an Italian war. Garvin's comment was 'That last letter could not well be read as meaning anything else.' He cabled his relief, adding, 'At least one year's postponement for re-arming might and main is indispensable ... Heaven grant us time. That's the grim doubt henceforth. Blessings. Garve.'

## V

Heaven, the saying goes, helps those who help themselves. That was precisely what Garvin believed we were not doing. When Hitler reoccupied the Rhineland, Britain had replied by appointing a Minister for the Coordination of Defence, but left him without a department. Garvin jotted down in a notebook his opinion of the principal members of Baldwin's government. It was not flattering:

*Baldwin* is lethargic, heavy, lazy, sentimental . . . His appointments are as poor and misplaced as his habits are dilatory. The touch of action is not in him. He is masterly in tactics for parliamentary and electioneering management; but . . . has never shown any mark as a statesman . . .

Lord North had many talents and virtues. Stanley Baldwin is as capable, to say the least, as any statesman we have had since of becoming the Lord North of a greater catastrophe.

*Neville Chamberlain* [Chancellor of the Exchequer] : a limited though cool and clear-cut man with nothing in him [at 66] to rival the energies of the dictatorships headed and served by men in the prime of their vigour. Still he might reunite the Unionist Party and construct a stronger combination.

*Sir John Simon* [Home Secretary] : neither popular nor strong.

*Lord Hailsham* [Lord Chancellor] : has ceased to count.

*Ramsey MacDonald* [Lord President] : exhausted.

*Malcolm MacDonald* [Dominions] : promoted prematurely and above his ability.

*Oliver Stanley* [Education] : weak and vacillating.

*Walter Elliot* [Agriculture] : always over-ingenious and misled by it . . . though perhaps the cleverest of them, lacks fundamental good judgment.

*Kingsley Wood* [Health] : a first class administrator but no leader.

*Duff Cooper* [War] : indolent and superficial.

*Halifax* [Lord Privy Seal] : ideas more exalted than sure, and more spacious than clear.

*Runciman* [Board of Trade] : a stale minister.

*Inskip* [Defence] : a fine lawyer but solidly commonplace politician, the appointment a ludicrous mistake.

*Ernest Brown* [Labour] : a better Boanerges than administrator.

*Anthony Eden* [Foreign Secretary] : has hereditary infirmities of rashness, provocativeness, anger, obstinacy. He is morbidly sensitive under criticism and as avid of flattery, has been a disastrous failure.

## VI

In July the League called off sanctions. All that Churchill and Garvin had foreseen a year before had come to pass. The League had proved a paper tiger. Britain, her bluff called, counted the cost. She had willed the end, but shied (as well she might) at the means. Hitler and Mussolini took note. In November Mussolini formally buried the Stresa front: 'The Berlin-Rome line is ... an axis around which can revolve all those European States with a will to collaboration and peace.' Haile Selassie was in exile. This chapter may close with words Dr Johnson wrote to pay for his mother's funeral:

Ye who listen with credulity to the whispers of fancy, and pursue with eagerness the phantoms of hope, who expect that ... the deficiencies of the present day will be supplied by the morrow; attend to the history of Rasselas, Prince of Abyssinia.

I

Three days after the League had admitted defeat over Abyssinia General Franco crossed from Morocco into Spain. The Spanish Civil War had begun. Readers of the *Observer* must have expected the editor to write at once and often about events that were dividing not only Spain but Europe. On the contrary, week after week went by without any word from him. Part of the reason no doubt was the fact that Garvin had only just settled down to his summer stint on *Joe*. There was a more personal reason. Edward Goulding, his friend for thirty-three years, had been seriously ill. He died the day before Franco rebelled. The loss affected Jim as though Edward had been a member of his own family. It was not like him, however, to let either business pressure or private sorrow prevent him speaking out in a crisis. He felt it his duty; he found it a pleasure. Neither tentative explanations really explains his silence. One looks elsewhere for a sufficient reason, and looks in vain.

It was mid-October before Garvin resumed his Articles in the *Observer*. By that time Italy and Germany were actively supporting Franco, whose troops were already outside Madrid. France and Britain had persuaded Germany and Italy to talk about non-intervention but not to stop intervening. Garvin summed up the situation in this way. To save themselves, Nazi Germany and Fascist Italy must stop Franco being overthrown by the help of Communist Russia: 'Prevent it, at need, they will. Shrewd men might wager any money that Moscow will think better of it.' Shrewd though he was, Garvin would have lost his bet. The intervention of all three dictatorships, however, was limited to a stake which each could at need afford to lose. For the Axis, Spain provided battle practice. For Soviet Russia it was a theatre where men could watch a revolution. What they saw there would whip up support for the Popular Fronts of Socialists and Communists which best suited Russia's own needs in Britain and France.

Certainly in England the Spanish Civil War brought a sharp change in sentiment and emotional mood among young men of the left. The great wave of anti-war pacifism, dominant since 1929, suddenly receded. Some who had signed the Peace Pledge in 1934 tore up their cards and enlisted in the International Brigade which went to Spain to fight the left's battle, one and indivisible, against Nazis and Fascists wherever they might be. Of course these men were a tiny minoriry – these were only two thousand British volunteers all told – but what the few did, many dreamed of doing. In spirit they were akin to Garvin, but on the other side of a deeper divide than England had known for generations. For the young men of the thirties, as A. J. P. Taylor has said, the Spanish war provided 'the emotional experience of their life-time . . . No foreign question since the French Revolution has so divided intelligent British opinion or, one may add, so excited it.'

The outlook of liberal-minded thirty-year-olds had been shaped to a considerable extent by Garvin's *Observer* in the dozen post-war years when he had demanded social reform, reconciliation in Europe and political advance in India. Later they had rejoiced in his denunciation of Hitler and all his works, and on that account had been willing to shrug off his weakness for Italy, even for Fascist Italy, as a great man's pardonable foible. At least that was so until the invasion of Abyssinia, and even then the Nazis were not directly involved. But when Garvin wrote that 'the true Government of Spain is already the Government of Burgos', they felt that in supporting Franco, Garvin was supporting Franco's ally, the arch-villain, Hitler. They had had enough.

It is likely that their disenchantment was reflected in the circulation of the *Observer*. At the outbreak of the Spanish Civil War the net weekly sale was 217,000, the highest figure since the early days of the First World War. In 1937 there was a drop, small but disquieting. Garvin's explanation was that he had taken too much time off for *Joe*. It is true that the circulation always fell when Garvin was long away, however gifted his substitutes. It is probable, however, that this drop was partly caused by a growing difference of opinion between the editor and his readers. The decline might, one feels, have been more serious if the *Sunday Times* had not been politically even less to their liking.


## II


'Il n'y a plus de Pyrénées,' said Louis XIV when his grandson became King of Spain. Two centuries later the British Left made a similar mistake. They thought that Franco was the puppet of Hitler and Mussolini. On the contrary, as Garvin perceived, he took what he wanted but gave little back. Only if Britain and France took sides with the increasingly Communist-dominated Spanish Republicans would Franco lose the independence he valued. We refrained. Within nine years Mussolini was murdered and Hitler had killed himself. Franco remained ruler of Spain till his death thirty years later. Garvin's attitude may have lost readers, but it made sense.

His interest in Spain was long standing. It began when he taught himself Spanish in order to write his firm's business letters, his first step up from a junior clerkship. Being Garvin, he had not been content with a smattering of commercial Spanish but had gone on to read widely. He knew little of Spain at first hand beyond a memorable fortnight with the Northcliffes at Seville, but he was steeped in its history. He knew that the Pyrenees were not just a good natural frontier between states, but a continental divide between civilisations. The Iberian peninsula was a world of its own, or rather several worlds. There was a separatist, syndicalist Spain which Garvin neither liked nor understood. His Spain was a land of antique values and virtues which he appreciated even when he could not share. The lapsed Irish Catholic responded to the still living legacy of the Most Catholic Kings. Garvin took delight in his membership of the Spanish Academy. 'Indeed he had a certain arrogance in this matter,' according to his stepson.

A pedant at table once told him that he was wrong in his pronunciation of Armada. 'Yes,' replied Garvin reflectively, 'I know that a Spaniard says Ar-ma-da. But then, he flashed, I'm a member of the Spanish Academy and I can pronounce it how I like.'

His fellow Academician, Franco's representative in London, would have smiled. The 17th Duke of Alva and 10th of Berwick was Garvin's good friend. Nothing could be more natural. They liked each other. They liked the same things. Both had a profound sense of history. They shared a common interest in Louis XIV's wars. The Duke was a natural Anglophil. He had little sympathy with the brashness of the Third Reich and the new Roman Empire. The two men agreed sufficiently in politics for Garvin to see Spain largely through Alva's eyes, and for the Duke to approve of what he read in the *Observer*. All the same he could be touchy when a reviewer wrote slightingly about his Spain. He took exception when A.G. MacDonnell appeared to belittle the epic defence of the Alcazar by Franco's men. The Duke's protest was written on the day Pétain took over the government of France. The moment when Hitler's troops were about to reach the

Pyrenees was not the time to offend Franco's representative. Mac-Donnell was sent no more books on Spain. Hitler was never able to say, 'Il n'y a plus de Pyrénées.'

I

In September 1936 Goebbels accused Czechoslovakia of harbouring Soviet aircraft. Garvin took his notebook and wrote:

Germany: War? When? How?

Czechoslovakia may become acute in 1937. But it would appear on the balance of the psychological reasons by which Hitler is swayed and sways that the ideal time for his great anti-Bolshevist crusade to make Germany supreme would be 1938-9 − twenty years after the Armistice and the Treaty of Versailles . . .

There is the possibility that Hitler and Stalin might make it up . . . This would make sense of the recent destruction of the Trotskyists.

Consistently with his internal influence and strength Hitler cannot for long pursue a tame course. He *is* a Pan-German. He must be a 'Vermehrer des Reiches.' It is probable that his next objective . . . will be autonomy for the Sudeten Deutsch in Czecho-slovakia . . . Hitler in spite of the Nürnberg thunder is still *free to settle* with Russia (if Russia in fact renounces Communist prop-aganda in other countries) and *to direct his power against France and England.*

Garvin had visited Prague with his son when it was still part of the Dual Monarchy. Then the Germans had dominated the Czechs; in 1919 the Czechs dominated the Germans. He quickly realised that 'new presbyter was but old priest writ large'. Benes had promised to satisfy the ethnic minorities by organising the new state on the Swiss model. That had not been done. The failure was one of the dragon's teeth sown at Versailles.

The crop was ripening. The Sudeten Germans turned towards Hitler; the Czechs to Hitler's enemies. Czechoslovakia negotiated pacts with France and Russia. The internal instability of Czechoslovakia and, as Garvin saw it, the resulting instability which its alliances brought into the European situation, were uppermost in his mind when he resumed his *Observer* articles after a three months' break. Arm, rearm, might and main, he insisted. Seek a German settlement − perhaps by colonial concessions, but above all get rid of the Soviet Pacts. 'They are the real war danger.' In a later article he explained that the Czech-Soviet Pact was 'the very plague-carrier of European politics' because it provided a corridor nearly six hundred miles long through which Russian air-power could strike straight into Germany. But, before that could happen, Hitler would see to it that there would be no Czechoslovakia.

Ivan Maisky had become Soviet ambassador in London at the time Hitler gained power. He and Garvin became friends. Garvin visited him in London; Maisky came to Gregories. At the height of the Hoare-Laval crisis their Sunday lunch extended to five hours of serious talk. Maisky used to read his *Observer* with care and bombard Garvin with a running commentary in which a morsel of wholesome criticism was served in a batter of almost fulsome praise. Their letters and meetings continued until November 1936. At that point Garvin's attack on the Soviet Pacts was too much for Maisky. He told Garvin that the line he was taking was 'the surest way of bringing about a new world war'. There were no more letters until the day when, as Garvin had prophesied, there was no Czechoslovakia. Then they began again.

If the young Garvin of 1901 with a copy of the *Fortnightly* in his hand could have seen what the elderly editor of 1936 had just been writing in the *Observer*, he would have been tempted to agree with Maisky. Which was right − young Garvin who had been foremost in advocating a Triple Entente of Britain, France and Russia, or old Garvin who believed that the Soviet Pacts were 'the real war danger'? Or could they both conceivably be right? In 1936 what threatened Europe was not just a war over territory as in 1914 but a European civil war, something more like the wars of religion in the seventeenth century. To Garvin, Nazis and Communists were equally hateful. He believed Germany was likely to start a war, but he feared the Communists too much to treat them as possible allies. What they were doing inside the Republican part of Spain to eradicate their non-Communist partners was a warning of what liberals must expect wherever Communists got a sufficient foothold.

In the Europe of 1936 Garvin could see no substitute for our lost Italian partner in the Stresa Front. That left only England and France, and France was in a near-revolutionary situation. Still, it was the best ally we had. So far Garvin's thinking was not far from Baldwin's. Garvin was driven back on his positive and passionate belief: 'Arm, rearm, might and main.' Only then would the world believe us; only then could we secure allies. Baldwin may well have agreed, but he was never the man to hurry.


## II


In 1936 people asked, When will Baldwin go? The answer was, Not before Edward VIII's Coronation, which, as Grigg complained to Garvin, would mean 'fifteen critical months of further fumbling'. Worse befell. Edward was determined to marry Mrs Simpson, and Baldwin was determined that Mrs Simpson should not be Queen. Although Garvin had met Mrs Simpson, he relied heavily on Grigg in making up his mind on the personal issue. He wrote compassionately about the King and the divorcée as ill-starred lovers, not merely as cases in a manual of ethics or a text-book of constitutional law which it was their fate to be. In the last week of Edward's reign, he saw the King as 'drawn closer to us by all that may take him from us'. Though Garvin saw the drama in personal terms, he knew it must be decided on public grounds. For once he thought Baldwin was right. Edward must either give up the idea of marrying Mrs Simpson or abdicate. Edward chose to abdicate.

The five months that remained before George VI's coronation were a time of intense introspection. The monarchy monopolised attention. Garvin made doubly sure of every word he published. He asked Grigg to write a 'Crown and Empire' supplement. Grigg had no difficulty in getting the King's private secretary to clear it; he found Garvin more difficult to satisfy. He was told that Mrs Simpson must not be mentioned by name. Then, Garvin did not like a reference to Edward's 'incompatible mentality'. It might provoke those, 'neither few nor insignificant', who felt that Edward had been shabbily treated. Nothing must disturb the support of the country for the new King: 'The Duke of Windsor reads the *Observer* . . . is acutely sensitive. Wise for all concerned not to anger him. In Rothermere's and Beaverbrook's press little counter-effects or little comments might follow.' Grigg agreed, but insisted that the 'incompatible mentality bit' was true:

His father said to me in January, 1920 that the Prince of Wales would never in his opinion stand the life of a sovereign with the restraints of a constitutional throne, and the Prince of Wales himself told me the same thing time and again.

When Garvin saw the supplement in proof he still had qualms. He cut out a reference to the Protestant oath 'which has done infinite harm' in the Empire. Five days later he took out a paragraph about 'a shadow on the throne'. 'The *Observer* could not for the world print that . . . the whole of the rest as it swings now is inspiring and makes me leave you even your reference to Republics under the Crown.'

One might think from the time he spent on the supplement that Garvin was fiddling with the furniture while Hitler was preparing to burn down the house. The inference would be unjust. He could not ignore the distress and perplexity which the whole Empire had experienced in the crisis of the monarchy. The *Observer* was much read and quoted overseas as well as widely read at home. Its words needed to be just right. That took time.

## III

George VI was crowned on 12 May 1937; on 28 May Neville Chamberlain succeeded Baldwin as Prime Minister. He included in his Cabinet all but one of the men on whom Garvin had written such tart comments the year before. He left Churchill out.

It was the time of the 'Cliveden Set', that imaginary 'kitchen Cabinet' of Claud Cockburn's concoction. Cockburn's newsletter, *The Week*, was required reading for all journalists and any radicals who could get hold of it. Its news − some real, some invented − coloured the views of newspapers and periodicals which were left of centre. There have been few more influential papers.

At Cliveden, according to Cockburn, Waldorf and Nancy Astor gathered a group of friends and relations through whom they organised important diplomatic moves behind the Foreign Secretary's back. The most notable was said to be 'bad' Lord Halifax's private visit to Hitler with proposals for giving Germany a free hand in the East, proposals to which 'good' Anthony Eden would never have agreed.

The allegations of conspiracy were nonsense though they were widely believed. They were believed because they satisfied the need for a scapegoat. The 'Cliveden Set' fitted the bill. Philip Kerr, Geoffrey Dawson, Robert Brand and Lionel Curtis had all been members of Milner's 'Kindergarten' in South Africa. Waldorf Astor, their host at Cliveden, became in effect an honorary *Kind* and all were deeply attached to the fascinating Nancy. Waldorf owned the *Observer*, Dawson edited *The Times*, which Waldorf's brother owned. Brand was a merchant banker. Waldorf was an active member of the House of Lords, Nancy of the Commons. Five other Astors or near relations by marriage sat in Parliament. So did Philip Kerr as Marquess of Lothian. In 1938 he became ambassador designate to the United States. It was unfortunately easy to imagine Tom Jones as a *Cagoulard*, a hooded man, the nickname for the French Fascists which Cockburn applied to the Cliveden Set. 'T.J.', who had been very close to Lloyd George, Ramsay MacDonald and Baldwin, struck Michael Astor as one who

> had about him a little of the wizard, whose wizardry was Welsh, persuasive and devious ... He combined a considerable political knowledge and cunning with a form of outward detachment appropriate to the office of a senior and responsible civil servant. My father always trusted him. My mother never did.

Barrington-Ward and Garvin were also pilloried as members of the nefarious set. Barrington-Ward had become deputy editor of *The Times* in 1934 and was largely responsible for formulating in detail the paper's German policy. He too was a friend of the Astors, and shared much of their outlook on Germany. Like many survivors of the 'lost generation', he was determined that there should never be another Somme. It was ridiculous to suppose him a conspirator. Incidentally, from 1927 until 1941 he never stayed at Cliveden.

The idea of a conspiracy between Garvin and the Astors in the later thirties is laughable. They were busy fighting about the editorial control of the paper. Waldorf had revived his idea of an editorial council. Reluctantly Garvin agreed to give it a trial (he never did) but added,

> if there comes to be any question of muzzle, gag or pinion in it, I must be free to leave and tell the country why ... And I listen to no gossip whatever about myself and Lady Astor. But I know beyond 'Yea' or 'Nay' what the situation has been ...

She wanted Garvin out, and he knew it.

*The Week* made it easy to believe that these men exercised an illegitimate and sinister influence over British policy. Easy, but unnecessary and wrong. Certainly Garvin had no influence with Chamberlain. 'Joe's Torso' threw a shadow between them. 'I *never* ask to see Neville,' he told Mrs Amery. He knew it would be useless. Nancy Astor, of course, did frequently meet Chamberlain. She admired him, entertained him and shared his views. That, however, is irrelevant. Neville Chamberlain made up his own mind. The responsibility for British policy from 1937 to 1939 is his alone.

## IV

It would be tidy to classify Garvin as a hawk or a dove during the last two years of peace, but it really cannot be done. He was both. Garvin was neither surprised nor astonished when Hitler ended Austria's nominal independence in March 1938. In Parliament the *Anschluss* was compared with the rape of Belgium in 1914, whereas, as Garvin noted, 'the majority of the Sabine victims in this case felt the call like magic, and gloried in the espousals'. On Austria, Garvin was a dove because the hawk's opportunity had disappeared when sanctions shattered the Stresa Front.

The *Anschluss* led straight into the Czech crisis. It divided Europe. It parted friends. Once again it separated Churchill and Garvin. The day after the *Anschluss* Churchill spoke in the House:

> To English ears, the name of Czechoslovakia sounds outlandish. No doubt they are only a small democratic State, . . . but still they are a virile people; they have their treaty rights, they have a line of fortresses, and they have a strongly manifested will to live freely.

'What is Czechoslovakia?' Garvin replied in the *Observer*.

> It is a nonesuch State like no other on earth . . . The Czechs proper − a brave and stubborn breed no doubt − are a minority . . . ruling and rather lording [it] over a mixed majority of other peoples. Is this democracy? . . . What we are really asked to guarantee is the racial ascendancy of the Czech minority over the rest.

Churchill wanted a Grand Alliance, centred round Britain and France, and sustained by the moral sense of the world. Strict adherence to the League Covenant would secure the goodwill of all peaceable nations. Garvin replied: Call the League together and see what happens. 'Not a quarter of it will agree now to stake themselves in arms for Czech domination.' For political or religious reasons none of the Dominions would fight for Czech ascendancy or for Republican Spain. 'Rather than do this more than one of the Dominions would secede.'

On Czechoslovakia, Garvin was a dove.

In the summer Churchill published a volume of his speeches. He sent Garvin a copy of *Arms and the Covenant*, telling him that 'the differences which have emerged between us on the supreme issues to which our lives have been devoted are very much less than the great body of doctrine and knowledge which unite us still in a common cause'. It was a fine pacific gesture since Garvin had just been warning his readers to beware of Churchill's 'gorgeous sophistry and air-rapt visions'. The gesture could be made and welcomed because in truth the two friends did differ only on calculating the odds, on tactical decisions. They both believed that Britain must be willing as well as armed to fight in a sufficient quarrel, and that this must be made known to potential enemies. Neither was an isolationist as their friend Beaverbrook was. Both were agreed that the independence of France and the Low Countries was a sufficient cause. Both were agreed that Britain's defences had been shamefully run down and were not being made good with anything like sufficient vigour. As Garvin put it, 'Only when the strong speak to the strong can there be a better European order.' On armaments, then, Garvin was a hawk. Overall, he is perhaps best described in 1938 as a hawk compelled to behave like a dove until its talons were fully developed.

V

Dove-like Garvin's isolation from his hawkish friends reached a dramatic climax on the night of 29 September 1938. Chamberlain was at Munich arranging with Hitler, Mussolini and Daladier for the partition of Czechoslovakia; Garvin was dining with The Other Club at the Savoy. Churchill turned savagely on the two Ministers present that night, Duff Cooper and Walter Elliot. 'It was a stormy meeting,' as Robert Boothby remembered. 'Garvin got up and walked out when I said that one good article didn't make up for twenty lousy ones; and Churchill tried in vain to dissuade him.'[1] That was kind of Churchill.

A few days later Oliver Locker-Lampson wrote:

Dear, dear Jim, Just one line of affectionate goodwill to you after the rude horseplay the other evening at the Savoy ... But you proved not merely the most cool and collected of disputants, but a deadly dialectician whose politeness froze the foolish into silence.

In fact the tide had already turned in Garvin's favour. Even Boothby had not attacked his last article but the previous 'twenty lousy ones'. And when Wickham Steed read his *Observer* he sat down and wrote:

You have lifted a load from my heart this morning. It has lain there many a long day. Often when driving through Beaconsfield on my way to and from this place[2] I have wished I could turn the wheel to right or left and drop in on you. It was impossible ... To see you in the same camp as certain people at Printing House Square was an abiding grief to me. Now, thank goodness, you have recaptured your old self.

Garvin, of course, did not see himself as a returning prodigal. He continued to look with anxiety at commitments in Eastern Europe which could not guarantee the safety of our allies but only hold out the hope of a possible resurrection. He remained desperately worried by the deep divisions inside France. He believed that the pace of our war effort (it was that in effect after Hitler's annexation of all Bohemia in March 1939) was still far too lethargic. He had been saying so ever since 1933.

This chapter began with the note Garvin made on 21 September 1936 — 'Hitler is still free to settle with Russia . . . and to direct his power against France and England.' On 21 June 1939 he noted: 'These people here ought to have secured Russia first. Without that the Polish engagement would be the worst blunder in the history of our foreign policy except the sanctions against Italy in 1935.' In August Hitler and Stalin agreed to divide Poland between them.

I

In July 1939 Garvin told his readers that a National government with-out Churchill must be 'as bewildering to foreigners as it is regrettable to his fellow-countrymen'. For once the Astors agreed, but Chamberlain thought the article 'insufferably dull and boring'. He was not worried since four-fifths of his back-benchers did not want Churchill back — or so Hoare told Bill Astor. It needed war itself to recall Churchill to the Admiralty. Grigg got an under-secretary's job; Amery was still excluded. He appealed to Garvin for help. Sadly but honestly, Garvin told him, 'The P.M. reacts against any suggestions of mine. Since he attained his present position he has never once asked me to see him.'

In the dark days of May 1940 Amery's famous philippic in the Commons[1] helped to topple Chamberlain's government. His bogus National government was replaced by a truly national coalition under Churchill, the statesman Garvin most admired and loved. Amery returned to office as Secretary of State for India. Garvin had reason to feel content, faith to believe that all would yet be well. That too was England's mood.

At the beginning of November Churchill offered Garvin the CH, knowing that he had twice refused it but hoping that this time he would accept it on behalf of the press, 'especially the worthy part of it'. 'May I also remind you', he added, 'that by accepting you will become a Member of an Order to which both our friend Smuts and I have the honour to belong.' Garvin would have been a curmudgeon to refuse. Brendan Bracken was probably right when he guessed, 'I don't think you would have accepted an honour from anyone save Winston.'

The fact that Churchill included Garvin in his first Honours List made no special appeal to the Astors. Rather the reverse. On the morning of Christmas Day 1940, so Garvin stated,

Lord Astor sent over to Mr. Garvin's house a letter dwelling on the Prime Minister's faults and failings. Mr. Garvin replied in a letter which ... championed the Prime Minister out and out for the great balance of his genius over his defects and urged that, instead

270

of crabbing him, we should all thank God on our knees for raising up his genius for us in this war.

The Astors' dissatisfaction with Churchill went on growing throughout 1941. They now lived mainly in Plymouth, where Waldorf was Lord Mayor throughout the war. In March it was the target on two successive nights for raids which virtually destroyed the centre of the city. Plymouth was obviously a legitimate and prime target, yet it was not an evacuation area. Its defences, both active and passive, were inadequate. The Astors had tried privately to get things put right. They had failed. After the March raids they carried the fight to Parliament. 'Supposing you had a general who had lost twelve battles, would you not begin to wonder whether you ought to get rid of him?' Nancy Astor asked. She added Herbert Morrison, the Home Secretary, to her list of least liked politicians.

A little later the *Observer*'s parliamentary correspondent was rash enough to praise him. Waldorf told Garvin that it must not happen again. Garvin exploded:

Your letter is an insult, almost unique, to the traditions of honest journalism in this country. Is it possible that you and Tom Jones, so far as the *Observer* is concerned, want it to be nothing but an obsequious annexe to Cliveden and a pliable appanage of your big money? . . . I refuse to rebuke or suggestionise our parliamentary correspondent in that sense . . . I am sick of these personal feuds that you are extending right and left from the Prime Minister down. I will have nothing to do with it. But the implications of your letter touch as well the standards of British journalism as they have been and shall be maintained by me. Shall be, so long as Responsible Editorship belongs to Your affectionate, Garve.

## II

Garvin's contract had only six months to run. No decision had been made about what was to happen after the last day of February 1942. There was bound to be tough, disagreeable bargaining as there always had been on these occasions. It was unfortunate that this time it took place against a background of growing political estrangement.

Garvin's wish to remain as editor was unqualified. He might be old and overburdened, but he would do his duty to the *Observer* and the country as long as God gave him strength, and Waldorf permission. Besides he needed the money.

Waldorf on the other hand now wanted to replace Garvin, or at least to relieve him of everything but leader-writing. He was anxious about the future of the paper after Garvin retired or died. He probably read more than was justified into the recurrent rest cures and complaints of failing eyesight. He found it hard to believe that in 1938 Lord Horder had really given Garvin a medical age of between 55 and 60. Yet in December 1940 he wrote nearly all one Friday night, got to bed at a quarter to five on Saturday morning, was up again at a quarter to eight, and kept at it until the evening. He was then 72; Waldorf 61. The older man was the tougher. Even so he was mortal. He might fall sick or be killed in an air raid. There was nobody to take his place.

Waldorf knew that something must be done. He did not know what to do. Ought he to appoint a new editor or to insist on a deputy fit, as Barrington-Ward had been, to be heir apparent? Perhaps Garvin was now too old and difficult for this to work? Waldorf felt that this was so, but then he had always found him difficult. Garvin declared that he was ready to appoint such a deputy, but was there indeed one single person whom both men would accept?

## III

Two of Waldorf's sons saw their future linked with the *Observer*. Bill, the heir to the title, expected to succeed his father as chairman. He had spent two years on the paper and got on well with Garvin. In 1941 in the Middle East he felt that Garvin had 'had a new lease of life. Never has he written better, and I find his writing a breath of fresh air.' That was not his father's view, but then Bill was far enough away to see things in a different perspective. When eventually he got home, Garvin was no longer editor and he himself was to be passed over for the chairmanship. It was not a simple case of out of sight, out of mind. His father doubted whether he was 'sufficiently imaginative to deal with the situation ahead of us'.

By Christmas 1940 David Astor was confident that he would become editor of the *Observer*. He was serving in the Royal Marines, stationed usually within reach of London. If the two brothers' postings had been reversed, it is possible that Garvin might have remained editor of the *Observer*. As it was, the brother who thought Garvin 'a conceited humbug' was in a position to influence his father's decision; the brother to whom Garvin's writing was 'a breath of fresh air' was out of reach.

David Astor, with the support of Tom Jones who had now become a director of the *Observer*, collected a group of able young radicals with whose help he hoped to give the paper the leftward course he intended to set when Garvin had gone. He managed after considerable difficulty with Garvin to secure a regular weekly space for their contributions in a new feature called 'Forum' over which the editor had only a negative control. It was a compromise that could not possibly last. The situation in 1941 had certain points in common with that at the *Outlook* in 1904 and the *Observer* in 1907 when Garvin had been the impatient young man knocking at the door.[2] Then Goldman and Northcliffe in turn had had to dislodge, or edge out, existing editors to make room for Garvin with his radical, revolutionary ideas. Now David Astor with his parents' backing was in Garvin's former role, and Garvin was in the uncomfortable position that Filson Young and Austin Harrison had then occupied. The wheel had come full circle.

## IV

The cards seemed stacked against Garvin. His own friends, powerful though they were, were powerless to help him. It was because he stood up for Churchill, Beaverbrook and Bracken that he was in trouble with the Astors. Garvin thought Waldorf was a changed man and perhaps he was right. In April he had a heart attack which was probably a stroke. When Bill Astor returned from the Middle East the following year he noticed a change for the worse in Waldorf's relation to Nancy. He later told Christopher Sykes that the explanation might well be a personality change of the kind which a stroke can cause. This might equally explain the worsening of Waldorf's relation to Garvin which had somehow survived so many storms but was now doomed to shipwreck.

Moreover, not only was Bill Astor in the Middle East and David in England; not only was Tom Jones a director of the *Observer*; not only was Lady Astor threatening Garvin on the telephone – 'If you go on the way you are going, Waldorf will not support you'; but, worst of all, Lord Lothian was dead. He had been closer to Waldorf and Nancy than any other of their circle, and he was also Garvin's trusted but not uncritical friend. He, if anybody, could have prevented the threatened head-on collision. Garvin told the tribunal, to which in August Waldorf referred his problem, that 'after Lothian's death[3] some reconciling influence (to which much had been owing for years) seemed to be removed'. He told his stepson, 'Philip's death was the end of the old conditions.'

Lothian had been a member of the tribunal which in 1938 had drawn up Garvin's current agreement. It had given Garvin what he most desired, the feeling of ownership, by transferring to him 10 per cent of the ordinary shares in the *Observer*. Taking a partner was so contrary to the Astor tradition that one feels that the finally persuasive voice must have been Lothian's. If he had been alive, could he have performed a similar miracle in 1941? I suppose anything is possible.


## V

Only Edward Grigg survived from that 1938 tribunal. Waldorf suggested Tom Jones to fill one vacancy, but substituted Geoffrey Dawson when Garvin protested. Garvin consulted Brendan Bracken about the other vacancy. Lord Bennett, the former Canadian Prime Minister, and Arthur Mann, who had been editor of the *Yorkshire Post*, were both willing to serve. Mann was appointed.

The tribunal met on 18 September to consider a memorandum from Waldorf which stated: 'Mr. Garvin should not be asked to continue as Editor, but should be invited to continue as a Director of the *Observer* and contribute signed articles.' He gave as reasons Garvin's health, the time it took him to recuperate each week, and the way he shut himself up in Gregories. Probably Waldorf did not realise that Garvin now spent each Saturday in London. Certainly he did not know that Garvin had been lunching with Churchill and Bracken just before Nancy launched her attack on Herbert Morrison, and had urged them 'to let the cliques bust themselves by expressing themselves'. Garvin was not living the life of a 'dug out' or 'has been'. If Waldorf hoped to persuade him to resign it was tactless to refer to 'Field Marshals and Generals [who] join the Home Guard regardless of rank'. Garvin underlined the sentence 'It is inconceivable that Mr. Garvin should prefer or be willing to write for a rival paper.' He wrote in the margin, 'If war-time restrictions on paper did not exist Mr. G would take away two-thirds of the readers. Prefer? – No; Willing; – Yes.'

Waldorf's memorandum did not mention politics. It was the real issue. There were no valid business grounds for getting rid of Garvin. The *Observer* had recovered from the slump which hit all newspapers at the beginning of the war and was again making a profit. Its circulation was greater than ever before. The omission of political differences deceived neither the tribunal nor Garvin. On Waldorf's memorandum Garvin wrote: *'Cherchez la femme*. The Winston feud – too much support to the government.' In his oral evidence he developed the theme. Waldorf counter-attacked. Garvin decided that as a contributor he would not have a free voice; for that reason he refused Waldorf's offer.

It was a head-on collision. Grigg, both men's intimate friend as well as chairman of the tribunal, was caught in the middle. The tribunal met and met again; it listened to Waldorf and it listened to Garvin; it read further memoranda which enlarged rather than narrowed the points at issue. Waldorf elaborated his proposal that Garvin should become a contributor in a way that made it even less acceptable. He wanted to leave it to the new editor and the directors to arrange the terms. Garvin's reaction was predictable: 'This could not be fair "negotiation" for any kind of free voice and sure scope.' The growing personal difficulty was admitted by both Waldorf and Garvin, though each, of course, attributed it to the other.

Garvin's chance of survival seemed remote. On the *Observer*'s 150th anniversary that December the *Manchester Guardian* pointedly remarked, 'England will be a poorer place when the *Observer* ceases to speak the mind of a man unmoved by greed or fear.' Yet somehow, by a remarkable feat of diplomacy, the tribunal managed to produce an acceptable draft agreement. Garvin would remain editor till the end of the war, but cease to be manager. He would write his Articles and keep an interest in the book reviews, thus safeguarding his daughter Viola's position. An associate editor would plan and direct the paper as a whole. The two men would discuss policy with the directors or their representative, presumably Waldorf or T.J., 'to ensure that there is no divergence on major questions of policy and in particular on the prosecution of the war, the leadership of the Government and the organisation of the executive'. Garvin was to be paid £2,600 a year, roughly half his current salary, and receive a pension of £2,000 on retirement. He was to have a car allowance of £500.

Meanwhile Geoffrey Dawson, Arthur Mann and Tom Jones had been helping Waldorf look for a suitable associate editor. Garvin was not consulted. They considered Grigg, but decided that it might be difficult to get rid of him after the war. It does not seem to have occurred to them that it would look decidedly odd if the chairman of the tribunal appointed to adjudicate between editor and proprietor ended up as editor. Nor does anyone seem to have asked whether Grigg would give up his place in Churchill's government.

David Astor obviously could not work with Garvin as associate editor. There was a case for getting rid of Garvin altogether and making David editor in his place. It would have meant a revolution in the *Observer*'s political outlook, but presumably a revolution was what Waldorf wanted. He felt, however, that David had not had sufficient experience to take complete control in wartime, so he plumped for an interregnum. A wiser man than Waldorf would have risked David, or put up with Garvin.

## VI

On Friday, 20 February Garvin's new contract was ready for signature. A cooling off period was needed. In the past, it had worked wonders. This time it was denied. Throughout January and February the war news from every theatre had been consistently bad. Worst of all was the surrender of Singapore on 15 February, the Sunday when by chance the *Observer* carried a Forum article demanding that Churchill should give up the Ministry of Defence. Waldorf had approved the article, which underlined what he had written in a letter to *The Times*. Churchill's government was in serious political danger. He carried out a major reconstruction. Beaverbrook retired; Churchill remained Minister of Defence as well as Prime Minister.

Garvin got the news at the same time that he heard about his contract. He put that to one side, and concentrated on what he should write about the government changes. Probably his mind went back to that wretched day in 1916 when he had to tell Mrs Churchill that 'Waldorf does not want the *Observer* to run Winston. It means that I shall have to remember that the *Observer* is not my paper.' Then Garvin had conformed. He could not do so now. No editor could refrain from comment on a major Cabinet reshuffle without making his paper ridiculous. Garvin, being Garvin, could only write what he believed. He knew that it would make trouble with Waldorf. He took pains to minimise their differences. He stressed the need to lighten Churchill's load. So far, so good. Waldorf had said so himself. Churchill had chosen to delegate 'the general run of domestic business'. Garvin

pointed out that this was what Chatham and Lloyd George had done —
and Waldorf's admiration of his old chief of Garden Suburb days had
not faded.

It was the best Garvin could do. It was not good enough for Waldorf.
He read the *Observer*, then sent Grigg a telegram: 'Article today runs
directly counter to my known policy and makes future cooperation
impossible stop desire tribunal to meet to consider fundamental divergence Astor.' Grigg rang up Waldorf to find out what his objections
were. He was furious about the passage on the Ministry of Defence and
about Garvin's hope that Beaverbrook would soon return to the government. Waldorf was inflexible. Grigg's patient diplomacy had failed. He
had to act alone because the two other members of the tribunal were
both seriously ill. 'Deeply grieved', he had to settle the financial terms
of severance. He awarded Garvin six months on full salary, followed by
a pension of £2,000 a year. Waldorf would buy back Garvin's shares in
the paper for £8,250. There was a post-script to his letter: 'It is, of
course, understood that as your Editorship will cease on Saturday
next, the 28th, the *Observer* of next Sunday, March 1st will be produced by whomsoever the Directors may appoint.'

A. P. Herbert, who had never been one of Garvin's circle, wrote in
*Punch*:

To J. L. Garvin

The little fellows laughed that you were long;
    The feeble fellows never like the strong;
The crooked fellows do not love the straight —
    But all, I think, agreed that you were great.

You did not always rollick or rejoice,
    But all the time you spoke with England's voice.
Though rude men talked about 'The Cliveden Set'
    Nobody asked 'Which way does Garvin bet?'

Newspapers get new masters in a night
    But it takes more to teach a man to write,
So we shall miss the thunder and the flame,
    And Sunday morning will not be the same.
A.P.H.

**I**

Oliver Woods was serving in the Middle East when a cable told him that his stepfather had been thrown out of the *Observer*. It was a tantalising cable — 'shall very soon resume elsewhere with same free voice'. Oliver had to wait eight weeks for the promised airgraph with details of what had been happening. When it came, he read:

> I never told you before you left and never told your Mums until the convulsion had happened that the struggle there [at the *Observer*] had been a misery night and day for six months before you went out. Lothian's death was the end of the old conditions. Cliveden wanted the thing to be its own — especially under David's influence and Her's — and wanted me, ceasing to be editor, to write under the direction of a committee . . .
>
> I couldn't do what they wanted if I would, and wouldn't if I could. Beaverbrook was the only real friend in the whole business. At the worst he said to me: 'Jim if they do this to you, I offer you a place for your article on the centre page of the *Sunday Express* to write as freely as Low draws for one year at £5,000.' I said 'Yes'. It was all done in less than half a minute. Max has kept his word in every way never seeking to influence.

There were four good reasons why Beaverbrook backed Garvin: he was generous; it was good business; it annoyed the Astors; and he liked Garvin — they had been in close touch throughout Beaverbrook's time at the Ministry of Aircraft Production. His offer, however, was triggered by Brendan Bracken and Churchill. Bracken had become Minister of Information in July 1941. Throughout the autumn and early winter he and Garvin met frequently and wrote often. Churchill needed Garvin's unhesitating, but not altogether uncritical, support instead of what he might expect if Waldorf had his way with the *Observer*. Bracken had encouraged Garvin to stand firm:

> It would take a lot more than the decadent descendants of Wall Street toughs to fray your nerves. Stand like the rock you are,

always remembering that your friends are more embittered than you are by the way you have been treated.

Long afterwards Barrington-Ward recorded in his diary how Bracken told him (what he had guessed) that he had got Winston to speak about a job for Garvin when he and the *Observer* parted company.


## II


Garvin relished the fact that a million and a half people bought the *Sunday Express*. He did not ask how many read him. In the *Observer* his Article had been, so to speak, the main course in an epicure's *table d'hôte*. The editor of the *Sunday Express* ran an *à la carte* newspaper. He provided both James Douglas and J. L. Garvin. Few readers can have liked, or read, both.

Working for the *Sunday Express* was depressingly lonely. Garvin was left 'without the faintest word or suggestion ever from anybody – but with no human intercourse either in connection with it'. He still went to London on Saturdays to deliver his 'copy', but he missed his old office and his familiar colleagues. Occasionally he saw Beaverbrook, and once or twice he lunched with Churchill, though there was a black time when he felt himself discarded. One day Barrington-Ward found him 'much disillusioned with Winston. Thinks he has changed. Reports on telephone conversation in which he was incredibly pompous . . . No thanks to Garve for the great sacrifice he has made for him.' The black time passed. He told Oliver how:

Mums and I on 'Armistice Day' last week lunched at No. 10 with P.M. and Mrs. C. They were kindness itself to us both. Marvellous how any man can support that mighty and still growing weight. One *can't* see him often but now and then does a lot of good.

In the First World War people sought Garvin out; in the Second, one feels they took him out.

It was men's company that Garvin missed most. His doctor son-in-law was in India; his stepson in Africa. After the Eighth Army reached Sicily, Oliver's letters got through in three weeks. That was long enough, but it seemed to Garvin 'like a magical reduction of the distance between us and worked like an elixir to one who, being rather Crusoed here, is almost starved for man society as yours used to be'.

With the loneliness went gnawing anxiety. 'The other day I got hold of an Iliad,' Oliver wrote. 'It's very interesting reading some of the really bloody passages when you've had a little practical experience.' Garvin was worried too about his daughter Katharine who was on her way to Turkey through submarine-infested seas. His youngest daughter, Ursula, had married an Italian engineer, Leo Slaghek Fabbri, and settled in Italy. She had contracted tuberculosis:

> One wonders and wonders about Ursula knowing nothing but that she has recovered and left the Sanatorium; and that he has been very good; and they are wretchedly poor. The other day a cable came: 'Am fit and well don't worry Garvin.' Some censorship, I couldn't tell which, had suppressed the place of origin. At first I thought it might have been really Ursula. But perhaps Kit.

There was another kind of anxiety about his eldest daughter's future. Viola had lost her job on the *Observer* in the wake of her father's dismissal, 'thrown out as the only real way of hurting me'.

Garvin's old power of recovery and rising to an occasion remained. He told Oliver how in August 1942

> I very nearly, within an inch or so, broke my neck by being catapulted out of bed in my sleep and coming crash upon the edge of a piece of furniture. X-rayed next morning at Windsor Hospital. No bones broken, thank God, but otherwise a severe knock. I determined to write my Sunday article next day and did somehow, and have kept it up.

## III

Garvin lovingly followed Oliver's movements, as once he had followed Ged's, by the aid of large-scale maps, historical knowledge and guess-work:

> Every inch I know — and the cactus and the prickly pears as well as the lemons, oranges and red wine. To my crammed historical mind, it's maddening under the paper restrictions not to be able to say much more about Syracuse, Centuripe, Agrigento and Palermo itself and so forth than if they were Balham and Tooting.

Oliver may have smiled at Garvin's ineradicable habit of telling him what he already knew, and knew far better; but he carefully kept all his letters. Ged had done the same. There was between Garvin and his two boys an unusually warm affection. Oliver, of course, was only a stepson, but they were 'Father' and 'Son' to each other. It speaks for itself.

## IV

Early in January 1945 Garvin told Oliver:

> My connection with the *Express Newspapers* has come to an abrupt end. No quarrel with Beaverbrook or communication. Editor of the *Sunday Express* insisted on my changing to a popular column about anything but the war. Of course impossible with a rag of self-respect.

He added a postscript. 'Mums and I just bidden to Chequers for next Sunday.'

Wheels began to turn. On Tuesday Garvin lunched with Bracken, who spoke to Camrose. A week later Camrose arranged for Garvin to write a weekly column for the *Daily Telegraph* for £5,000 a year plus a car allowance of £1,000. The *Telegraph* had given him his start in Fleet Street when he was thirty-one. He rejoined the paper a month before his seventy-seventh birthday. Molly Hudson, Northcliffe's widow, was one of the first he told. She replied:

> Oh, Garve dear, what wonderful news! ... Back in your own element, your own milieu, and with one of the dearest and kindest men it has ever been my good fortune to know. And I am just as happy for him too! — and for all of us. It is just as much his gain.

Garvin's work for the *Telegraph* was uneven in quality. The peaks were fewer, the laborious plains longer. He exercised little influence on politicians or parties — he was not close enough to the daily battle for that — but he made his readers think in ways that might not otherwise have occurred to them about how the world was changing. And he still had the gods' gift of a memorable phrase.

His thinking ran parallel with his work in the great years that followed 1918. What he wrote then he repeated, not of course word for word but spirit for spirit, in his *Telegraph* articles. The world had to be re-made for the second time in his lifetime. Of course there was in 1945 a question mark in his mind over human nature, especially German human nature, which had been lacking in 1918:

> We do not yet know how far the decivilisation of the German heart has gone while, by an appalling paradox, the German technical brain has developed for evil. The same person may be like Jekyll and Hyde — individually humane yet a robot of collective cruelty.

When the Allies met at Potsdam Garvin saw their task in terms very like those that he had put forward in 1919:

> About the complicity of the bulk of the German people ... you may hold any theory you please. You cannot act on theory. You cannot punish the mass of men, women and children by slaughtering and starving them wholesale or by enslavement in chain gangs or by setting up concentration camps of your own ... To safeguard them, if you can, from famine next winter you must help them to make the most of their soil.

And he went on to advocate a policy of 'guarded fraternisation' by our troops in order 'to effect by degrees a large extent of moral disarmament'.

In 1945, as in 1919, Garvin believed that it was even more important to organise peace than to enforce it. Then he had looked to the allied economic cooperation in war as a preparation for world economic cooperation through the League. In 1945, faced by the much greater challenge of the Atomic Age (which had rekindled his scientific curiosity), he demanded

> a Scientific and Technical Council equal to the Security Council itself. Its real importance would be greater ... We shall abolish war when this kind of world cooperation offers advantages to every society such as none of them by itself could achieve ... In that sense, this crisis of all time is not the modern world's last chance, but its first.

Meanwhile Garvin was clear that it was folly for one Power or group of Powers to keep the atomic secret to itself, as the West was then doing: 'It would lend an unholy fascination to rival research and counter-secrets ... Some day flash-point and finis would come of themselves.'

Garvin developed his old theme of American partnership at a time when England was hanging back in spirit. In a comment on Churchill's Fulton speech he wrote: 'The way of life and liberty we share with America is about as much nearer to us than Communist dictatorship as the skin is nearer than the shirt.' Yet he refused to think of America as 'globally centric'. Russia was twice as large, and an even newer Third World was being called into existence to redress the balance not only of the Old World but the New. Russia and India, 'strange conjunction', had combined to prevent South Africa incorporating what we now call Namibia: 'This incident, as touching the British Commonwealth so nearly, may serve as a small but vivid symbol of a transformation so sweeping and astonishing that it has no parallel in history.'

# V

Garvin's daughter Kit, 'gay, witty, civilised and kind' as A. P. Ryan remembered her, got back from Turkey in January 1945. When they met there was need to think seriously about her future. James Gordon, Garvin's third grandchild, was born on 15 March.

Ursula was still lost somewhere in northern Italy. Letters and cables went astray, but some sort of contact was established. Finally Oliver got leave from his regiment and crossed the Brenner on a relief expedition bearing 'champagne, paté de foie, chocolates, and books'. He brought back what was substantially good news. It was the spring of 1946, however, before Ursula was fit to travel. There at Gregories she found her father in tender, reminiscent mood.

Garvin's last years were a time of reconciliation as well as home-coming. In August 1946 he and Waldorf dined with The Other Club. Garvin went up to shake hands. Waldorf welcomed the gesture. Garvin drove home to Gregories and told Ursula: 'I think he meant it.' Waldorf did.

# VI

Two people who met Garvin for the first time in 1946 have left pictures of him in his old age. Frank Waters had been managing director of the

*News Chronicle* and was now on *The Times*. They met at lunch at a Greek restaurant in Bloomsbury. The proprietor asked Waters whether the gentleman he was about to join was Professor Gilbert Murray; but 'at the name of Garvin he raised his hands in delight and drew in a deep breath and exclaimed: "Ah! it is indeed Mr. J. L. Garvin" — as though Byron himself had arrived having just swum the Hellespont'.

Waters expected to meet 'a sombre, verbose, pontifical' political commentator. He found 'an alert mind of infinite comprehension and resource, astonishing in its vitality and refreshing in its fervour and zeal', a man moreover who 'understands newspapers through and through, being primarily a working journalist, a master of his trade'.

As they talked, Waters became aware that

> Garvin has all the ability of a Churchill in depicting panoramic-ally a world situation, and something of the bombast. The egoism is as great, if not greater, but the knowledge behind it a great deal more encyclopedic thus providing a more effective and convincing basis and justification for an overwhelming forthrightness of man-ner. His fervour moreover has a fine, moral ring. He speaks neither for party, nor nation, but for the world. And when he speaks it is with the dignity of an Olympian whose argument is unanswerable. What would you reply when Zeus himself says earnestly: —
>
>> 'You see I did not want this war, but I saw that it had to be. I realised that the sacrifice that had to be made by the present generation was infinitesimal compared with the calamity con-fronting the world a few years hence when the chasm that divided humanity would be insurmountable . . .'
>
> Or again, with a twinkle-in-the-eye, explaining his reasons for refus-ing to meet Hitler when it was suggested he might be the means of bringing about a settlement:
>
>> 'I would not do so; I would not allow myself to be shouted at. I knew that as soon as he started shouting, I would shout back, and I have never been shouted down in my life.'

Later that year Frank Waters and his wife Joan met the Garvins at a cocktail party. She described the scene in a letter to me:

> Looking across the room I remember feeling intense compassion at the sight of that tired, ungainly old man by the door. The 'aura of wisdom and experience' was there; but he also looked frail and vulnerable.

Viola stood at his side. She was wearing the black tricorne hat, large crucifix, and the long, dark, shapeless dress which you have seen so often in the photographs. But her distinctive, natural grace survived the theatrical emphasis of the clothes ... Viola's romantic outlook, fierce loyalties and her wonderfully untarnished and often child-like mind, must have both fascinated and irritated Garvin ... Anyway, there they stood together by the doorway — Garve and Viola. They didn't seem a pair — yet they were complementary to each other ...

From that lengthy observation across the room, to come into close contact was like moving from the view in a long mirror to the reflection in a shaving glass ... His skin was greyish white and flaccid; it was lined and pouched. He hadn't much hair — not enough to improve his looks. He had a paunch which sloped from his chest. His physique showed no signs of any effort towards physical fitness, except the possible flexing of those large, well shaped ears. The brow was noble and the features strong. His hands were large, capable; and swollen with rheumatism. He looked old, tired, ill — and intensely vital. Those remarkable eyes were his glory.

What I had not expected was the Celtic web of poetic fantasy ... I think the talk started with me making some silly joke about the exertions attendant upon Holidays Abroad and the alternative delights of a Holiday at Home reading about other people's Holidays Abroad. This he seized upon gleefully, and extolled the delights of his favourite Edwardian hotel in Studland Bay ... He was extremely funny, and he encouraged all my flights of fancy with his own bright plumage. I think we travelled as far as Bognor. There was nothing of the monopolist/monologue in his talk. No shred of it.

Garvin's last article appeared in the *Telegraph* on 16 January 1947. That day he fell ill. Camrose told him not to hurry back to work: 'You have your public — they will wait for you.' Garvin seemed to be making good progress. Then he had a relapse. He was too ill to be moved from the Shepherd's Kitchen. There he died on the day his next article would have been published.

Barrington-Ward wrote in his diary that evening:

*January 23, 1947*: Soon after noon Oliver Woods rang me up with the staggering news that Garve had died a few minutes before. Can't take it in. What has he not meant to me and my family? He is one of the people to whom I owe anything I have done.

A great human figure. It is hard to think of my world without him . . .

Next morning in the *Telegraph* Churchill wrote of 'Jim Garvin . . . a friend of fifty years in whom courage, generosity and faithfulness shone in private and in public life as they shine in few'. Of all the obituary tributes Garvin himself might have relished most a fellow Irishman's. St John Ervine wrote, 'I hope there are newspapers in Heaven, and that I may write in Garve's.'

# NOTES AND REFERENCES

J. L. Garvin has been the subject of two books, a short intimate memoir by his daughter Katharine, *J. L. Garvin*, published in 1948, and a detailed authoritative study of the years when he first became a national figure, *J. L. Garvin and the Observer 1908 to 1914: A Study in a Great Editorship*, by A. M. Gollin, published in 1960. References to him abound in political and newspaper biographies dealing with the period 1903 to 1947.

There is a very large collection of Garvin's letters, papers, memoranda and notebooks in the Humanities Research Center of the University of Texas at Austin. These provide the main material on which this biography is based. The notes to the chapters which follow indicate in outline, and where necessary in detail, the use that has been made of them and other sources such as, to name only four of the more important, the Northcliffe Papers in the British Library, the Astor Papers in the University of Reading, the Sandars Papers in the Bodleian and the Barrington-Ward Papers in the possession of his son, Mark, who wrote the article on Garvin in the *Dictionary of National Biography*. It will be noticed that sometimes the authority for statements in the early part of this book is a letter written very many years after the event. That Garvin's memory was not only prodigious but accurate can be checked whenever it is possible to compare his recall of events which took place forty or fifty years before with what he or others wrote at the time. Where such a comparison is impossible I have therefore relied on his recollection with reasonable confidence.

Apart from the three volumes of his *Life of Joseph Chamberlain* (3 vols, 1932-4), Garvin's writings are to be found almost entirely in the files of newspapers and periodicals accessible only in specialist libraries. I have read widely in, but quoted sparingly from, the *Daily Telegraph*, the *Observer* and the *Pall Mall Gazette*; the *Outlook*, the *Fortnightly Review* and the *National Review*. To have done otherwise would have turned a biography into an anthology, much of which, without copious footnotes, could be fully understood today only by professional historians. It is sad that so powerful a writer should have to be represented by so little of his writing. I have, however, given the date of all Garvin's articles referred to in the text so that those who wish, and are in a position to do so, may read them for themselves.

**Book One: North Country Apprenticeship, 1868-1899**

*1 An Irish Boy on Merseyside, 1868-1884*

Note: In correspondence references Garvin is referred to as G.

This chapter rests mainly on family tradition recorded by Katharine Garvin, *J. L. Garvin*, and on enquiries made in Birkenhead after Garvin's death by his daughter Viola with a view to a biography she never wrote. Garvin was extremely reticent about his father, but see his letters to Northcliffe (19 Aug. 1909), Frances Colvin (11 Aug. 1919) and to Christina Garvin (Thursday inc. d. 1914). For his early religious experience see his Notebook 52 (28 Mar. 1899), his letter to his son (28 Apr. 1916) and a letter from Father Dallow (30 Aug. 1908). His childhood reading is remembered in an interview with J. P. Collins (*Book Monthly*, March 1913) confirmed by a letter from his brother Michael (23 Apr. 1913). See also Garvin to his son, 22 Sept. 1915.

*2 Tammany Teenager, 1884-1889*

Garvin's political activity and thinking are to be found in his contributions to the Hull newspapers and to the *Dublin Weekly Freeman* preserved in a newspaper cuttings book. For Joseph Chamberlain's visit to Hull see Garvin, *Life of Joseph Chamberlain*, vol. II, pp. 56, 60. For his contact with J. A. Spender see Wilson Harris, *J. A. Spender* (1946), pp. 5, 8, 16, 17; Katharine Garvin, *J. L. Garvin*, p. 29; and J. A. Spender, *Life, Journalism and Politics* (1927), vol. I, p. 44. Garvin's office life in Hull is described in a MS sketch of his fellow clerks. Garvin's attempts to enter the Civil Service are described by him in letters to the *Civil Service Aspirant* (Cuttings Book). For J. H. Tutin and Wordsworth see *Book Monthly* (March 1913). Garvin's letters to C. P. Scott, 4 Nov. 1926, and J. L. Hammond, 10 Mar. 1942, mention his early addiction to the *Manchester Guardian*, and a letter to Barrington-Ward, 28 Sept. 1942, recalls the start of his reading of *The Times*.

*3 Garvin Finds a Guru, 1889-1899*

1. Garvin was a naturally good linguist, but, because self-taught, an uneasy and reluctant speaker.

*I* Garvin's Cuttings Book contains examples of his writing in *United Ireland*. See also Jeremiah MacVeagh in Hansard, 8 May 1912, cols. 473-5, and A. G. Gardiner in the *Daily News*, 5 Oct. 1912, quoting Peter Fanning of Jarrow. Five letters from George Mackie written between 1899 and 1927 give echoes of Garvin's 'Jacobinical past'. Mackie was a fellow employee of J. W. Holmes and Co. who died in 1929 aged ninety. The news of his death was endorsed by Garvin: 'Alas, dear old friend for forty years.' Notebook 52 (14 May 1898) records Garvin's contact with working-class culture in the North-East. Arthur Henderson's speech at a lunch given by the *Spectator* for Garvin on 14 Nov. 1929 refers to their early days in Newcastle.

*II* Katharine Garvin, *J. L. Garvin*; information from Mark Barrington-Ward. Garvin's account of Parnell's funeral in the *Newcastle Chronicle* is in his Cuttings Book.

*III* William Duncan, *Joseph Cowen* (1904); Cowen/G, 23 Dec. 1898; 21 June, 13 July 1899; G/Cowen, 17 Dec. 1899 (unposted); G/Christina Garvin, 29 June 1899; Notebook 52; *Economic Foundations of Peace* (1919), p. 440 (Ruskin and free trade); *Fortnightly Review* (Jan. 1901), 'Can Britain Last the Century?'.

*IV* 'Ideas for Improving the Newcastle Daily Chronicle' (title supplied by his daughter Viola), MS.

## 4 Marriage, 1894

1. Actually the poem was by John Hoskins, but from 1711 to 1912 it was attributed to Donne.

This chapter is based largely on the 73 letters from Garvin to his wife written during his Newcastle period. Notebook 52 contains a journal for 1898-9. Garvin's pocket diaries for 1893 and 1894 survive. The self-portrait in verse is in his Cuttings Book. The story of the spilt milk was told me by Mrs Eileen France, a childhood friend of the family in London. It is referred to in G/Gerard Garvin, 5 Oct. 1915. There is much family tradition in Katharine Garvin, *J. L. Garvin*.

## 5 London Bound, 1893-1899

*I* *The Sun*/G, 22, 26 July 1893; G/Christina Garvin, 9, 11 Oct. 1893; *Irish Independent*/G, 15, 16, 23 Sept. 1896; Redmond/G, 16, 23 Sept. 1896.

*II* J. E. Courtney, *The Making of an Editor: W. L. Courtney 1850-1928* (1930); *Fortnightly Review* (May 1895), 'Future of Irish Politics'; (Sept. 1895), 'A Party with a Future'; Courtney/G, 24, 26 July 1895.

*III* Viola Meynell, *Francis Thompson and Wilfrid Meynell* (1952), pp. 55, 99-103; *idem, Alice Meynell: A Memoir* (1929); *The Bookman* (Mar. 1897); G/Christina Garvin, Easter 1897; 22 Apr. 1897; 16, 24 May 1898; W. Meynell/G, four undated letters; 3 Dec. 1922; Alice Meynell/G, 9 Feb. 1897; *Fortnightly Review* (Feb. 1897), 'Coventry Patmore'; MS article on Meredith's poetry, Courtney/G, 9 Mar. 1899, Notebook 49.

*IV* G/Christina Garvin, 28, 31 May 1898; Courtney/G, 8, 11 July 1899; *Fortnightly Review* (Mar. 1898), 'The End of the New Unionism'; (Dec. 1898), 'Parnell and his Power'; (Jan. 1899), 'The Disraeli of Liberalism'.

**Book Two: Empire Day in Fleet Street, 1899-1906**

## 6 His Master's Voice, 1899-1904

Nearly 150 of Garvin's letters to his wife were written during his five years on the *Daily Telegraph*. Their profusion, of great value to the biographer, is due to the illness of their eldest daughter, which separated husband and wife for considerable periods. Another major source for this period is the letters from Sir Edward Lawson (1st Lord Burnham), his son (1st Viscount Burnham) and Sir John Le Strange, the managing editor of the *Daily Telegraph*. Many of Garvin's leading articles for the *Daily Telegraph* can be identified from these sources.

*I*   G/Christina Garvin, 19 July 1899; G/Cowen, 17 Dec. 1899; Michael MacDonagh/G, 22 July 1899.

*II*   Lord Burnham, *Peterborough Court: The Story of the Daily Telegraph* (1955); G/Christina Garvin, 3 Oct. 1900; 22, 24 Jan. 1901; Ed. Lawson/G, 22 May 1900; Le Sage/G, 27 Dec. 1901.

*III*   Katharine Garvin, *J. L. Garvin*; Notebook 60, 17 Dec. 1899; G/Christina Garvin, 22, 28 Nov. 1900 (Irish Literary Society); 8 Jan. 1901 (Viola's leg); 4 Jan. 1901 (friction with Garvin's mother); 2, 7 Dec. 1900 ('the little breviary'); 11, 16 July, 2, 9, 13 Aug., 9, 11 Oct. 1900 (money difficulties).

*IV*   Notebook 60, 8, 9 Dec. 1899.

7   *What Calchas Foresaw, 1899-1902*

*I*   *Fortnightly Review* (July 1900), 'The Crux in Foreign Policy' (Anon.); (Dec. 1900), 'A Cabinet of Commonplace' (Calchas); Courtney/G, 17 Dec. 1900; Maxse/G, 15, 31 Aug. 1900; *National Review* (Oct. 1900), 'The German Danger in the East' (X). Homer, *The Iliad*, trans. E. V. Rieu (Penguin Classics, 1950), pp. 25, 48. Copyright © the Estate of E. V. Rieu, 1950. Reprinted by permission of Penguin Books Ltd.

*II*   *Fortnightly Review* (Jan. 1901), 'Will England Last the Century?' (Calchas); *National Review* (Oct. 1900), 'The German Danger in the Far East' (X); *Fortnightly Review* (Dec. 1901), 'The Crisis in Germany and its Results' (Calchas); (June, July 1901), 'Russia and her Problem' (Calchas).

*III*   G/Stanley Morison, 1, 6, 21 June 1943; Morison/G, 4 June, 5 July 1943.

8   *Indian Interlude, 1902-1903*

This chapter is based on the 21 long letters Garvin wrote to his wife during his visit to India. The last (5 Feb. 1903) ends thus: 'I sincerely believe that I have written you the equivalent of a page and a half of the paper – the longest letter ever written by mortal man to his love.' His messages to the *Daily Telegraph* were of comparable length.

9   *Chamberlain's Man, 1903-1904*

*I*   G/Frances Colvin, 18 May 1909; G/Northcliffe, 23 Dec. 1908.

*II*   *Fortnightly Review* (Nov. 1903), 'Mr Chamberlain: The Protagonist and the Future' (reference to F. C. Gould); *Daily Telegraph*, 16 May 1903 and daily thereafter; Lawson/G, 25 June 1903; Maxse/G, 14 Sept., 17 Oct. 1903; Chaplin/G, 20 Oct. 1903; J. Amery, *The Life of Joseph Chamberlain* (1951), vol. IV, p. 275 (Chaplin/Chamberlain), vol. V, pp. 421, 422 (Amery's diary); G/Bonar Law, 20 Nov. 1906.

*III*   Duncan, *Joseph Cowen*, p. 232; *Fortnightly Review* (Jan. 1901), 'Will England Last the Century?'; (Sept. 1901), 'The Eve of the Campaign'; Maxse/G, 30 Jan. 1907.

*IV*   L. S. Amery, *My Political Life* (1953), vol. I. pp. 238, 264-5; *The Times*, 18 July 1936; G/Gerard Garvin, 14 Sept. 1915.

*10 Garvin's* Outlook, *1904-1906*

Garvin's participation in Chamberlain's imperial preference campaign made him a political figure in his own right and is reflected in a marked broadening of the sources available to a biographer. The first of the 97 letters from L. J. Maxse was written as early as 1900. There now followed the beginning of eight other long-running correspondences. In 1904 Garvin received the first of 76 letters from L. S. Amery and of 266 from Admiral Fisher; in 1905 the first of 95 from Bonar Law, of 138 from Lord Roberts, and of 342 from Edward Goulding; and in 1906 the first of 95 from F. S. Oliver, of 109 from Oliver Locker-Lampson, and 138 from Lord Northcliffe. Nineteen hundred and six also brought the first of 111 letters from Sidney and Frances Colvin, and of 126 from Sybil and Arthur Colefax.

*I*   Sir William Beach Thomas, *The Story of the Spectator: 1828-1928* (1928); G/Maxse, 6 Oct. 1904; Maxse/G, 8, 15 Oct. 1904; Amery/G, 4 Oct. 1904; G/Amery, 6 Oct. 1904; Robinson/G, 26 Sept., 1, 8, 15 Oct. 1904; Goldman/G, 6, 8 Oct. 1904; for Filson Young, see David Ayerst, *Guardian: Biography of a Newspaper* (1971).

*II*   G/Maxse, 13 Nov. 1904; Goldman/G, early Nov. 1904 (front page missing); Filson Young/G, 4 Jan. 1905; 1, n.d., 14 Mar. 1906; G/Walter Guinness, 8 Dec. 1906; Amery, *My Political Life*, vol. I, pp. 266, 267.

*III*   G/Amery, 8 Jan. 1905; Grigg/G, Wed. (Jan. 1905); Fiennes/G, 15 July 1906; Beach Thomas/G, 5 Dec. 1906; Whibley/G, 4 Feb. 1905; G/Christina Garvin, 30 Jan., 3, 5, Feb., 12 July 1905; *Outlook* (11 March 1905), 'Nelson's Year and England's Duty' (Chamberlain); (19 Oct. 1905), Meredith's threnody for Nelson who 'lives in the immortality That poets dream and noblest souls desire'. Housman/G, 11 Oct. 1905; Hardy/G, 12 Oct. 1905; Meredith/G, 15, 17 Oct. 1905.

*IV*   *Outlook*'s weekly circulation and profit and loss data (MS); *Outlook*, Estimates for business deal prepared for Chamberlain (typescript), 17 Mar. 1906; G/Christina Garvin, 13 Feb. 1905; G/Goldman, 6 Jan., 3 Apr. 1906; Goldman/G, 10 Jan., 6 Feb. 1906; Chamberlain/G, 6 Apr. 1906.

*V*   G/Christina Garvin, 15, 19 Oct. 1904; 31 Jan., 2, 6 Feb., 2, 9 June 1905; Goldman/G, 3 Jan. 1905.

*VI*   Willoughby/G, 7, 21 June 1906 (Goldman's third partner was Col. the Hon. H. A. Laurence); G/Northcliffe, 20 June 1906 (they met 18 and 21 June); Northcliffe/G, 19 Dec. 1906; G/Christina Garvin, 24 Aug. 1906; Arbuthnot/G, 4 Apr., 3, 4 Nov. 1906; Guinness/G, 9, 10, 15, 24 Nov. 1906; G/Guinness, 14 Nov. 1906 (Garvin's interviews with Guinness were on 4 and 5 November); Long/G, 10 Nov. 1906; Frewen/G, 1 Sept. 1907; G/Maxse, 29 Nov. 1906.

**Book Three: The Northcliffe Years, 1908-1911**

Essential for Chapters 11 to 17 are *The History of The Times: The Twentieth Century Test 1884-1912* (1947); R. Pound and G. Harmsworth, *Northcliffe* (1959); and Gollin, *J. L. Garvin and the Observer* (1960).
G's letters to Northcliffe are in the British Library; those from Northcliffe at Austin.

*11 Northcliffe's Partner, 1907-1911*

*I*   G/Northcliffe, 20 June, 1, 8 Dec. 1906; Northcliffe/G, 4 Dec. 1906; G/Maxse, 8 May 1905; information from Mrs Ursula Slaghek.

*II*   H. Lawson/G, 6 Jan. 1907; E. Lawson/G, 21 Dec. 1907; Courtney/G, 6 Nov. 1906; 11 Feb. 1907; G/F. Colvin (summer) 1907; Northcliffe/G, 17 Aug., 14 Sept. 1907; G/Northcliffe, 7, 12 Sept. 1907; 25 Jan. 1908; G/Maxse, 6 Oct. 1907; G/Goulding, 25 Oct. 1907; Gollin, *J. L. Garvin and The Observer*, pp. 20, 21.

*III*   *Observer*, Circulation and profit and loss data, 1907-1913 (MS); Pound and Harmsworth, *Northcliffe*, pp. 291, 341; H. Hobson, P. Knightley and L. Russell, *The Pearl of Days: An Intimate Memoir of the Sunday Times* (1972), pp. 51-8; Northcliffe/G, 2, 10 Jan., 2, 11 Mar. 1908; G/Northcliffe, 7 Jan. 1908; Butes/G, 30 Apr. 1909.

*IV*   G/Northcliffe, 10 Jan. 1908; 5 Feb., 10 May 1909; Pearson/G, 28, 30 Jan. 1908; *History of The Times*, vol. III, p. 553; Russell/G, 18 May 1909; G/Christina Garvin, 9 Apr. 1910.

*12 Greville Place, 1908-1922*

*I*   G/Northcliffe, 2 Feb. 1908; *Observer*, 2, 9, Feb. 1908.

*II*   G/Christina Garvin, 7, 20 July 1905; Katharine Garvin, *J. L. Garvin*, pp. 62-5, 68, 83; information from Mrs Slaghek, Mrs Wildblood, Mrs France.

*III*   W. Meynell/G, 13 Nov. 1924; F. Colvin/G, 6 June 1915; T. Morison, *Sir Edward Fitzgerald Law* (1911), p. 354; Viola G. Garvin/G, n.d. (May 1931); Northcliffe/G, 18 May 1908.

*IV*   G/Maxse, 23 Dec. 1908; Fisher/G, 18 Nov. 1908; Lady Northcliffe/G, 25 June 1909; G/F. Colvin, 6 Sept. 1907; 16 June 1909; G/Maxse, n.d. It is not possible to say precisely when Mrs Garvin's heavy drinking bouts began. In a letter to Sidney Colvin on 21 March 1919 Garvin refers to his 'seven years' crucifixion' which would put the onset in 1912. It may well have started earlier.

*13 The Defence of Britain, 1908-1911*

1. Prothero was joint editor of the *Cambridge Modern History*.
2. A fairer translation than 'a contemptible little army of mercenaries'.

*I* *Quarterly Review* (July and Oct. 1908); Garvin, *Life of Joseph Chamberlain*, vol. III, p. 501; Prothero/G, 3 June, 8, 9, 11, 16 Oct. 1908; *Daily Telegraph*, 28 Oct. 1908; G, 'Note of Conversation with Lord Burnham 3 January 1928'.

*II* Admiral Sir Reginald Baron, *Lord Fisher* (1929), vol. I, p. 241 (Garvin on Fisher); G/Northcliffe, 1 Dec. 1908; Fisher/G, 28 Jan., 4, 10 Feb., 19 July 1908; 11, 14, 19, 20 Mar. 1909; *Observer*, 2, 9 Feb. 1908; 21 Mar. 1909; *Daily Mail*, 22 Mar. 1909; G/Edward Grey, 22 Mar. 1909; Grey/G, 22 Mar. 1909; McKenna/G, 2 June 1915.

*III* Fisher/G, 16, 28 Dec. 1907; 4 Apr., 26 Nov. 1908; Roberts/G, 18 July 1906; 24 Nov. 1907; 1, 5 Jan., 15 Feb. 1908; *Fortnightly Review* (Jan. 1901), 'Can England Last the Century?'; *Quarterly Review* (July 1908), 'The German Peril'; John Wilson, *CB: A Life of Sir Henry Campbell Bannerman* (1973), pp. 180-1; *Observer*, 15 Mar., 9 Aug., 29 Nov. 1908.

## 14 The Lords and the Budget, 1909

1. Since Queen Victoria's death her birthday (24 May) had been kept as Empire Day. It was renamed Commonwealth Day in 1958.

2. The title Garvin gave to a collected reprint of his *Observer* articles.

For this and the following two chapters there is an important new source available in the brisk exchange of letters between Garvin and J. S. Sandars, Balfour's intimate friend and personal assistant, now in the Bodleian.

*I* Memorandum 'Upon the Necessity, the Method and the Limits of Social Reform Considered as part of Unionist Policy', dated 17 Sept. 1909. This survives in three versions – MS draft partly in Garvin's and partly in Mrs Garvin's hand, a typescript, and a revised version of the typescript. An envelope in Garvin's hand shows that the memorandum was intended for Balfour. It was probably also sent to Walter Long (see Long/G, 6, 8 Oct 1909) in a vain attempt to convert him. *Observer*, 21 Feb., 21 Mar., 15 Aug. 1909.

*II* *Observer*, 22 Aug. 1909; G/Northcliffe, 27 May, 4, 19 Aug. 1909; Northcliffe/G, 30 Dec. 1909; Pound and Harmsworth, *Northcliffe*, pp. 376, 377; Balfour/Sandars, 6 Aug. 1909; Sandars/G, 12 Aug. 1909; G/F. Colvin, 9 Aug. 1909.

*III* Lloyd George's speech at the National Liberal Club was on 3 Dec. 1909; Oliver/G, 3, 6 Dec. 1909; *Manchester Guardian*, 8 Dec. 1909; Election forecasts, *Observer*, 7 Nov. 1909; 'A year ago 200 Conservative gains would have been certain.' G/Northcliffe, 3 Jan. 1910: '150-170 Conservative gains'.

## 15 A Truce of God

*I* G/Christina Garvin, 22 Mar., 10, 15 Apr. 1910.

*II* *Observer*, 8 May 1910; G/Northcliffe, 29 Apr., 13 June 1910; G/Sandars, 9 May 1910; Oliver/G, 23, 24, 26 May 1910.

*III* *Observer*, 15 May 1910; G/Sandars, 3, 5 May 1910; Kennedy Jones/G, 10 May 1910; Marlowe/G, 14 June 1910; W. T. Stead/G, 18, 26, 27 May 1910;

Oliver/G, 24 May 1910; Brooks/G, 30 May 1910; G/Northcliffe, 13 June 1910.

*IV*   G/Northcliffe, 13 June 1910; Oliver/G, 23 May, 6, 8, 9 June 1910.

*V*   G/F. Colvin, 6 Oct. 1910. The Sandars Papers contain Balfour's notes of his negotiations with Lloyd George and an endorsement by Sandars explaining how he met Balfour's train. G/Northcliffe, Sunday, 6 Nov. 1910: 'On Wednesday there was a serious little row about leakages. "Who else knew about these things?" said A.J.B. "Garvin knew everything, but he gave nothing away," said Lloyd George.' G/Balfour, 17, 25 Oct. 1910; A. Chamberlain/G, 21, 24 Oct. 1910; Oliver/G, 11 Oct. 1910.

*VI*   G/Northcliffe, 2, 3, 6 Nov. 1910; Sandars/G, 4, 5, 8 Nov. 1910; Elibank/G, 3 Dec. 1910.

## 16 The Battle Resumed, 1910

1. Highbury was the Chamberlain home in Birmingham.

*I*   Oliver/G, 11 Nov. 1910; *Observer*, 13 Nov. 1910; W. R. Holt/G, 17 Nov. 1910; *Manchester Guardian*, 28 Nov. 1910; Sandars/G, 11, 13, 15 Nov. 1910; G/Northcliffe, 15 Nov. 1910; Austen Chamberlain/J. Chamberlain, 13 Nov. 1910 (Austen Chamberlain, *Politics from Inside* (1936), p. 298.

*II*   G/Northcliffe, 21 Nov. 1910; W. R. Holt/G, 17 Nov. 1910.

*III*   *Textile Mercury*/G, 26 Nov. 1910; *Observer*, 27 Nov., 4 Dec. 1910; *Manchester Guardian*, 28 Nov. 1910; Sandars/G, 27 Nov. 1910; G/Sandars, 30 Nov. 1910.

*IV*   W. T. Stead/G, 14 Oct. 1909; Lloyd George, speech at East Ham, 15 Dec. 1910.

## 17 Exit Northcliffe, 1910-1911

*I*   Northcliffe/G, 11 Jan. 1908; G/Christina Garvin, 1, 9 Apr. 1910; Russell/G, 26 May, 24 June, 8, 12, 20 Oct., 5 Nov. 1910; Sutton/G, 26 Apr. 1910.

*II*   Northcliffe/G, 31 Jan., 2, 3 Feb. 1911; G/Northcliffe, 1, 2 Feb. 1911; *Daily Mail*, 28 Jan. 1911; *Observer*, 5 Feb. 1911; Northcliffe/Cornford (resigning directorship), 6 Feb. 1911; Gollin, *J. L. Garvin and the Observer*, pp. 287-97; Pound and Harmsworth, *Northcliffe*, pp. 414, 415; A. J. P. Taylor, *Beaverbrook* (1974), pp. 90, 91; Lady Northcliffe/G, n.d. (Feb. 1911).

### Book Four: Garvin and the Astors, 1911-1914

At this point a torrential stream of Astor letters begins to flow towards Garvin. There arè 1,194 from Waldorf Astor to Garvin in the Humanities Research Center at Austin besides 43 from his wife and 30 from his father. In addition the Humanities Research Center holds 109 from Sir John Coode Adams, the Astor man of business, to Garvin. Garvin's letters to Waldorf Astor are in the University of Reading.

Christopher Sykes in *Nancy: The Life of Lady Astor* (1972) and Michael

Astor in *Tribal Feeling* (1963) help greatly to an understanding of the Astor setting of Garvin's life for the next thirty-one years.

*18 Enter the Astors, 1911*

*I* Taylor, *Beaverbrook*, p. 85; Aitken/G, 8 Feb. 1911; Roberts/G, 10, 11, 17, 18 Feb. 1911; Goldman/G, 23 Mar. 1911; Gollin, *J. L. Garvin and the Observer*, pp. 297-8, 303-4.

*II* Russell/G, 5, 13, 28 Apr., 15 June 1911; Coode Adams/Russell, 10 Mar. 1911; G/Coode Adams, 11 Mar. 1911; G/W. W. Astor, 11 Mar. 1911; J. W. Robertson Scott, *The Life and Death of a Newspaper* (1952), pp. 379, 380; G/Gerard Garvin, 5 Sept. 1915.

*III* Lady Edward Cecil/Milner, 23 Dec. 1912 (Gollin, *J. L. Garvin and the Observer*, p. 366); Sykes, *Nancy*, p. 95; G/Christina Garvin, 21 Nov. 1911; Nancy Astor/G, inc. d. (Dec. 1911); G/Astor, 2, 6 Aug. 1911; Astor/G, 4 Aug. 1911.

*19 Politics in No Man's Land, 1911*

1. *The Flying Inn* was published in 1914.
2. Presumably the *Telegraph* leader was written with Waldorf's permission.

*I* Sir Colin Coote, *The Other Club* (1971).

*II* Sandars/G, 4, 8 Mar. 1911; G/Sandars, 28 June 1911; G/Astor, 2, 6 Aug. 1911; 8 Jan. 1912; Astor/G, 4 Aug. 1911; *Observer*, 7 May, 30 July 1911; Elibank/G, 3 May 1911.

*III* Sykes, *Nancy*, p. 176; typescript of speech to Unionist Social Reform Committee, 27 Oct. 1911.

*IV* *Daily Telegraph*, 9 Nov. 1911; Sandars/G, 7, 9 Nov. 1911; Maxse/Nancy Astor, 10 Nov. 1911; Taylor, *Beaverbrook*, pp. 104-6; Gollin, *J. L. Garvin and the Observer*, pp. 349-63; G/Astor, 10, 12 Nov. 1911; G/Goulding, 12 Nov. 1911.

*20 Garvin's Tandem, 1912-1914*

1. Among the 1,500 drowned was W. T. Stead.

*I* The inscription on the table was transcribed by the writer while working at it. The *PMG* is the subject of two books by J. W. Robertson Scott: *The Story of the Pall Mall Gazette* (1950), dedicated to 'all the editors who gave up their posts and salaries for their opinions', and *The Life and Death of a Newspaper* (1952). G/Coode Adams, 20 July 1911; Oliver/G, 15 Jan. 1912; Whibley/G, 8 Apr. 1911; 4 Feb. 1912; E. T. Cook/G, 29 Jan. 1912; W. T. Stead, 18 Jan. 1912; *Punch*, 7 Feb. 1912.

*II* Robertson Scott, *Life and Death of a Newspaper*, p. 394; G/Bonar Law, 8 Jan. 1912 (really 1913); MS, memoranda on circulation and profit and loss by Garvin.

*III*   G/Coode Adams, 20 July, 6 Dec. 1911; 24 Feb. 1913; 6 Jan., 21 Nov. 1914; G's private memoranda; G/W. W. Astor, 16 Apr. 1912; W. W. Astor/G, 3 Mar. 1914.

*IV*   Oliver/G, 20, 22 July 1914; Roberts/G, 29 July, 2 Aug. 1914; Astor/G, 11 Aug. 1914; W. W. Astor/G, 31 Aug. 1914.

*21 The Covenanter, 1912-1914*

*I*   Bonar Law spoke at the Albert Hall on 14 November and at Ashton-under-Lyne on 16 December 1912. G/Astor, 19 Dec. 1912 ('You can never establish the food tax without direct authority from the people'); 28 Dec. 1912; Oliver/G, 31 Dec. 1912; *Observer*, 5 Jan. 1913; Taylor, *Beaverbrook*, pp. 112, 113; Astor/G, 6 Jan. 1913; Goulding/G, 8 Jan. 1913.

*II*   Astor/G, 7 Nov. 1912 (with endorsement by Garvin); *Observer*, 10 Nov. 1912; G/Gerard Garvin, 25 May 1915 (reference to coalition); Fisher/G, 9 Nov. 1911; G/Astor, 19 Dec. 1913; Haldane left the War Office on 10 June 1912; Roberts/G, 10 Oct. 1913.

*III*   G/S. Colvin, 19 Oct. 1910; H. W. Nevinson, *Fire of Life* (1935), pp. 281, 282; *Observer*, 29 Sept. 1912; *Daily News*, 5 Oct. 1912; Hansard, 8 May 1912, col. 475; Oliver/G, 4 Dec. 1913; G/Astor, 18 Mar. 1914; speech to the United Empire Club, 30 Mar. 1914 (MS); G/C. P. Scott, 25 Nov. 1913; 14 May 1914; Scott/G, 7 May 1914.

**Book Five: The First World War: Father and Son, 1914-1918**

*22 The Coming of War, 1914-1915*

1. Michael died in Cape Town on New Year's Eve. As Jim told his son, 'To fight a long battle as bravely as he did and leave all accounts square is no unworthy thing.'

2. Garvin's account was published in 1928 in Beaverbrook's *Politicians and the War* (1928) – without acknowledgement, as A. J. P. Taylor has pointed out.

The first two years of the First World War are probably the best documented part of Garvin's life thanks to the many letters that passed between Gerard Garvin and his parents – 221 from Gerard, 188 from Garvin and 148 from Christina.

From this time on Garvin's correspondence with Churchill is of great value. I am grateful to the Churchill trustees for permission to quote from some of Churchill's unpublished letters in the Humanities Research Center. Martin Gilbert's biography and its companion volumes, published by Heinemann, are indispensable (*Winston S. Churchill* (7 vols., 1971-83)).

*I*   Information from Mrs France (Eileen Macoun), a school friend of Garvin's eldest daughter; typescript of Garvin's lecture on Francis Thompson to the Poetry Society; G/F. Colvin, 7 July 1914; G/Gerard Garvin, 15 Feb. 1915; Morley/G, 3 July 1914.

*II*   PMG, 27 July 1914; Roberts/G, 2 Aug. 1914.

*III*   Mrs Denis (Bess) O'Sullivan, *Harry Butters, R.F.A.* (1919), pp. 273-9; Chidson/Christina Garvin, 23 Aug. 1916; E. Marsh/F. E. Smith, 17 Aug. 1914; Roberts/G, 1 Sept. 1914; Gerard Garvin/parents, 31 Aug. 1914 (he enlisted 28 August and was commissioned 19 September 1914); G/Gerard Garvin, 8 Feb. 1915; Gerard Garvin/G, 6 July 1915; Gerard Garvin/Christina Garvin, 2, 3, 14 Nov. 1914; 27 Mar. 1915.

*IV*   G/Gerard Garvin, 6 June 1916; W. S. Churchill, *The World Crisis 1911-1918* (one-volume edition, 1931), p. 227; G/Churchill, 23 Sept. (Gilbert); Fisher/G, 31 Oct., 3 Nov. 1914.

*V*   G/Law, 31 July 1914; Steel Maitland/Law, 9 Aug., 17 Oct. 1914; G/Sinclair, 16, 17 Sept. 1914; Benson/G, 18, 27 Nov. 1914; G/Benson, 19, 29 Nov. 1914; Lord Grey/G, 11 Nov. 1914; Astor/G, 28 Nov. 4, 8, 13 Dec. 1914; G/Astor, 17 Jan., 11 Feb. 1915; C. P. Scott/G, 7 Dec. 1914; 22 Mar. 1915; *Manchester Guardian*, 7 Jan. 1915; G/Gerard Garvin, 12, 25 Jan., 4 Mar., 23 Aug., 2 Sept. 1915; Christina Garvin/Gerard Garvin, 15 Feb. 1915; Rothermere/Law, 27(?) Feb. 1915; Law/Rothermere, 3 Mar. 1915; Coode Adams/Astor, 17 Feb. 1915; W. W. Astor/Astor, 25 Feb. 1915; Sackville/G, 28 Sept. 1915.

*VI*   Christina Garvin/Gerard Garvin, 4 Mar. 1915; G/Gerard Garvin, 4, 10 Mar., 25 May 1915.

### 23   *The Flowers of the Forest, July 1915-July 1916*

1. The evacuation of Gallipoli had just been announced.

2. Fisher never was recalled. Garvin, at Churchill's and Goulding's suggestion, helped Fisher prepare his written evidence for the Dardanelles enquiry. The report distributed blame, but gave enough support to Fisher's enemies to prevent his return to power.

3. What did Ged mean by 'entering the Catholic Church'? To a boy at a public school 'entering the Church' would naturally mean being ordained. Probably Ged used it in that sense.

*I*   Gerard Garvin/G, 25 June, 19 Sept. 1915; Gerard Garvin/Christina Garvin, 20 Sept. 1915; Gerard Garvin/parents, 20, 22 Sept. 1915; Julie Heynemann/ Gerard Garvin, 27 Sept. 1915.

*II*   Christina Garvin/Gerard Garvin, 16 Oct., 14 Nov. 1915; G/Gerard Garvin, 18, 20, 21, 25 Oct., 8, 12, 18 Nov. 1915; G/Churchill, 14 Nov. 1915 (Gilbert); G/Lady Randolph Churchill, 15 Nov. 1915 (Gilbert); Churchill/G, 4 Dec. 1915 (but cf. G/Gerard Garvin, 25 Dec. 1915).

*III*   G/Gerard Garvin, 8 Dec. 1915; Garvin's MS interview note; *Observer*, 8 Dec. 1915.

*IV*   G/Gerard Garvin, 14, 26 Dec. 1915; 13 Mar. 1916; Christina Garvin/Gerard Garvin, 14 Dec. 1915; G/C. P. Scott, 8 Dec. 1915; Trevor Wilson (ed.), *C. P. Scott's Political Diaries 1911-1928* (1970), with further details from British Library Add. Mss 55, 903), pp. 161, 162; G/Fisher, 25 Dec. 1915 (Gilbert).

*V* Gerard Garvin/Christina Garvin, 16/17 Nov. 1915; 8 Jan., 13 Mar. 1916; Gerard Garvin/G, 28 Nov. 1915.

*VI* G/Gerard Garvin, 9, 13 Mar. 1916; Christina Garvin/Gerard Garvin, 11, 12 Mar. 1916; Gerard Garvin/Christina Garvin, 15 Mar. 1916; *Scott's Political Diaries*, p. 189; *Observer*, 12 Mar. 1916; Astor/G, 13 Mar. 1916; G/Mrs Churchill, 28 Mar. 1916 (Gilbert).

*VII* Gerard Garvin/G, 23, 29 Apr., 11 May 1916; G/Gerard Garvin, 26 27 Apr., 15 May 1916.

*VIII* G/Gerard Garvin, 3, 5, 8, 12 July 1916; Christina Garvin/Gerard Garvin, 12 July 1916; Gerard Garvin's Diary; B. R. Mullalay, *The South Lancashire Regiment*, p. 206; Gerard Garvin/G, 8 July 1916.

*IX* Gerard Garvin/G, 12, 20 July 1916; 20 Dec. 1915; Narratives of 2/Lts John Wolfenden and Douglas Sharp (typescript); Spender Clay/G, 25 July 1916; Vellacott/G, 26 July 1916; Winser/G, n.d. (July 1916); *Observer*, 30 July 1916.

*24 De Profundis, 1916-1918*

   1. Max Aitken had become Lord Beaverbrook in 1917.

During Garvin's visit to the Western Front in 1917 he filled ten notebooks (Nos. 94-103). On his return typescript copies were made which form the main material of sections I and II. The Narrative runs to some 75,000 words.

*I* Churchill/A. Sinclair, 15 Sept. 1916 (Gilbert); Wordsworth, 'Peele Castle'; *Observer*, 22 July 1917; Christina Garvin/G, 4, 6 July 1917.

*II* Narrative, fos. 165-72 *passim*; fo. 137 (anger with Germany); fos. 194, 195 (Sir William Robertson); fos. 371, 436, 452, 453 (Alsace).

*III* *Observer*, 22 July 1917.

*IV* G/S. Colvin, 25 Mar. 1918; *Observer*, 2, 9 Dec. 1917.

*V* G/Astor, 4 Jan., 1 Mar., 24 Apr. 1918; Astor/G, 29 Apr., 3, 7 May, 23 July 1918; Goulding/G, 7 Jan., 16, 18, 21, 25 Feb. 1918; *New York Tribune* (A. S. Draper)/G, 25 Dec. 1915; 27 Jan., 23 Oct. 1916; G/Gerard Garvin, 21 Dec. 1915; 10 Jan., 18 Feb. 1916; Oliver/G, 10 May 1918; Paine/G, 16, 21 May, 19, 28 June, 12, 19 July 1918.

*VI* Goulding/G, 16, 27 Feb. 1918; Austen Chamberlain in the Commons, 19 Feb. 1918; Astor/G, 6 Mar. 1918 (enclosing letters to and from Sir Hedworth Meux).

*VII* Astor/G, 18 Feb. 1917; 29 Apr., 11 May 1918; G/Astor, 20 Feb., 22 Aug., 20, 24 Sept. 1917; Basil Thomson (Scotland Yard)–S. W. Harris (Home Office) with information for Astor, 20 Feb. 1917; G/S. Colvin, 6 June 1918, saying Bottomley had bought *National News* which, after attacking Lloyd George throughout April, had backed him against Maurice on 12 May. The week before this it announced that its financial backer had withdrawn. *New Statesman* (Nov. 1917); *Times*, 7 May 1918; *Observer*, 12 May 1918.

*VIII* G/S. Colvin, 6, 12 June 1918; Christina Garvin/Gerard Garvin, 23, 25 Jan. 1916; G/Lady Lee of Fareham, 16 July 1918; Lady Lee/G, 14, 24 July 1918; Lord Lee/G, 18 July 1918.

*IX* *Observer*, 8 Dec. 1918; G/Astor, 25 Dec. 1918; G/F. Colvin, 31 Dec. 1918; information from Mrs Ursula Salghek.

**Book Six: A Second Spring, 1919-1927**

*25 Peace and Dragon's Teeth, 1919*

1. Greenwood was thirty-nine.

*I* G/Astor, 1 Jan. 1919; *Observer*, 30 Mar. 1919; J. L. Garvin, *Economic Foundations of Peace* (1919), p. x.

*II* Page references to the *Economic Foundations* are given in the order followed in this chapter: pp. 5, 15, 86 (need for a League); pp. 32, 445 (reparations); p. 183 (Germany and Russia); p. 481 (disarmament); pp. 369, 370 (Russia); pp. 493-5 (America and Britain); pp. 443-5 'developing countries'.

*III* *Observer*, 23 Mar., 4, 11 May 1919; Smuts/G, 26 June 1919.

*IV* Greenwood/G, n.d. (1919).

*V* *C. P. Scott's Political Diaries*, p. 371, 21 Feb. 1919.

*26 The Second Mrs Garvin, 1919-1921*

1. It passed the Lords, but was withdrawn in the Commons. The law remained unchanged until 1923.
2. Garvin was just under six foot and weighed thirteen stone.

Behind this chapter lie three unpublished memoirs written by three successive generations of the Woods family. The first, 'The Dancing Slope', by Mrs. M. L. Woods, is in the Bodleian. The second, 'Remembering like Anything', by her daughter-in-law, Mrs Viola Woods Garvin, Garvin's second wife. The third, 'The Chequered Board', is by her son, Oliver Woods, and is the beginning of an auto-biography cut short by his death.

All three, of course, were written long after the events with which we are concerned. Fortunately there survive 72 letters from Viola Woods to Garvin written during the nine months before her divorce was made absolute.

*I* Sackville/G, 1 Jan. 1919; G/S. Colvin, 21 Mar. 1919; G/Lee-Mathews, n.d. but obviously same day.

*II* M. Woods/G, 11 Mar. (1911); V. Woods/G, 18 Mar. 1911; G/Christina Garvin, 23 Nov. 1911; Christina Garvin/Gerard Garvin, 10, 25 Jan., 16 Apr. 1916;

G/Gerard Garvin, 6 Jan. 1916; M. L. Woods, 'The Dancing Slope', fos. 107, 112.

*III*  V. Woods/M. Woods, 28 May 1919; M. Woods/V. Woods, 29 May 1919; Petition for restitution of conjugal rights, 30 May 1919; Lady Sackville, Diary Lilly Library Univ. of Indiana), 11 June 1919; Katharine Garvin, *J. L. Garvin*, pp. 92, 93; G/F. Colvin, 23 June, 11 Aug. 1919; 18 Nov. 1920; Viola (Woods) Garvin, 'Remembering Like Anything', fos. 21, 22; Viola Woods/G, 14 Dec. 1920.

*IV*  Lovat Dickson, *Radclyffe Hall at the Well of Loneliness: A Sapphic Chronicle* (1975), *passim*; V. (Woods) Garvin, 'Remembering Like Anything', fo. 22; V. Woods/G, 1 Mar. 1920; V. Woods *v.* M. Woods, Decree *nisi*, 31 Jan. 1921.

*V*  Viola Woods/G, 30, 31 Mar. 1921; Oliver Woods, 'The Chequered Board'.

*VI*  V. Woods/G, 17, 21 Dec., 2 Mar. 1921; V. (Woods) Garvin, 'Remembering Like Anything'.

*VII*  V. Woods/G, 5, 7, 9 Mar., 8, 11 Apr. 1921.

*VIII*  V. Woods/G, 26, 29 Mar., 19 Apr. 1921; G/Lee-Mathews, 21 Nov. 1921; Oliver Woods, 'The Chequered Board', fo. 11.

*IX*  V. Woods/G, 16 Apr. 1921; V. Woods *v.* M. Woods, Decree absolute, 10 Aug. 1921. After Maurice Woods' death 'they remarried each other according to the Catholic rite in the presence of Canon Westlake at Worthing. The date was the anniversary of their legal marriage.' Katharine Garvin, *J. L. Garvin*, p. 197, who, however, wrongly gives the year as 1928 instead of 1929.

### 27  The Coming of Barrington-Ward, 1919

Immediately after the First World War an abundant new source of information becomes available in the correspondence and diaries of R. M. Barrington-Ward, who became editor of *The Times*. For the first nine inter-war years he was Garvin's right-hand man; he remained a confidential friend until Garvin's death in 1947, a year before his own. See Donald McLachlan's biography, *In the Chair* (1971), especially Chapters 6 and 7. Barrington-Ward's diaries and Garvin's letters to him are in the possession of his son.

*I*  G/Grigg, 23 Jan. 1923; Astor/G, 7 Feb. 1919; McLachlan, *In the Chair*, pp. 42, 53-5; G/B-W, 23 Oct. 1924; B-W Diary, Sept./Oct. 1919; 27 Dec. 1930.

*II*  B-W Diary, 31 Aug. 1920; B-W to his mother, 30 Aug. 1921; 23 Feb. 1922; B-W Diary, 17 May, 20 June 1924.

### 28  Garvin and Lloyd George, 1922

1. Memorable to Lina because Garvin had declaimed Shelley's 'Ode to the West Wind' while it whistled round his head.

2. Rathenau, a Jew, was murdered by a German Nationalist a month after the Conference.

3. Tchitcherin kept up an occasional correspondence with Garvin as long as he was Commissar for Foreign Affairs.

4. Frances Stevenson, Lloyd George's secretary and mistress, had been lunching with R. W. Child, US ambassador to Italy at the time of the Genoa Conference.

Lina Waterfield, a family friend as well as the *Observer*'s Rome correspondent, is a major source for the period 1922-36. Over a hundred personal letters between editor and correspondent survive from these years. I am much indebted to her son, Gordon Waterfield, for the loan of those in his possession and for permission to quote. Her autobiography, *Castle in Italy* (1961), gives a lively impression of the relations between two distinguished and unusual people.

*I*  G/Viola Woods, 9 Feb. 1920; Waterfield, *Castle in Italy*, pp. 179-85; Lina Waterfield/Gordon Waterfield, 28 May 1922; Viola (Woods) Garvin, 'Remembering Like Anything'; *Observer*, 16, 23, 30 Apr., 4, 7, 21 May 1922.

*II*  G/Lee-Mathews, 1 Sept. 1922; G/B-W, 15 July 1922; MS notes for Northcliffe obituary; *Observer*, 20 Aug. 1922; C. Harmsworth/G, 1936 (n.d.).

*III*  G/B-W, 21, 26 Sept. 1922.

*IV*  *Observer*, 15 Oct., 19 Nov. 1922; Frances Stevenson, *Lloyd George: A Diary*, ed. A. J. P. Taylor (1971), 7 Apr. 1934.

*29 Gregories, 1921-1947*

1. A translation of Francis Jammes' sonnet, *Avoir une Maison*.

*I*  Viola Woods/G, 20 Dec. 1920; 3 Mar., 15 Apr. 1921 and *passim*; G/Astor, 11, 12 Jan. 1923; G/Kindersley, 19 Jan. 1923; *Observer*, 15 Apr., 27 May 1923 (Garvin's boastful assessment of his scoop was written on an envelope containing press cuttings about Law); Amery/G, 4 Sept. 1931.

*II*  Oliver Woods, 'The Chequered Board'; Andrew Boyle, *Poor Dear Brendan: The Quest for Brendan Bracken* (1974); C. E. Lysaght, *Brendan Bracken* (1979); information from Douglas Woodruff. From 1923, when Bracken's address is pencilled in Garvin's engagement diary, onwards, Bracken played an important part in Garvin's life, and his fifty odd letters to Garvin are a valuable biographical source. Unfortunately only one of Garvin's letters survived the wholesale destruction of Bracken's papers after his death, and that only in a MS copy in Garvin's handwriting.

*III*  Based on Oliver Woods 'The Chequered Board', and Katharine Garvin, *J. L. Garvin*; G/Viola (Woods) Garvin, 15 Sept. 1927.

*IV*  Oliver Woods, 'The Chequered Board'; information from Ivor Brown.

*V*  Oliver Woods; Katharine Garvin, *J. L. Garvin*; information from Mrs Slaghek.

*30 The Loss of Barrington-Ward, 1925-1927*

1. Two days later France ratified the Locarno treaties.

*I*   B-W Diary, 5 Dec. 1925; 20 Jan., 28 Feb., 12, 13 Mar., 16 Apr. 1926.

*II*   McLachlan, *In the Chair*, pp. 62, 63; B-W/G, 6 May 1926.

*III*   Garvin wrote *These Eventful Years* (2 vols.) for the *Encyclopaedia Britannica* in 1924. He edited the 1926 three supplementary volumes which, with the existing 1911 edition, were marketed as the thirteenth edition. On 29 April 1927 F. H. Hooper confirmed his offer to Garvin of the appointment of editor-in-chief of the completely new fourteenth edition. B-W Diary; G/B-W, 6 Sept. 1926; 6, 8 Apr. 1927; Astor/G, 2 Apr. 1927; G/Astor, 5 Apr. 1927.

*IV*   Duff Hart Davis, *Peter Fleming: A Biography (1974)*, pp. 145, 146; Astor/G, 21, 29 Nov. 1927 (Barry); 4 Oct. 1927 (Atkins); F. Meynell/G, 11, 20, inc. d. (July 1927) (Postgate); Bracken/G, 26 July, 2 Aug. 1927 (Mottram); G/B-W, 18 Aug. 1927 (Woodruff).

**Book Seven: Appearance and Reality, 1929-1938**

*31 High Water, 1929-1930*

*I*   G/Astor, 25 Feb., 10 Apr. 1929; G/Viola (Woods) Garvin, 8 Apr. 1929; H. Macmillan, *The Past Masters* (1915), pp. 158, 159; *Observer*, 7 Apr. 1929; Bracken/G, 2 June 1929.

*II*   Guest list of *Spectator* lunch, 14 Nov. 1929; E. A. Jenkins, *From Foundry to Foreign Office* (1933); *Observer*, 17 Nov. 1929; Bowen-Rowlands *v. Observer*, 8 Feb. 1926; Gould/G, 2 Nov. 1929; Ervine/G, 25 July 1929.

*III*   Guest list, 25 June 1930; MS of Garvin's speech; Lady Astor/G, 5 June 1930; Beaverbrook/G, 12 July 1929; Taylor, *Beaverbrook*, p. 300; G/Una Ledingham, 3 July 1930.

*IV*   Speech at Beaverbrook dinner; G/Christina Garvin, 11 Nov. 1902; 23 Nov. 1911 (on Philip Kerr); Lothian/G, 25 Dec. 1930 and 9 other letters Dec. 1930- Nov. 1931; Morison/G, 27 May, 15, 18 Oct. 1930. The extent of Garvin's involvement with the princely and Muslim members of the Round Table Conference may be gauged from the fact that there are 19 letters from Sir Akbar Hydari and 40 from Sir Sha'afat Ahmad Khan in the Garvin papers. G/B-W, 28 Oct. 1931; Dr Ambedkar/G, 23, 24 Sept. 1914; Hoare/G, 11 Apr. 1932 and 10 others up to Dec. 1934; Churchill/G, 29 Apr., 16, 19, 24 May, 1, 3 June, 12 July 1933.

*V*   C. P. Scott/G, 17 July 1929; 16 Dec. 1930; Stamfordham/G, 17 July 1929; MacDonald/G, 10 Dec. 1930; Churchill/G, 13 Dec. 1940.

*32 The Tide Turns, 1928-1933*

1. Lord Burnham, the 'Mr. Harry' of Garvin's time on the paper, sold to William and Gomer Berry and Lord Iliffe, who took control on New Year's Day, 1928.

2. Garvin signed the contract on 28 February 1930.
3. In fact MacDonald remained Prime Minister for another four years.
4. Viola's nickname for Wolfe: Humbert-Hummingbird-Bird.

*I* Dawson/G, 13 Jan. 1928; Astor/G, 28 Feb., 5 Mar. 1928; G/Astor, 29 Feb., 1 Mar. (memorandum).

*II* Bryant/G, 27 Apr. 1927; W. J. Cox/G, 29 Apr. 1927; G/Astor, 27 Feb. 1926; Oliver Woods, 'The Chequered Board', fo. 5; *Encyclopaedia* 'bible' (MS).

*III* G/Astor, 2 June 1927; W. Berry/G, 4 Jan. 1928 with Garvin's endorsement on envelope; Bracken/G, 17 Dec. 1928; Locker-Lampson/G, 26 Nov. 1928.

*IV* Draft contract endorsed by Garvin, 1 Nov. 1929; Astor/G, 17 Nov., 1 Dec. 1929; G/Astor, 30 Nov. 1929.

*V* Blanch/Astor, 18 Mar. 1921; A. P. Wadsworth, *Newspaper Circulations 1800-1954* (1955); Hobson, Russell and Knightley, *The Pearl of Days*, p. 73; G/Lee-Mathews, 17 Sept. 1933; T. E. Lawrence/G, 15 July 1934; Astor/G, 3 Mar., 2 Dec. 1928; 9, 10 Jan. 1931; Garvin's memoranda for Astor, 19, 26 Feb. 1931.

*VI* A. J. P. Taylor, *English History 1914-1945* (1965), p. 285; MacDonald/G, 25 Aug. 1931; Henderson/G, 25 Aug. 1931.

*VII* G/Viola G. Garvin, 4 Nov. 1930; 1 July, 28 Sept., 21 Oct. 1931.

*33 The Chamberlain Torso, 1932-1938*

1. Marjorie Pollard, the hockey international, was then a sports reporter on the *Observer*. She recalled that on Saturdays a scout was posted at the corner of Tudor Street to give warning of the editor's approach.

*I* A. Chamberlain/G, 23 Mar., 17, 26 Oct. 1932; N. Chamberlain/G, 25 Nov. 1932; 6 Jan. 1933; N. Chamberlain/Goulding, 11 Feb. 1932; Volumes I, II and III were published in 1932, 1934 and 1935 respectively; B-W Diary, 23 July 1934; *Manchester Guardian*, 29 Nov. 1932.

*II* Henry Harrison, *Parnell Vindicated* (1931); Henry Harrison, *Joseph Chamberlain, Parnell and Mr. Garvin* (1938); G/Harrison, 1931, quoted from Harrison, *Joseph Chamberlain*, p. 22; *Observer*, 21 Aug. 1938; Garvin, *Chamberlain*, vol. II, p. 378.

*III* G/Oliver Woods, 10 Sept. 1934; G/Waterfield, 3 Oct. 1934; 30 Aug. 1935; G/B-W, 22 Sept., 12 Nov. 1934; B-W Diary, 3 Oct. 1937; A. Chamberlain/G, 13 June 1935; G/Macmillan, 8 Nov. 1937.

*IV* B-W Diary, 30 Sept. 1925.

**Book Eight: A Diversity of Dictators, 1933-1947**

*34 Calchas Redivivus, 1933-1935*

*I*   *Observer*, 5 Feb., 26 Mar., 9 Apr., 17, 24 Sept., 13 Oct. 1933; Sir Horace Rumbold/G, 12 Apr. 1933; P. Beaumont Wadsworth/*Observer*, 11 Oct. 1933 (telephoned).

*II*   White Paper on Defence, 4 Mar. 1935; *Observer*, 5 Nov. 1933.

*III*   *Observer*, 22 Mar., 14 May 1933; G/Amery, 23 Nov. 1933; G/Waterfield, 4 May 1923; 9 Nov. 1926.

*IV*   *Observer*, 18 Feb. 1934; Waterfield, *Castle in Italy*, pp. 241, 242; Waterfield/G, 11 Apr. 1935.

*V*   Sir Edward Grigg, who had been Garvin's assistant editor on the *Outlook*, returned to England in 1931 after being Governor in Kenya. Two years later he became MP for Altrincham. From this time he became a principal contributor to the *Observer* and a trusted confidant of Garvin. There are over a hundred letters from him to Garvin in the University of Texas. His son, John Grigg, kindly gave me access to Garvin's letters to his father and to other papers relating to the *Observer* in his possession. Together they provide a main source for the latter part of Garvin's life. G/Grigg, 28 May, 5 June 1935; Notebook 31, entry for 21 Sept. 1936; Engagement Diary 1935, entry for 1 June; *Observer*, 3 June 1935; Nancy Astor/Baldwin, 17 Nov. 1935 (Gilbert, *Winston S. Churchill*, vol. V, p. 686); Notebook 24, note on Baldwin's cabinet.

*35 The Mountains of Rasselas, 1935-1936*

1. 'Hoisting the Standard of St. George on the Mountains of Rasselas': Disraeli on Napier's victory at Magdala in 1868.
2. The present wars in the Horn of Africa support Garvin's view.
3. The Emperor Haile Selassie.

*I*   Waterfield, *Castle in Italy*, pp. 239, 242; G/Waterfield, 30 Oct. 1934.

*II*   The Peace Ballot result was published 27 June 1935. *Observer*, 7, 14 July 1935; Churchill/G, 1 Sept. 1935; Sadler/G, 27, 29 Aug. 1935; B-W Diary, 27 Sept. 1936; Steed/G, 22 Nov. 1936; Katharine Garvin, *J. L. Garvin*, p. 190.

*III*   Beevor/Waterfield, 30 Dec. 1935.

*IV*   Notebook 33.

*V*   Notebook 24.

*36 Odd Dictator Out, 1936-1940*

*I*   On 5 July Garvin wrote on the centenary of Joseph Chamberlain's birth. He did not write again until 18 October when he called his article 'The Red Rout: Spain and its Sequel'. The previous week Salvador de Madariaga had written on 'Spain's Ordeal: A Conflict of Legitimate Wills'. During Garvin's absence Edward Grigg and Lord Lothian had each written the principal article three times. *Observer*, 25 Oct. 1936; Taylor, *English History 1914-1945*, p. 395; G/Astor, 12 June 1936; G/Lothian, 8 Feb. 1938.

*II* Oliver Woods, 'The Chequered Board'; Viola G. Garvin/G, 17 June 1940.

*37 'The Nonesuch State', 1936-1939*

1. Colin Coote (*The Other Club*, p. 90) states that Garvin kept away from The Other Club until April 1945. In fact Garvin's engagement diary for 1939 shows four Other Club entries. In 1945 there are three similar entries before April. He may not have attended all, but he certainly intended to.
2. Eynsham Hall, Witney.

*I* Notebook 33, 21 Sept. 1936; *Observer*, 1, 21 Nov. 1936; Maisky/G, 14 Dec. 1935 (with endorsement by Garvin); 2 Nov. 1936.

*II* Grigg/G, 20 Mar., 8, 10 Apr. 1937; G/Grigg, 8, 12, 18 Apr. 1937; Nigel Nicolson (ed.), *Harold Nicolson: Diaries and Letters 1930-1939* (1966), 22 Apr. 1936; *Observer*, 6 Dec. 1936.

*III* Michael Astor, *Tribal Feeling* (1963), p. 81; information from Mark Barrington-Ward; G/Astor, 12 June 1936; G/Mrs Amery, 4 Oct. 1938.

*IV* Churchill in the Commons, 14 Mar. 1938; *Observer*, 20 Mar. 1938; Churchill/G, 15 June 1938.

*V* C. Coote, *History of The Other Club* (1971), pp. 88, 89; Lord Boothby, *Memories of a Rebel* (1978), p. 129; Gilbert, *Winston S. Churchill, The Wilderness Years*, p. 234, gives a different version: 'Duff Cooper insulted Garvin who left in a huff; then everybody insulted everybody else.' Locker-Lampson/G, n.d.; Steed/G, 25 Sept. 1938; G/Grigg, 20 June 1939.

*38 Shipwreck, 1939-1942*

1. Amery quoted Cromwell's words to the Rump of the Long Parliament: 'You have sat here too long for any good you have been doing. Depart, I say, and let us have done with you. In the name of God, go!'
2. See above, pp. 57, 69.
3. Lord Lothian died on 12 December 1940.

*I* *Observer*, 3 July 1939; Hoare/William Astor, 11 July 1939 (Gilbert); N. Chamberlain to his sister, 23 July 1939 (Gilbert); G/Amery, 5 Sept. 1939; Churchill/G, 13 Dec. 1939; Bracken/G, 2 Jan. 1941; Astor/G, 25 Dec. 1940 (according to Garvin's oral evidence to tribunal), 22 Sept. 1941; G/Astor, 14 Aug. 1941; Lady Astor, speech in Commons, 19 May 1941.

*II* Horder quoted in Garvin's memorandum, 21 Sept. 1941; G/Oliver Woods, 18 Dec. 1940; Astor's memorandum, 16 Sept. 1941.

*III*   William Astor/Viola G. Garvin, 31 Jan. 1940; Astor/T. Jones, 21 Feb. 1943; Astor/William Astor, 10 Mar. 1943.

*IV*   Sykes, *Nancy*, p. 451; Garvin's oral evidence, 22 Sept. 1941; G/Oliver Woods, 14 Oct. 1942.

*V*   Astor/Hollis Walker, 18 Aug. 1941; Bracken/G, 3, 9 Sept. 1941 (with enclosure from Arthur Mann); G/Bracken, 5 May 1941; Memoranda from Astor, 16 Sept., 1, 28 Oct. 1941; 4 Feb. 1942; Garvin, 21 Sept., 25 Nov. 1941; David Astor, 13 Oct. 1941; oral evidence by Garvin, 22 Sept. 1941; Garvin's comments on proposals by the tribunal, 20 Dec. 1941; Draft contract, 27 Jan. 1942; *Manchester Guardian*, 8 Dec. 1941; Astor/William Astor, 3 Mar. 1943; Astor/T. Jones, 8 Aug. 1941; Grigg/G, 18 Nov., 10, n.d. Dec. 1941; 4, 5, 9, 13, 17, 20 Feb. 1942; G/Grigg, 21 Sept., 21 Dec. 1941.

*VI*   *Observer*, 22 Feb. 1942; Astor/G, 22 Feb. 1942; Grigg/G, 23, 24, 26 Feb. 1942; G/Grigg, 24 Feb. 1942; *Punch*, 11 Mar. 1942.

*39 Afterglow, 1942-1947*

*I*   G/Oliver Woods inc. d. (Mar.); 19 Aug., inc. d. (Oct. 1942); Bracken/G, 4 Nov. 1941; B-W Diary, 16 Apr. 1946.

*II*   G/Oliver Woods, 4, 17 Aug., 15 Nov. 1943; B-W Diary, 11 Aug. 1942; Ursula Garvin's marriage was in 1936.

*III*   G/Oliver Woods, 17 Aug. 1943.

*IV*   G/Oliver Woods, 6, 12 Jan. 1945; 1945 Engagement Diary shows entries for Churchill (14 Jan.); Bracken (Jan. 16); and Camrose (23 Jan.); Lady Hudson/ G, 27 Jan. 1945; *Daily Telegraph*, 26 Apr., 4 July, 8 Nov. 1945; 14 Mar. 1946; 2 Jan. 1947.

*V*   Oliver Woods/G, 10 Aug. 1945; Katharine Garvin, *J. L. Garvin*; information from Mrs Ursula Slaghek.

*VI*   F. Waters, Diary, 1 Mar. 1946; Mrs Joan Woods/Ayerst, 6 Feb. 1979; Camrose/G, 21 Jan. 1947.

# INDEX

Note: Garvin is contracted to G; *Observer* to *Obs.*